W9-CBH-400

DISCARDED

Write a

Business
Plan

...me

Frank Fiore

800 East 96th Street
Indianapolis, Indiana 46240

Write a Business Plan In No Time

International Standard Book Number: 0-7897-3372-2

Library of Congress Catalog Card Number: 2004117326

Printed in the United States of America

First Printing: May 2005

08   07   06   05   4   3   2   1

Trademarks

Warning and Disclaimer

Bulk Sales

Que Publishing offers excellent discounts on this book when ordered in quantity for bulk purchases or special sales. For more information, please contact

U.S. Corporate and Government Sales
1-800-382-3419
corpsales@pearsontechgroup.com

For sales outside the United States, please contact

International Sales
international@pearsoned.com

Executive Editor
Candace Hall

Development Editor
Lorna Gentry

Managing Editor
Charlotte Clapp

Project Editor
Tonya Simpson

Production Editor
Heather Wilkins

Indexer
Ken Johnson

Technical Editor
Gina Woods

Publishing Coordinator
Cindy Teeters

Interior Designer
Anne Jones

Cover Designer
Anne Jones

Cover Illustrator
Nathan Clement, Stickman Studio

Page Layout
Michelle Mitchell

Write a Business Plan ...In No Time

Contents at a Glance

Table of Contents

III Where and How?

IV When and How Much?

V The Pitch

VI Helpful References

About the Author

Frank Fiore is a business expert and accomplished author of seven e-business books: *The 2005 Shopping Directory for Dummies, The Complete Idiot's Guide to Starting an Online Business, eMarketing Strategies, Successful Affiliate Marketing for Merchants, TechTV's Starting an Online Business, How To Succeed in Sales Using Today's Technology,* and *Dr. Livingston's Online Shopping Safari Guidebook.* He has written numerous columns on e-business and has appeared on numerous radio and TV shows discussing e-business and the future of e-commerce. He is an assistant professor at Western International University in Phoenix, Arizona and teaches several ground and online courses on e-business. He lives in Paradise Valley, Arizona with his wife and their Scottish sheepdog.

Dedication

To my sister Joan

We Want to Hear from You!

As the reader of this book, *you* are our most important critic and commentator. We value your opinion and want to know what we're doing right, what we could do better, what areas you'd like to see us publish in, and any other words of wisdom you're willing to pass our way.

As an executive editor for Que Publishing, I welcome your comments. You can email or write me directly to let me know what you did or didn't like about this book—as well as what we can do to make our books better.

Please note that I cannot help you with technical problems related to the topic of this book. We do have a User Services group, however, where I will forward specific technical questions related to the book.

When you write, please be sure to include this book's title and author as well as your name, email address, and phone number. I will carefully review your comments and share them with the author and editors who worked on the book.

Email: feedback@quepublishing.com

Mail: Candace Hall
Executive Editor
Que Publishing
800 East 96th Street
Indianapolis, IN 46240 USA

For more information about this book or another Que title, visit our website at www.quepublishing.com. Type the ISBN (excluding hyphens) or the title of a book in the Search field to find the page you're looking for.

Introduction

There's an old saying about businesses. "They don't plan to fail. They fail to plan." That adage is still true today and holds whether you're a seasoned businessperson, aspiring entrepreneur, or the person pitching a new revenue-producing idea for your company. Planning to succeed in today's competitive business world takes preparation and a lot of forethought.

And that's where a business plan comes into play.

When you say *business plan* to most people, they think of a dry tome used to raise lots of money that's packed with market statistics and financial data with mysterious terms like *balance sheet*, *cash flow*, and *profit and loss statements*. It's true that, in most cases, these are necessary parts of most business plans. It's also true that if you're seeking a capital investment for your business, a sound business plan is necessary for approaching funding sources. If you're in need of company resources for an in-house project, then a business plan is necessary for that, too. But that's only half the story.

A business plan is also a planning tool and a road map to success. One that can organize your thoughts, formalize your intentions, and help sell your project. The real power of a business plan is that it forces you to think about the important aspects of your business, whether it's an ongoing operation or a startup.

Writing a business plan is no easy task. Ask anyone who has done it. Even you might have struggled to create a business plan or company strategy for your marketplace. In your quest for guidance and instruction, you probably have seen or read a number of books out today on writing business plans. You might even have contracted the services of a consultant or two. But in the end, the books (long on theory, short on how-to), consultants, and web resources came up short and, at best, left you in a state of confusion. The final product, a working, professional business plan, seemed to elude you.

It takes time and energy and much thought to write an effective, workable business plan. And even though you may have a good idea of what your business enterprise wants to do, the single hardest part about writing a business plan is where to begin. What do you do first? second? third?

That's why this book is for you! It walks you through each step of creating a professional business plan.

Who Should Read This Book

Whatever your situation or whatever your objective, writing a business plan goes a long way in helping you succeed. If you're an entrepreneur looking to start a new business, this book is for you. If you're an existing business in need of a new plan to move your company forward, this book is for you. And if you're a manager or supervisor of a department at your company and need an internal plan to promote and execute a new idea, then this book is for you.

You'll find that no matter what your business goal may be, *Write a Business Plan In No Time* is organized to help you write a plan for it.

How This Book Is Organized

The purpose of this book is plain and simple: *to help you write a business plan in no time.*

Unlike other books of its kind that talk more about business theory or describe what needs to be in a business plan, this book is organized to teach you how to write the correct plan for your business objective; part by part, section by section, and step by step. When you finish this book, you will have a finished plan ready for presentation and/or implementation.

Business plans come in all shapes and sizes and are used for a multitude of purposes and in a variety of businesses. There is no simple formula or one-size-fits-all approach to writing a business plan. But most business plans fall into three major types:

- Startup business plan
- Full business plan
- Internal business plan

What sets this book apart from other business plan how-to guides is that it recognizes these different types of business plans and walks you through the process of writing the type of plan that's right for *your* business.

Remember, the end result of working through this book is having in your hands a completed plan for whatever business objective you had in mind.

How the Information Is Organized

Every journalism student is taught early on the proper way to write a news story. They are told to answer these simple questions in every story they write:

- Who?
- What?
- Where?
- When?
- Why?
- How?

Answering these simple questions (and one other, how much?) is also a way to ensure the business plan you write covers all the necessary and important bases. The parts of this book are organized to help you do just that. In addition, this book teaches you how to summarize and pitch your plan to investors, bankers, and/or management.

Part I, "Get a Plan!," introduces you to the world of business plans. Before you can start the actual writing of your plan, you need to know what a business plan is and why it's necessary to have one. This part also provides you with an understanding of the different types of business plans and how to avoid some common business plan errors—some of which play a role in the major reasons businesses fail. Part I also asks and answers the essential questions of a business plan and discusses the different elements that make up a successful plan.

In Part II, "Who and Why?," you start to write your individual plan. The chapters in this part answer the questions Who is your business? and Why is it a business?—in other words, What human need does it solve? This part helps you introduce your plan, identify the mission and goals for your company, prepare your company overview, explain your product or service, and describe your management team. Each of these chapters ends with a series of questions that prompt you to write the first parts of your business plan.

Part III, "Where and How?," leads you through the process of describing your marketplace, crafting your marketing strategy, listing your distribution channels, describing your competition, and outlining the risks and opportunities of your business. These chapters also end with questions that prompt you to write these parts of your business plan.

Part IV, "When and How Much?," shows you how to create your implementation plan. It also explains and describes what you need to know in order to detail your capital requirements and write your financial plan. As in Parts II and III, questions at the end of each chapter in this part prompt you to write the relevant sections of your business plan.

In Part V, "The Pitch," you learn how to write one of the most important parts of a business plan—the Executive Summary. A series of questions at the end of the Executive Summary chapter walk you through the process of completing this last, important part of your business plan. The book's final chapter helps you create your short *elevator pitch*, and gives you tips on how to present your plan to investors, bankers, and/or management. By elevator pitch, I mean an extremely concise summary of your business idea delivered to a potential funding source. Your pitch should last only a few minutes, or the duration of an elevator ride.

Basic Tools and Special Elements

All the information in this book is important for the formulation of an effective business plan. But certain parts of the text are important enough to bring to your attention. The book does that through the use of a series of special elements, including sidebars, tips, notes, cautions, and graphic icons.

The sidebars in this book offer interesting insights and expanded information related to the chapter topic. In addition to traditional tips, notes, and cautions, you'll also encounter a series of graphic icons unique to *Write a Business Plan In No Time*. These icons are used to draw your attention to text related to recurring themes or important issues you must keep in mind throughout the process of writing your plan.

The ***Plan to Succeed*** icon points out information you need to know in order to cover all of your bases as you write a particular section of your business plan. This icon might mark text advising you to pull together information before you start the section, or it might indicate particularly important advice to help you succeed in writing a good plan.

The ***Errors to Avoid*** icon points out common errors or mistakes people make when writing specific sections of the business plan. Take these warnings to heart. Many of the errors you'll read about have sunk a potentially successful plan.

The ***Budget It*** icon points out items in the text you need to remember when preparing the financial sections of your business plan. This icon gives you a sort of heads up and can help you quickly find the information in the book that helps you take the mystery out of the balance sheet, cash flow, and profit and loss statements you add to your plan.

note   As I mentioned earlier, *Write a Business Plan In No Time* teaches you how to write three different types of business plans. Most of the writing chapters in this book relate directly to a specific section of those plans. Look for special notes in the introductions to these chapters that explain how each type of plan uses the related section, so you'll know how to apply the chapter's topic to your own work.

The *Find It Fast* icon points to additional resources that help you write that section of your business plan. There are all types of informational resources on the World Wide Web that can help you when formulating your business plan. These are referenced in many of the chapter sections.

The *Check It Out* icon marks cross-references to specific examples in the sample business plan and business plan sections located in Appendices A and B of the book. Follow these references to see actual examples of the business plan elements as you learn how to write your own.

How to Use This Book

I wrote this book to make it easy to end up with a completed plan ready for presentation and implementation. Using this book to write your business plan is an easy five step process.

1. **Read** chapters 1 through 3.
2. **Determine** what type of business plan you need to write.
3. **Check** the notes at the beginning of subsequent chapters to determine which parts of the sections discussed in the chapters are relevant to the type of plan you're writing.
4. **Study** the chapters as they relate to your plan.
5. **Answer** the questions at the end of the relevant chapters. Your answers to the questions create your business plan. Answer the questions on a paper pad, index cards, or directly into your word processor as you move through the chapters.

That's it. Follow this quick and easy process and by the end of the book you will have a professional business plan ready for presentation and implementation.

Some Tips Before You Start

Here are a few basic tips to keep in mind even before you start thinking of your plan. These tips are especially useful if you're looking to fund your business plan:

- It pays to take a class or two on running a business. You should have a general knowledge of the different aspects of a business before you sit down to start your plan. There are many fine courses offered by your local community college, seminars offered by non-profit organizations, and small business programs offered by the government. Take advantage of these and spend a little time learning the ins and outs of running a business.
- Check out SCORE, "Counselors to America's Small Business." They provide entrepreneurs with free, confidential, face-to-face, and online business counseling. Counseling and workshops are offered at 389 chapter offices nationwide by experienced business volunteers.

- Line up your credit. If you're looking for someone to finance your business idea or loan you money, you better have your credit rating in good shape. No one is going to loan money to someone who bounces checks or makes late installment payments. Get a copy of your credit report (it's free) and look it over. Make sure there are no bad ratings and if so, get them cleared up. Pay down your debt so your personal financial statement looks solid. Then check your credit cards. Pay those balances down so you can use them as an alternative way to fund your business or in case of emergencies.
- Open a separate business checking account with the name of your business on the checks. Ask your bank about getting a credit card merchant account so you can accept credit cards in your new business. You may be required to provide a deposit to get a merchant account. This is normal for a new business without a track record. So make sure you have the cash for this.
- Polish your résumé. You'll need it for your business plan. If you have others on your management team, make sure their résumés are updated too. Also, include the names of any professional advisors, a law firm, or accounting firm on your résumé. It enhances your credibility and shows investors and bankers you have professional guidance on hand.

Now come with me, your humble guide, and I will lead you step by step through the process of creating an effective and usable professional business plan.

Part 1

Get a Plan!

Business Plan Basics

1

An old friend and colleague of mine had an interesting approach to evaluating a business concept. He would comment, "That's a great idea! But is it a business?" Ideas are a dime a dozen, he would say, but turning those ideas into an executable business is another matter all together. So what's the secret of an idea's success?

Writing a business plan is the best way to discover if your innovative idea that might shake up the business world could be a real business. But if you think writing a business plan, to paraphrase Woody Allen, is like spending an evening with an insurance salesman or watching 2004 presidential election campaign ads, then you're not alone.

All things considered, writing a business plan is a necessary and important process for you to analyze your business idea, your customers, your competition, and your marketplace. It also supplies one other thing—a plan to execute your business idea. So, if your business plan is to just plan to be in business, you might find that approach a recipe for failure. Plan your work—then work your plan.

So, just what is this creature called a business plan? Let's track it down and find out.

To do list

- [ ] Learn the two primary functions of a business plan
- [ ] Learn how to use your business plan

What Is a Business Plan?

You wouldn't think about hiking into the back woods without a map, compass, food, and clothing. If you're Grizzly Adams or one of those mountain men survival types, you can do it, but why make it hard on yourself? The same goes for business. Writing a business plan can make planning and executing your business idea a lot easier.

Pure and simple, a business plan is two things:

1. An organizing tool to simplify and clarify your business goals and strategy.
2. A selling document that sells your business idea and demonstrates that your product or service can make a profit and attract funding and/or company resources.

As an organizing tool, think of a business plan as a navigation chart that guides you to where you want to go and details how to get there. But a business plan is not set in stone. It's a flexible document. Like any journey, there are occasional detours, but a good solid plan helps you avoid costly mistakes that might sink your business before it even starts. A business plan that is complete and well thought out also acts as a touchstone or litmus test against the reality of your business operations once you open its doors. It should be a guidebook for your business that is used along the way, telling you what you should be doing and how well you're doing it.

If used as an internal plan, a business plan can be written to define new business opportunities, manage a company better, or reset its objectives or goals in reaction to a more competitive market environment.

Finally, a business plan acts as a dry run of your business even before it starts. It's actually a written description of your business's future.

As a selling tool, your business plan should sell *you* on your business; sell others on your business; give you confidence that your hard-earned money, or that of your investors or company (in the case of an internal business plan), is well spent; and tell you that your business idea can succeed. A business plan should convince at least one other person of

note If you've created a good solid business plan and your plan tells you your idea will not work and will not make a profit, then trust the plan. Paper is cheaper than cash! Throw away the plan and start over. It's lots cheaper than throwing money at an ineffective business idea.

the value of your business idea. If not, then you should either reconsider your idea or rewrite your plan.

Writing a business plan focuses your thoughts and helps you refine your goals, identify risks, organize your thinking, set priorities, allocate resources, focus on key points, and prepare for problems and opportunities. It also shows those who may fund your business idea—investors, bankers, and management—that your idea is worthy of financial or management support. It also proves you have the skill, talent, and team to execute your business idea.

Finally, a business plan can be used as a device to more effectively communicate with suppliers, advertisers, auditors, business consultants, lawyers, and accounts.

FINDING INFORMATION FOR YOUR BUSINESS PLAN

If you're stumped for information for your business plan, and need to study more background material on your type of business before you begin writing, try these tips.

First, look at magazines that focus on your business. Get a few copies and look for company reviews. Go to the library and research articles written about your business or business idea.

Next, find similar businesses in your area and talk to them. Locate them by using the Yellow Pages. Talk to the owner and find out as much as you can. People love to talk about their business. Then check out the businesses for sale in your area. Find those that are similar to yours. Interview the broker and find out as much about the businesses as you can. Who knows? You might even decide to buy one instead of starting your own. At the very least, you might get access to their financial data—something you need when writing your business plan. And the information you gather provides you with a good idea of how the industry works.

Getting the Most Benefit from Your Business Plan

Many people think business plans are used only to start a new business. That's not true. Yes, business plans are used to raise capital from investors or borrow money from a bank. But business plans have other uses, too. For example, they can be used to improve the operations of existing businesses, propose a new direction for a department or business unit, or reset a company's priorities.

Different business plans can also be written for different audiences. Writing a plan to borrow money from a bank is different from writing a plan to attract investment from venture capitalists. Although, like the investor, the bank manager is interested in management, he primarily is looking to see if your financial assumptions are realistic. For example: Will your cash flow be sufficient enough to make the payments on your loan? Venture capitalists are looking for different things in your plan. Though they too are interested in financial assumptions, they're also concerned with your management team. In real estate, the three biggest criteria are "location, location, and location." For venture capitalists, it's "people, people, and people." The venture capitalist wants to know how experienced the management team is in running a business. Does your team have knowledge of the industry you plan to do business in? Have they started or run successful businesses in the past?

Then again, suppose you're writing a plan for management. You might have an idea to expand the company's current business or have a new product or service idea. The focus of that plan may be more operational than financial.

Briefly, the reasons for writing a business plan include

- Defining a new business venture
- Determining whether your business will make a profit
- Providing an estimate of your startup costs
- Devising an effective marketing strategy
- Helping you compete in the marketplace
- Anticipating potential problems
- Supporting a loan application
- Raising investment funds
- Expanding a current business or product line
- Defining new goals and objectives for an ongoing business
- Measuring your business performance
- Tracking your growth
- Setting a value on a business for sale or for legal purposes

American Express identifies a number of ways to achieve business success, each of which is directly connected to writing a business plan. For example, productivity and success are tied to using your mind's creative process to full capacity. Writing a business plan forces you to think about a business in creative ways that you haven't before. A business plan also forces you to set goals and provides the tools to control the outcome. In short, it translates ideas into actions.

A proper business plan lists your strengths while at the same time preventing you from ignoring your weaknesses. It makes you analyze your competition, build the right team, know your customer, and define your product.

The consequences of not writing a business plan are many. Dun & Bradstreet tells us that some of the many reasons why 80% of new businesses fail within five years are

- Running out of money
- Failure to make accurate financial projections
- Lack of adequate funding
- Poor location
- Poor cash flow

One of the things a good solid business plan does is to take these mistakes into consideration and prepare for them with good financial projections and a realistic sales and distribution strategy.

A good plan that is well thought out reduces the odds of failure and increases the chances of success. Without a business plan, you leave far too many things to chance.

To do list

- ☐ Learn the three types of business plans used by most businesses today
- ☐ Learn the functions and format of each type of plan

Understanding the Three Types of Business Plans

As we've seen in the introduction, business plans come in a variety of flavors. Business plans are as varied as businesses, and there isn't one business plan format or content that covers all occasions. Other types of business plans include strategic plans, investment plans, expansion plans, operational plans, annual plans, internal plans, growth plans, product plans, and feasibility plans, just to name a few.

The type of business plan you write depends on how you will use your plan and your specific situation. A plan's appearance, contents, and length depend upon the emphasis it places on the different parts of your business. For example, if your plan's purpose is to raise money, the management team becomes very important for investors, though your financial history is more important to bankers. If you're developing an internal business plan, you don't need to include a lot of background on company that your intended audience already knows.

A plan's purpose also affects its length. If you're asking for millions of dollars, your plan better be long on detail and full of convincing information and data. On the other hand, if your plan is for internal purposes, such as managing an ongoing business, a shorter version is fine.

Remember, page count is less important than readability. When you're writing your plan, use plenty of helpful graphics. If they apply to your plan, use charts and tables to clarify numbers and data and use photographs and drawings to show locations, products, sample menus, product pictures, and other illustrations.

The key here is to make your plan match its purpose.

Even with all the varied uses of a business plan, they have many things in common, such as business objectives, product and customer descriptions, market analyses, marketing plans, cash flow projections, and pro formas. A *pro forma* is an estimate of how the business will turn out if certain assumptions are achieved. These assumptions, which you create later in your financial plan, are the basis of your financial projections.

Basically, business plans fall into three types.

- The startup business plan
- The full business plan
- The internal business plan

Let's take a closer look at each one.

note Palo Alto Software, whose sample plans are used in this book, runs an annual business plan contest. They usually have several hundred plans enter the competition. Palo Alto has found the finalists have never had fewer than 20 pages or more than 50 pages. Most run 30–40 pages.

Startup Business Plan

Sometimes called the miniplan, the *startup* plan is generally used to define the steps needed to start up a new company. Those types of plans consist of approximately 10 pages and can be a valuable start to a full-length plan later on.

A startup plan is used to quickly test a business concept or measure the interest of an individual investor. It includes a succinct description of a company and its objectives, the product or service being sold, the customer and market niche being served, market strategies, executive team, and financials. The financials include projected sales, profit and loss statements, and cash flow for only the first year, along with an Executive Summary.

Do not use a startup plan as a substitute for a full business plan. Before you send a plan to a venture capitalist firm, make sure you find out if it requires a full plan for review.

The key purpose of a startup plan is to present a summary of the business that provides a brief overview of the mission of the company, its keys to success, and the market and break-even analysis. It's a good tool to see if the idea is a business worth doing (answering the question, "It's a good idea, but is it a business?"), but a startup plan isn't detailed enough to actually run a business.

The Full Business Plan

The *full* business plan is what most people think of when you say "business plan."

These types of plan are sometimes called *working* plans because they are written to actually run a business. Full plans consist of 20–40 pages and, like the startup plan, they include a mission statement, descriptions of the company and its objectives, the product or service being sold, the customer and market niche being served, market strategies, implementation plan, management team, and financials. But the financials are projected out 3–5 years, and the description of the executive team is expanded to include key members of management and staff. Full plans also include a detailed description of the company's sales and distribution channels, a balance sheet, an analysis of competitive threats and risks, and an implementation plan and time line.

This is the type of plan used to raise millions of dollars from investors for your business idea or to borrow large sums of money from a bank. That said, a full plan should look and feel professional. It should be printed on quality paper by a color laser printer. Full plans should also include graphics, such as graphs, tables, and illustrations and must be bound in a durable fashion and easy to read.

The Internal Business Plan

An *internal* plan is written to seek resources from the company itself. Used to plan for growth, a new product, or a business expansion, these plans focus primarily on one part of a business. An internal plan can be used to update a business as well. For example, if your market is changing fast, you might want to update your business plan yearly, semi-yearly, or even monthly.

These plans are for internal use only and can be as short as 20 pages or as long as 40 pages or more. It all depends on the objective of the plan. Internal plans don't include a detailed background of the company or its executive team. Their financial projections are limited to the department or division the plan is written for and may not be as detailed as those in the presentation and standard business plans. Internal plans also include a break-even analysis and cash flow statement, but typically don't have a pro forma or balance sheet that goes out three to five years. The format of these plans is somewhat simple and may use bullet points to cover the main points instead of pages of detailed copy.

No matter how well-established your business, you may have multiple opportunities to write an internal plan. If you're looking for additional funding, investors or bankers might need to see an updated plan. If your firm has developed a new product or is entering a new market niche, an internal plan might be necessary. Or perhaps your business has outgrown its old plan due to success in the marketplace and doesn't reflect reality anymore. That would be a time to write an internal plan.

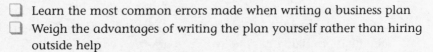

To do list

- ☐ Learn the most common errors made when writing a business plan
- ☐ Weigh the advantages of writing the plan yourself rather than hiring outside help

Avoiding Common Business Plan Errors

No matter which type of business plan you choose, there are a few cardinal rules that apply to all plans. Try to avoid these common errors and your business plan has a better chance of gaining funding and success.

- **Don't look like an amateur**—Create a professional-looking plan. I can't say it enough times. Your business plan represents your business idea—and *you.* Its purpose is to convince investors, bankers, and/or management to fund or support you and your idea. Print your plan on quality paper on a laser printer, with color-coded charts and graphs. Check it for spelling and grammar and make sure your numbers add up. Someone reading your plan who notices unprofessional errors will also wonder if you'll make similar oversights running your business.

- **Don't be a blowhard**—No matter the size of your plan, the reader should be able to get a good feel of your business idea in 15 minutes and read the entire plan in an hour. A business plan is not a doctoral thesis.

- **Don't be dull**—Jazz up your plan. Don't be afraid to add graphs, charts, and illustrations—in color!

- **Don't over- or underestimate your business idea**—Investors can smell a puff job. Tell them the facts and just the facts. Leave out the superlatives about being the best or mindless business jargon. Your idea doesn't have to blow their socks off. Just show you can produce results. Remember, there are very few new ideas. What makes a business a success is in its execution of that idea. Besides, a new idea is much harder to sell than one people are familiar with.

- **Don't be vague**—Tailor your plan to your business objective. One size plan does not fit all. Business plans can be used to start a business or run a business. In other words, keep your objective in mind when writing your plan. Who is your intended audience and why are you writing this plan?

- **Don't avoid the negatives**—Think competitively throughout your plan and *sell*! Anyone reading your plan knows you have competition. You also have risks. State them. Call them out. Too many plans shy away from these because it inserts a negative into the presentation. Show the reader how you will deal with these.

- **Avoid hockey stick financial projections**—Don't be blue sky with your financial projections. Stay conservative so you can defend them. Overestimate your expenses and underestimate your revenue.

Finally, should you consider using a professional to write your plan? Here's the problem with that. Too many people who outsource the writing of their plan don't understand it. They didn't put the necessary time and sweat of thinking about their business into the plan to actually create it. So, when asked by investors, bankers, or management to answer complex questions, they draw a blank. You need to be able to explain every portion of your plan and, if you didn't pull it together yourself, that is difficult to do.

MAJOR REASONS WHY BUSINESSES FAIL

Writing a solid business plan can help your business idea come into fruition. But it doesn't guarantee your business will be a success. The following are some of the common mistakes a business owner makes and should be avoided *after* the business plan is written:

* Many companies fail to anticipate the amount of working capital they'll need to operate their business.
* Many new business owners waste working capital on frivolous expenses. All your working capital should go for one thing—making sales!
* Too often, businesses fail to prepare for management turnover. Key personnel leave a business. Be ready to replace them.
* Businesses that don't pay their taxes on time become a target of the IRS. Pay your taxes first, before you pay any other expenses. The last thing you need is a lien against your business revenue. It's very tempting to save your tax payments and employee withholdings for last. Don't do it.
* Many businesses fail to plan for the highs and lows. Remember that most businesses are seasonal. Have enough cash on hand for the slow months or diversify to keep your doors open and your business humming along.

If you do run into trouble, here are some tips on how to overcome setbacks in your business.

First, keep the names of a good accountant and attorney handy. If you do run into problems, seek help from someone you trust, preferably someone in an industry like yours. Also, don't hide from the problem. Avoid meetings or phone calls with vendors or whomever raises a red flag in their minds and they might interpret it as a problem even more serious than it is. Always keep an upbeat attitude around your employees, no matter what the problems might be. You don't want your best employees to become anxious and start looking for work elsewhere.

Look at the problem. If it has to do with cash flow, look for ways to reduce everyday expenses. Cut back on entertainment and travel expenses. If your cash flow is seriously affected, consider cutting back on nonessential employees, beginning with administrative personnel. Keep those that generate the income for your company.

Most importantly, do everything you can to pay your bills on time. Your credit rating is the lifeblood of your business. If you can't make a payment on time, talk to your vendor and work out a plan to deal with the situation. Be proactive and be prepared to offer a payment plan when you call them. Above all, don't make promises of payment you can't make.

Finally, take a breather to relax and unwind. Take a walk or go to a movie. Then come back with a clear head to tackle the problem.

Summary

In this chapter, you've learned that writing a business plan is a necessary and important process for you to analyze your business idea, your customers, your competition, and your marketplace. It also supplies a plan to execute your business idea. Writing a business plan focuses your thoughts and helps you refine your goals, identify risks, organize your thinking, set priorities, allocate resources, focus on key points, and prepare for problems and opportunities. It also shows those who might fund your business idea—investors, bankers, and management—that your idea is worthy of financial or management support.

You also learned that a business plan is both an organizing tool and a selling document. This chapter outlined several ways that business plans can be used, and it discussed the three types of business plans, their structure, and their purpose.

You also learned some techniques for creating a professional looking plan by jazzing it up with graphs, charts, and illustrations, and by using high-quality printing and binding methods. Finally, this chapter provided a number of tips for writing a good plan, as well as a list of common errors to avoid, including over- or underestimating your business idea. You learned to tailor your plan to your business objective, to think competitively throughout your plan, and to use your plan to *sell*!

As you've learned in this chapter, a good plan that is well thought out reduces the odds of failure and increases the chances of success. Without a business plan, you leave far too many things to chance.

In the next chapter, you'll learn the essential questions to ask when developing a business plan and learn about the elements that make up a business plan.

Understanding the Elements of a Business Plan

There's an old maxim in the computer world called GIGO, which stands for "garbage in, garbage out," and means if you enter bad data into your system, you get faulty results. That goes double for a business plan. The outcome of a business plan depends on what goes into it. A successful implementation of a business idea starts with a solid and well-organized plan.

Simple, focused, realistic, and complete plans are the easiest to implement; such a plan also conveys your business idea, outlines a plan for managing your business, and provides a yardstick for measuring your progress.

Simply put, your plan must clearly communicate who you are, what you do, what your product or service is, what consumer or business need it solves, how you plan to implement your business, what markets you service, and how much money or how many resources you need to execute your plan.

So let's take a look at the essential questions every business plan must answer to help you succeed in your new endeavor. Your business plan must answer these questions whether you're seeking investors, applying for a loan, launching a new

In this chapter:

* Learn the essential questions to ask when developing a business plan
* Learn the elements that make up a business plan

product or business strategy, or just reorganizing your business to compete better in your marketplace.

To do list

- ☐ Learn to identify and describe yourself, your business partners, and your business.
- ☐ Learn to describe what your business sells.
- ☐ Prepare to answer the question "What need does your business fulfill and what problems does it solve?"
- ☐ Understand how to outline your implementation plan.
- ☐ Learn to define your business location and market.
- ☐ Learn to describe your marketing techniques.
- ☐ Plan to answer the question "How much money do you need to get your business started and running?"

Answering the Essential Questions

Much of life is a search for answers to essential questions. A business plan is no different. The introduction to this book listed a set of questions that should be answered by every plan. These questions include Who? What? Why? When? Where? How? and How much? Crafting the best answers to these questions is the foundation of writing a solid and effective business plan and the foundation of launching a successful business.

How you answer these questions is as important as the answers themselves.

Your responses to these questions should be simple, specific, realistic, and complete. They should be easy to understand and act on, with definite objectives in mind that include specific dates, people, and budgets. Your sales, expenses, and implementation targets should be realistic. And above all, your plan should be thorough and complete—include all sections of a business plan that apply to your particular company.

The following sections look at each of the essential questions in detail and describe how you should approach answering these questions within your business plan. If you answer these questions truthfully and objectively, you will end up with a focused, well-researched business plan that should serve as a blueprint that details how your business or venture will be operated, managed, and capitalized.

Who—Who Is Your Business?

To quote the caterpillar in *Alice in Wonderland*, "Who R U?" Anyone who reviews your business plan is looking for answers to the same question—just who are you? In your business plan, you have to clearly describe yourself, your business experience and qualifications, the other chief "players" in your organization, the roles they fill, and their qualifications and experience. For example, if you're going to seek funding for your business idea, investors and bankers surely want to know who they are dealing with. They want to know about your experience, your skills, and your role in the business you chose. In addition, they want to know who supplies the business experience and expertise you might lack and your plans on how to acquire that extra talent.

DO YOU HAVE THE TRAITS OF A SUCCESSFUL ENTREPRENEUR?

You should also know something about yourself. Do you feel you have what it takes to start and run a new business? Are you willing and able to put in the long hours and hard work a new enterprise entails? Are you financially able to survive through the tough startup months? And most important of all, do you have the traits of an entrepreneur?

Business Week lists 10 traits of a successful entrepreneur. Do you have them?

1. You must be willing to take calculated risks.
2. You must move toward the edge and almost step over it.
3. You must truly utilize out-of-the-box thinking and rat-like cunning.
4. You must be ready to lead by example and empower your teammates to make decisions and handle crisis situations.
5. You must have a management style that is flexible and can adapt to changing situations.
6. You must have passion for what you are doing. If you do, then you will spend as much time as is required to be successful.
7. You must learn to come up with new and innovative ideas that produce meaningful and perceptive differences, and you must be able to communicate that idea.
8. You must surround yourself with a great team.
9. You must constantly reinvent your business.
10. You must always be ready to "jumpstart your brain."

The Internet provides many resources that can assist entrepreneurs. A good one is entrepreneur.com. This website is packed with actionable information that helps you start and grow your business.

Finally, what form does your business take? What is the legal structure? Is it a sole proprietorship? A partnership? A corporation?

What—What Does It Sell?

The purpose of a business is to sell something. It may be a product, a service, or information. In any case, your business plan must be able to explain in detail what kind of product or service you plan to sell. You'll answer a number of questions in providing this information. What is your product or service? What makes it unique? How does it compare with your competition? Do they dominate your market niche? If so, can a newcomer break into the market? How do you plan to compete? Do you have a competitive advantage? What is it? Is your product as good as your competition? Better? Why?

Your business plan must also include information that demonstrates you're looking ahead. To provide that information, you'll want to answer a number of other questions, all within this "what" category. For example, what are the plans for the future of your company? Will you add new products or services? Enter compatible markets? Sell internationally? Once you're established in the marketplace, can a new company easily undercut your prices or your earnings with a newer product or service? Do you have a barrier to competition—some unique product or service that prevents other companies from competing successfully with you? For example, you might have a proprietary product only you manufacture or maybe a special relationship with vendors other businesses do not have. If so, that barrier to competition is part of your business, so describe it in your business plan.

Why—Why Is It a Business and What Need Does It Solve?

We've all heard the joke about the dumb salesman trying to sell refrigerators to Eskimos. As it turns out, it's not dumb at all. Refrigerators serve a real purpose in frigidly cold weather. They keep the food from freezing solid. This is an example of finding a need and meeting it. Your product or service must do the same thing. Your business plan must clearly describe the specific need your product or service fulfills or the problem it solves.

To clearly explain how your product meets a consumer need, you first have to identify your target customers and define just what their need might be. To do that, your business plan must answer a series of questions within this major "why" category. Who are you targeting? Consumers? Retailers? Wholesalers? The government? Is your product practical? Does it fill a need? What need?

As you explain precisely what makes your business a viable undertaking, you also need to identify how you are acquiring the things you need in order to produce whatever you're selling. To answer this question, you need to identify your suppliers and back-up suppliers, and—if you're manufacturing your own product—you also must identify the sources for your parts.

When—What Is the Implementation Plan?

As that esteemed professor of philosophy, Yogi Berra, once said, "If you don't know where you are going, you might wind up someplace else."

A business plan does you little good if you don't have a strategy to get your business up and running. An implementation plan lays out your company's objectives, the tasks or actions necessary to reach those objectives, a timescale of events or actions, and a way to monitor your progress. Your business plan must describe your implementation plan to answer this "when" question.

Things to consider when answering this question in your plan are how many months do you anticipate you'll be in operation before your business clears a profit? Do you have a phased plan for development that clearly lists what you wish to accomplish in each phase, a date for accomplishing each phase, and what must take place before each phase happens? What are your major milestones and decision points? What milestones do you want to hit and by when? What actions must you take in order to meet those milestones?

Your implementation plan and that of your *pro forma* (your projected balance sheet and income statement, based on your assumptions of how your business will perform) act as a yardstick to measure how well your plan is being executed. Investors and bankers who are funding your idea with venture capital or loans want to see an implementation plan and look at how well you're hitting your targets. Are your target goals realistic? Does your plan support your belief that the goals are achievable?

Where—Where Is Your Business and What Markets/Customers Will It Service?

Whether there is a market for your product or service is just as important as the product or service itself. The business landscape is littered with companies who thought they had a great product or service idea, brought it to market, and discovered few people were interested in buying it. Market research tells you whether there is a market for your product or service, and then you must use that information to answer this "where" question within your business plan.

Your business plan needs to provide a complete description of your marketplace, then answer a number of questions to demonstrate how your business functions within it. Who will buy your product? What are the demographics of your target market? What is the potential size of your market? How big a piece of the market can you capture? Where do your customers live, work, and shop? What types of online sites do they frequent? You also need to back up your assertions with real data from private, public, or government sources, such as census information, databases, and industry information.

If you've done your research well, you will have a very good idea of the size of your market, the makeup of its consumers, and the important information you need to create your marketing plan.

And finally, you'll need to describe the location and physical facility in which you plan to operate your business. To supply this information, you'll answer another series of questions: Where is your business located? What physical plant is necessary? Office space? Retail space? Warehouse space? A combination of some sort? Are you starting a home-based business? If so, do you have space in your home? Where are you locating it? What about your community's covenants, conditions, and restrictions (CC&R)? What are their conditions and restrictions on what you can use your home for? Do they allow a home business such as yours?

How—How Will You Market Your Business and Your Product or Service?

Marketing your company and what it sells is the cornerstone of a successful marketing plan. A good marketing plan is essential to your business development and success. All is for naught if you can't actually sell the product or service your company offers. To do that, you need to create a demand for what you sell. Demand is created through advertising, publicity, and promotional programs. When you write your business plan, you'll have to answer a number of questions as you describe how you'll market your business.

What are your plans for marketing your business? Are they realistic, based upon your proposed marketing budget? What is your overall marketing strategy? How does your choice of marketing vehicles help you reach your target market? What advertising media do you use? TV? Radio? The Internet? Some combination of them? Do you use direct mailing or telemarketing to reach potential customers? How do you use public relations in your marketing mix? Are trade shows, seminars, and workshops also included in your marketing plan? How do you use them? Where and when?

How well your business plan answers these questions determines the success of both your plan and your company.

How Much—How Much Money Do You Need to Get Your Business Started and Running?

Money and resources are the lifeblood of any business. How much of both do you need to breathe life into your business? Your business plan must include a financials section that outlines what funding your business requires for start up and operations. Your financials section must also identify the sources for those funds.

As you write the financials section, you'll provide a series of answers, all of which relate to the essential question "How much?" What is your source of funds and/or resources? Do you need financing? What kind? Equity? Debt? A combination of both? How much does your business need to reach break-even? How much money do you need to meet your sales and revenue projections? If your business is a startup, how do you compensate yourself? What are the personal resources you contribute to the business? If you're seeking a loan from a bank, your friendly banker wants to know what kind of financial risk you're personally taking.

You'll also need to describe the resources and their expenses that you must gather for your business. Who do you need to hire and how much do they cost? What technical resources do you need? Where do you buy them? How much do they cost? Do you need some special business insurance? What is it? What does it cost?

You'll answer all of these questions and more as you write your plan. If you answer them truthfully and objectively, you end up with a focused, well-thought-out business plan that details how your business venture will be operated, managed, and capitalized.

To do list

- ☐ Learn the functions of each element of a full business plan
- ☐ Understand how the elements are organized within the plan

Pulling It Together—The Business Plan Elements

As you've seen, a successful business plan must answer some essential questions; the answers to these questions are typically organized in parts that make up the elements of your business plan. Here are the basic elements that make up a business plan:

- Executive Summary
- Company mission and objectives
- An overview of the company
- A description of the company's product or service
- The management team
- The marketplace
- Marketing strategy
- Competition
- Risks of your business
- Implementation plan
- Capital requirements
- Financial plan
- Any supporting exhibits

Your plan may or may not include all of these parts, depending upon which of the three types of business plan you're writing. The following sections look at these elements in more detail and discuss how you'll organize them in your plan.

Understanding How the Elements Work Within Your Plan

Each part of your business plan serves a specific purpose. The *Executive Summary* is probably the most important section of your plan. Why? Because it is a short summary of all the most important parts of your business plan that's meant to sell your idea to the reader. If you can grab their interest, then they are more likely to read the details of your plan.

But remember, an Executive Summary is just that—a *summary*, not a foreword. In effect, it's your entire plan in a nutshell. Since it is a summary, you have to wait until you've written all the parts of your business plan before you write the Executive Summary. It's the first thing read but the last thing written.

The sections of your plan that deal with your company itself are the Company Mission and Objectives, Company Overview, and Management Team sections. The *Company Mission and Objective* section details your company mission and vision statements. It describes what your business does and why. It also lays out a vision of your company and where you want it to be in the future. The *Company Overview* section provides a description of your company—if it's a startup or existing company, the legal form, and the like—and its goals and objectives. The *Management Team* section lists the key personnel—executives and/or key management and staff—that you propose to use to manage and operate your company.

The focus of what you intend to sell and how you will sell it is in the *Product or Service Description* section of your plan. Here you not only describe what you intend to sell but also what human needs it fulfills. In other words, this section describes your product and service in detail and explains your unique selling position. Hand in hand with your product or service description is an analysis of the *marketplace* you sell within and the *marketing strategy* you use to market your product or service. Finally, the *Distribution Channels* section explains the distribution or sales channels you use to sell your product.

A Pollyanna approach to a business plan does not garner very much interest or support. Yes, there are opportunities now and in the future that will help your business succeed. But to ignore the risks is to invite disaster. There are companies in your marketplace that will compete with your business. Every business faces risks from them and those of the everyday operations of a company. The *Competition* and *Risks and Opportunities* sections of your business plan list and deal with these.

A business plan is not only a selling document but a planning one too. It represents a roadmap your company plans to follow to implement your business idea. That's the purpose of the *implementation plan*. This plan describes step-by-step how you plan to carry out your business plan.

The last few sections of your business plan deal with money and resources. It lists the *capital requirements* you need to launch and operate your company to reach the break-even point. Your *financial plan* provides a pro forma—or assumption—of revenue and expenses, and profits and loss.

Finally, you might include *supporting exhibits* in your plan. This might include your company or competitor's brochures, proposed advertising and promotion materials, industry studies, maps and photos of locations, magazine or other articles, lists of equipment owned or to be purchased, copies of leases and contracts, letters of support from future customers, and other materials that support the assumptions of your plan. This section also includes the résumés of your management team, the board of directors, and your advisors.

Organizing Elements Within the Plan

"Parts is parts," the saying goes. Not so when writing a business plan. The structure of a business plan is not random. It has a logical progression of thought. The marketing plan comes after the information that describes your product or service, but before your implementation and financial information. As for the other parts, the order they appear in your plan depends upon the best way you feel you can communicate and sell your business concept.

Certain parts of the full business plan may not apply to your business. Remember, there are three basic types of plans (the startup business plan, the full business plan, and the internal business plan), and the startup and internal plan types don't require all of the sections included in a full business plan. When you write your plan, you'll use the sections of the full business plan that apply only to your business venture.

For instance, if you're going to sell directly to the public as a retailer, then your plan needs to detail where and how you purchase your products but your distribution or sales strategy is pretty basic. On the other hand, if you're manufacturing a product to sell, then your plan needs to thoroughly describe your distribution strategy.

But all plans should answer two basic questions:

1. Is this a product or service people will buy?
2. Are you the right person to make your idea success?

Organizing your plan in a way that logically and thoroughly answers these questions determines how successful your plan is in garnering resources and support.

The chapters that follow walk you through the process of writing these business plan elements. Depending upon the type of business you propose, your responses to the questions at the end of the chapters can range from "not applicable" to a single sentence to a page or more. When you finish answering each of these chapter's questions, you'll have written all of the essential elements for a successful business plan.

Summary

What comes out of a business plan depends on what goes into it. A successful implementation of a business idea starts with a solid and well-organized plan.

Questions that should be answered by every plan include Who? What? Why? When? Where? How? and How much? Your response to these questions should be simple, specific, realistic, and complete.

The structure of a business plan is not random. It has a logical progression of thought. Certain parts of the standard business plan might not apply to your business. But all plans should answer two basic questions: "Is this a product or service that people will buy?" and "Are you the right person to make your idea a success?" Organizing your plan in a way that answers these questions determines how successful your plan is in garnering resources and support.

Now it's time to write your plan. The next chapter will help you answer the questions of Who? and Why? It will lead you through the process of formatting your plan and identifying your company's mission and goals.

Part II

Who and Why?

Getting Started: Introducing Your Plan and Identifying Your Mission and Goals

Now that you have the basics of a business plan under your belt, it's time to write your plan. We begin, where else, at the beginning. And the beginning is where you determine the basic format of your plan.

In Chapter 1, "Business Plan Basics," we spoke about the mechanics of formatting a business plan and how to create a professional-looking business proposal that captures attention and mirrors the credibility of your business concept. We spoke about the importance of using quality paper and printing, checking your spelling and grammar, and making certain the numbers in your financials add up. All of these factors play a role in your plan's format. But the type of formatting discussed in this chapter is different.

In this chapter you learn about creating a basic business plan format. You can also look at the sample business plan from Palo Alto Software in Appendix A, "Sample Business Plan," for a formatting example.

You might think the requirements of a title page, Table of Contents, and investment disclaimers; the treatment of graphics; and the inclusion of supporting documents are mere afterthoughts. In fact, these elements of a business plan are important and should not be taken lightly. They all contain important information for the reader and add to the success of your plan.

As I've noted in previous chapters, each of the three types of business plans uses its own combination of standard plan elements. Here's how the elements described in this chapter relate to each of the three plan types:

- All three plan types include a title page, Table of Contents, supporting documents, company or division mission statement, and objectives.
- The internal plan would not include an investment disclaimer or confidentiality agreement.

To do list

- ☐ Learn how to lay out and prepare your plan's title page
- ☐ Learn to write a Table of Contents
- ☐ Understand the important role of graphics in your plan
- ☐ Learn why your plan needs an investment disclaimer
- ☐ Determine what supporting documents you might need for your plan

Formatting the Plan

Every plan, no matter its type, has a title page and a Table of Contents page. The amount of information on these pages varies depending upon what you need to say about your company and the contents of the plan itself. Your plan should also include graphics and the type and formatting of these should be considered in each part of your plan.

Another part of a typical business plan format is the *disclaimers* and *supporting documents*. Your plan may or may not include these elements, depending upon the type of plan you are writing, whether you're looking for investments, and how much supporting documentation is needed to support your business concept.

Writing the Title Page

Every good book deserves a good title page and so does your business plan.

In general, the *title page* of your business plan should include information that identifies you and your proposed business. It's amazing how many business plans lack this critical element.

So what goes on a title page? It should contain these elements:

note The legal designation of your company is its legal structure, such as a sole proprietorship, partnership, or corporation. Chapter 4, "Preparing Your Company Overview," describes these designations or structures and their implications and helps you choose the one that's right for your company.

- The full name of your company including its legal designation
- The address of your business
- Your name, phone number, and website and email addresses
- The month and year in which the plan is issued
- A space for a control number or copy number of the plan

The last element of this list is important. Every plan you hand out should have a unique *control* or *copy number* on it (like BP001, BP002) to track the plan and inhibit people from copying it. Keep a simple distribution list of who has a copy of your plan and when you gave it to them along with the control number.

Here's an example of the contents of a title page (this information should be centered on the page:

Socks R Us, LLC

March 2005

Jim Andrews

29 Easy Money Lane

Any Town, USA 11111

602-555-1212

jandrews@yahoo.com

http://socksRus.com

Plan # BP027

Here are some other elements you might consider using on your title page, depending upon your circumstances:

- Trade names or doing business as (DBAs)
- A company logo
- The names, titles, addresses, and phone numbers of the other principals of the company or partners in your plan.

An informative title page is the first step to creating a useable and understandable business plan.

Creating a Table of Contents

The *Table of Contents* presents a listing of all major parts, sections, and subsections of your plan. A good Table of Contents includes all headings and subheadings within your plan, along with the page numbers of each.

Look at the Table of Contents in Appendix A as an example. It provides a quick overview of what your plan covers for the reader. It not only lists the plan sections but also lists the appendixes, addendums, and supporting documents you have in your plan.

A good Table of Contents helps the readers easily navigate your business plan to find the information they need. Your readers use the Table of Contents to find sections and, with the aid of cross-references within the plan, to find specific pieces of information within sections.

For example, suppose you're describing the use of a certain marketing vehicle, such as buying ads in a trade magazine. You want to support the expense of this marketing tactic by showing the reader the size of the market it will reach. To do this, you may point the reader's attention to a graph on a page of your Market Analysis section that shows the market segment you'll reach. Your reader can find this information by referring to your plan's detailed Table of Contents with page numbers.

Don't make the mistake that some plan writers make by leaving out the page numbers in your Table of Contents.

Using Graphics

The use of *graphics*—including tables, charts, pictures, and other visuals—is an effective means of driving home important points within your plan. For example, your title page could have your company logo, a photo of your present facility, or an artist's rendering of a future facility.

You can use pie charts to show present and projected share of market versus that of your competitors (as explained in Chapter 7, "Describing Your Marketplace"), or depict the demographics of your market and customer segment (see Chapter 8, "Crafting Your Marketing Strategy"). Your plan might include an organizational chart (see Chapter 6, "Presenting Your Organizational Structure and Management Team"), designating areas of responsibilities within your business and the chain of command. Photos and drawings of products in the product and services section of your plan may also help a reader visualize what you sell—especially if your product is new or unique.

You might include copies of renderings of potential ad copy in the marketing strategies section, and if you're manufacturing a product, you might show a layout of your manufacturing facility in the products and services section of your plan. And of course, graphics and charts depicting the numbers in your Financial Plan section is always a plus. As we proceed through the writing of your plan, I will point out where you might want to include graphics, tables, charts, pictures, and other visuals to support and clarify your facts and figures.

INSERTING GRAPHICS AND CHARTS

Many business plans need pictures or charts to better show or explain a product or visibly depict a business concept. You can create charts using a variety of software programs on the market today. Images of products can be found on the Web and copied and saved on your computer for insertion into your business plan document. If you manufacture your own product, use a digital camera to take a picture of the product, save the picture on your computer, and then insert it into your document.

A good place to learn how to insert images into a MS Word document can be found at office.microsoft.com/en-us/assistance/HP051898661033.aspx and www.clipsahoy.com/howto.htm

Stating Disclaimers

If the purpose of your plan is to raise money from private investors, a *disclaimer and confidentiality statement* should be included in your plan.

The disclaimer and confidentiality statement should appear after your title page and before your Table of Contents page. Its purpose is two fold. First, in its role as a disclaimer, this section alerts the reader that your business plan is not an offer to sell securities.

Second, a disclaimer and confidentiality statement also alerts the reader that information contained within the plan is confidential and is intended only for the person to whom it is delivered. This means the plan cannot be copied or reproduced.

Here is an example of a disclaimer and confidentiality statement:

This business plan is neither an offer to sell securities nor a solicitation of an offer to buy securities.

XYZ Company, Inc. has supplied the contents of this confidential private business plan including all pro forma financial data. No person is authorized in connection with any

caution

You cannot ask an investor to read your plan and, on that basis, write a check to you. That is illegal under the rules and regulations of the Securities and Exchanges Commission (SEC). If a potential investor is interested in funding your enterprise, you must work through a corporation lawyer to draw up the proper paperwork for investors to sign before you can collect any investment funds. The disclaimer within this section of the business plan clearly states that your plan is written in compliance with this SEC regulation.

offering made hereby to give or make any representations other than as contained in this confidential private business plan. All representations as to future prospects and earnings are based on certain forward-looking assumptions.

The information contained in this business plan is confidential and is intended only for the person to whom it is delivered by XYZ Company, Inc. Any reproduction of its contents in whole or in part without prior written consent of XYZ Company, Inc. is prohibited.

Another sample of a disclaimer and confidentiality statement can be found in the business plan in Appendix A.

Although the disclaimer and confidentiality statement is not a legal document (you should use a nondisclosure agreement or NDA for that), it does state upfront what the use of the business plan is and could keep you out of trouble with the SEC.

NONDISCLOSURE AGREEMENTS

If you're using your plan to seek investment capital or even to borrow money from a bank, it would be prudent to have each recipient sign a *nondisclosure agreement* or NDA. An NDA, or *confidentiality agreement*, is actually a contract between you and the recipient of your plan. Its purpose is to protect the confidentiality of the information in your plan. If you make a nondisclosure agreement with a recipient who then uses or makes public the contents of your plan without authorization, you can request a court to stop the violator from making any further disclosures and you can sue for damages.

According to Nolo Press (nolo.com), there are five important elements in a nondisclosure agreement:

1. Definition of confidential information.

2. Exclusions from confidential information. For example, if another company develops an invention with similar trade secret information before being exposed to the disclosing party's secrets, that company is still free to use its independently created invention.

3. Obligations of the receiving party. Under most state laws, the receiving party cannot breach the confidential relationship, induce others to breach it, or induce others to acquire the secret by improper means.

4. Time periods the NDA is in force.

5. Miscellaneous terms.

Miscellaneous terms (sometimes known as *boilerplate*) are included at the end of every agreement. They include such matters as which state's law applies in the event the agreement is breached and whether arbitration is used in the event of a dispute or attorney fees are awarded to the prevailing party in a dispute.

You can buy an NDA from Nolo's website (nolo.com) or download a free sample NDA from www.bitlaw.com/forms/nda.html.

Including Supporting Documents

Most business plans have an *Appendix*. Among other things, this is where you include any and all documents that are needed for the operation of your proposed or established business. You also include all documents and materials that you feel support your business concept and its execution.

Examples of these documents might include

- **Résumés of executives, key management, board of directors, and/or board of advisors**—All résumés should be limited to one page and include work history, educational background, professional affiliations, honors, and special skills.
- **Legal documents**—Include documents associated with the legal structure, licenses, proprietary rights, insurance, and so on.
- **Schedule of employee staffing**—Lists your personnel requirements. These personnel numbers should correspond with your estimates of payroll expenses on your projected financial statements.
- **Lease or purchase agreements**—Copy of proposed lease or purchase agreement for facilities.
- **Letters and testimonials**—Copies of letters of intent from suppliers, letters of support from future customers, and, if appropriate, customer testimonials.
- **Brochures and ad copy**—Sample brochures, dummy advertisements, announcements, or other promotional literature.
- **Literature**—Industry studies, and news, magazine, or other articles.
- **Equipment**—Lists of equipment owned or to be purchased.
- **Visuals**—Blueprints, plans, maps, and photos of business locations.

As you can see, many types of supporting documents and materials can be included in your plan. Take some time to think through the material you should include and which would best support you and your plan.

To do list

- ☐ Learn how to write a mission statement
- ☐ Learn how to create company objectives

Defining Your Mission Statement and Company Objectives

Business plans should tell your reader how to get from here to there, and you provide that information by outlining your short- and long-term business objectives.

But before you do that, you need to create your company mission statement. Your *mission statement* clearly states what your company stands for and what it intends to achieve. After all, how can you write a plan for your new business if you don't know what your business is and where you want it to go? Defining your mission and its objectives achieves this purpose.

So, let's look at the mission statement first.

Defining Your Company Mission

Abraham Lincoln once said to a friend that if he had more time, he would have written a shorter letter. Lincoln had the luxury of rambling in his letters to friends, but you can't do that in your company mission statement. Your mission statement must announce clearly and succinctly what you're in business to do—in just a few sentences. And, as Lincoln indicated, that's difficult to do. How, you ask, can you distill everything your company will do into 50 or fewer words?

A good and useable company mission statement needs to answer these three important questions:

- What does your company do?
- What customers does it serve?
- What makes you different from your competition?

A good example of a mission statement is McDonald's. "McDonald's vision is to be the world's best quick service restaurant experience. Being the best means providing outstanding quality, service, cleanliness, and value, so that we make every customer in every restaurant smile."

To better understand exactly what makes up a great mission statement, let's begin by looking at some examples of some famous company mission statements of the past:

- Ford Motor Company (early 1900s)—"Ford will democratize the automobile."
- Boeing (1950)—"Become the dominant player in commercial aircraft and bring the world into the jet age."
- Sony (1950s)—"Become the company most known for changing the world-wide poor-quality image of Japanese products."
- Wal-Mart (1990)—"Become a $125 billion company by the year 2000."

The authors of the above statements did a pretty good job of defining the goals of the company at the time, but they didn't really craft mission statements that would be successful in a business plan today.

Does Ford's early mission statement, "Ford will democratize the automobile," answer the question "What does Ford do?" Maybe. It did democratize the automobile, in that it made the automobile easy to own for most of the population at that time. But did Ford's mission statement define the customers it served and differentiate Ford from its competition? No, it doesn't.

A better mission statement for Ford at that time which answers all three of our questions might look something like this:

"Ford will democratize automobile ownership by making automobiles available at affordable prices unmatched in today's marketplace."

Let's look at Wal-Mart's mission statement. "Become a $125 billion company by the year 2000." Does it answer the question of what it does? No. It states only what it wants to become. Ditto on the questions of defining its target customers and differentiating itself from its competitors. We might change its mission statement to read something like this:

"Wal-Mart will offer a wide selection of quality merchandise to the price-conscience consumer at prices lower than those of its competitors."

Be careful not to regurgitate a description of your business with your mission statement. That's not its purpose. For example, let's take McDonald's. Look at its mission statement. If it just said the company is a restaurant that sells burgers and fries, that would be a description of the business, not a mission statement.

Finally, if you don't believe it, don't include it in your mission statement. Don't lie or claim to be something you're not.

Here are some more examples of good mission statements:

- J. Sainsbury: "Our mission is to be the consumer's first choice for food, delivering products of outstanding quality and great service at a competitive cost through working faster, simpler, and together."
- Big Binoculars: "Our mission is simply to offer our customers the most binocular aperture, at the highest quality, for the lowest price."
- The United Nations High Commissioner for Human Rights (OHCHR): "The mission of the Office of the United Nations High Commissioner for Human Rights (OHCHR) is to protect and promote all human rights for all."

> **tip**
> A well-thought-out and executed mission statement also serves another purpose. It's an excellent way to focus your attention on the priorities of your business. Your mission statement also clearly sets forth the guiding principle through which your company will function. Small companies, large companies, and even divisions within companies all need a mission statement when embarking on a new endeavor.

Defining Your Company Objectives

The second word in *business plan* is *plan*. But unless you know where you want to go, it's not really possible to plan at all. That's the purpose of the *Company Objectives* section of your plan. This section of your plan should take your company mission to the next step, by clearly stating where you want your company to be in the near term and in the future in terms of sales or revenue, additional markets, new products or services, or maybe expansion of the geographical territory its serves.

Writing this section is both an exercise of thinking about your short, intermediate, and long-term objectives of your company, and a way for the reader to see a broad overview of how you will get there.

Don't try to mimic your implementation plan when defining your company's objectives. The implementation plan for your business is much more detailed—including times and dates, an action plan of tasks to accomplish, who is supposed to accomplish the tasks, and when they'll be completed—than your company objectives.

Look at your objectives as your business intentions—where you would like to see your company's size, success, and marketplace position two, three, and five years down the road. Keep in mind that you want to make your objectives broad enough so as not to restrict the flexibility of your business plan. Start by looking five years into the future.

When determining your company objectives, ask yourself, "What will the company or business look like? What will it be doing? What will I need to do first, second, and third?"

Here's an example from one of my business plans. It was a proposal to create a premier home concierge service that would grow into a concierge service for business executives and their employees. The company's initial objective was to be a concierge service only to the home. The plan was to offer home owners a one-stop shop for purchasing any and all services for the home, including landscaping, pool cleaning, roof inspection, pet sitting, and so on. After that objective was reached, the service would leverage the business systems which were in place and expand into the business marketplace by offering concierge services first to company executives. After that second objective was reached, the company would offer its concierge services to all employees at its business customer locations, finally becoming a full-service concierge service meeting any and all needs of its customers.

In the Company Objectives section of the business plan, I explained these objectives and stated that they would be accomplished over a five-year period; I also stated that their phases of development were described in the Implementation Plan section of the business plan.

Like your mission statement, determining your business objectives up front helps you focus your attention on the future of your business and what you want it to become.

Write the Plan!

OK. Let's get started! Find the appropriate section below, then answer the questions in that section to write the elements of your business plan we've discussed in this chapter. Each of the three sections below applies to one of the three business plan types—startup, full, or internal plan.

Startup Business Plan

Answer these questions to write the title page of a startup business plan:

1. What is the full name of your company, including its legal designation?
2. Is it a sole proprietorship, partnership, limited liability corporation (LLC), or full corporation (subchapter S, C corporation)?
3. What are the name and address of your business?
4. What are your name, phone number, and website and email addresses?
5. What are the month and year in which the plan is issued?
6. Is there a place for a control number or copy number of the plan?
7. Are there any trade names or DBAs being used?
8. Are you including a company logo?
9. What are the names, titles, addresses, and phone numbers of other principals of the company or partners in your plan?

Answer these questions to write the investment disclaimer and confidentiality statement of your plan:

1. What information is considered confidential in your plan?
2. What are the exclusions from confidential information, if any?
3. What are the obligations of a receiving party?

Answer these questions to pull together your supporting documents:

1. Do you have one-page résumés for the key members of management, board of directors, or board of advisors?
2. Do you have any letters and testimonials from suppliers, letters of support from future customers, and, if appropriate, customer testimonials?
3. Do you have any industry studies and news, magazine or other articles that provide supporting information about your company's product, service, marketplace, or growth trends?

Answer these questions to construct your company's mission statement:

1. What does your company do?
2. What customers does it serve?
3. What makes you different from your competition?

Answer these questions to write your company objectives:

1. What are your company business objectives?
2. What will your company or business be in the future? What will it be doing? How will it be accomplishing its goals differently than now?
3. What will you need to do first, second, and third to get there? What are your goals for the year after that, in terms of sales or revenue, additional markets, new products or services, expansion of the geographical territory it serves, and so on?

4. Can you make a prediction of the share of the market, sales volume, and so forth that you might have at the end of the first year? Can you project those changes through the second, third, and even fifth year of your business?

5. What are your plans for geographic expansion? How will you grow locally, nationally, and/or globally?

6. Is your business going to remain independent and privately owned, or will it eventually be acquired or go public?

7. Will you use a graphic representation to show present and projected share of market, sales, and the like?

Full Business Plan

Answer these questions to write the title page of a full business plan:

1. What is the full name of your company, including its legal designation?

2. Is it a sole proprietorship, partnership, limited liability corporation (LLC), or full corporation (subchapter S, C corporation)?

3. What are the name and address of your business?

4. What are your name, phone number, and website and email addresses?

5. What are the month and year in which the plan is issued?

6. Is there a place for a control number or copy number of the plan?

7. Are there any trade names or DBAs being used?

8. Are you including a company logo?

9. What are the names, titles, addresses, and phone numbers of other principals of the company or partners in your plan?

Answer these questions to write the investment disclaimer and confidentiality statement of your plan:

1. What information is considered confidential in your plan?

2. What are the exclusions from confidential information, if any?

3. What are the obligations of a receiving party?

Answer these questions to pull together your supporting documents:

1. Do you have one-page résumés for the key members of management, board of directors, or board of advisors?

2. What are your legal documents, such as licenses, proprietary rights, and business insurance, that support your legal structure?

3. What are your personnel requirements?

4. What are your lease or purchase agreements?

5. Do you have any letters and testimonials from suppliers, letters of support from future customers, and, if appropriate, customer testimonials?

6. Do you have any brochures, ad copy, or other promotional literature?

7. Do you have any industry studies and news, magazine, or other articles that provide supporting information about your business, its marketplace, or projected growth trends?

8. What equipment will you need? Do you have a list of equipment owned or to be purchased?

9. Do you have any blueprints, plans, maps, and photos of business locations?

Answer these questions to construct your company's mission statement:

1. What does your company do?

2. What customers does it serve?

3. What makes you different from your competition?

Answer these questions to write your company objectives:

1. What are your company business objectives?

2. What will your company or business be like in the future? What will it be doing? How will it be accomplishing its goals differently than now?

3. What will you need to do first, second, and third to get there? What are your goals in terms of sales or revenue, additional markets, new products or services, expansion of the geographical territory its serves, and so on?

4. Can you make a prediction of the share of the market, sales volume, and so forth that you might have at the end of the first year? Can you project those changes through the second, third, and even fifth year of your business?

5. What are your plans for geographic expansion? How will you grow locally, nationally, and/or globally?

6. Is your business going to remain independent and privately owned, or will it eventually be acquired or go public?

7. Will you use a graphic representation to show present and projected share of market, sales, and the like?

Internal Business Plan

Answer these questions to write the title page of an internal business plan:

1. What is the full name of your division or department?

2. What are your name, phone number, and website and email addresses?

3. What are the month and year in which the plan is issued?

4. Is there a place for a control number or copy number of the plan?

5. Are there any trade names or DBAs being used?

6. Are you including a company logo?

Answer these questions to pull together your supporting documents:

1. Do you have one-page résumés for the key people involved?

2. What are your personnel requirements?

3. What are your lease or purchase agreements?
4. Do you have any letters and testimonials from suppliers, letters of support from future customers, and, if appropriate, customer testimonials?
5. Do you have any brochures, ad copy, or other promotional literature?
6. Do you have any industry studies and news, magazine, or other articles?
7. What equipment will you need? Do you have a list of equipment owned or to be purchased?
8. Do you have any blueprints, plans, maps, and photos of business locations?

Answer these questions to construct your mission statement:

1. What will your new division or department do?
2. What customers does it serve?
3. What makes you different from your competition?

Answer these questions to write your company objectives:

1. What are your division or department objectives?
2. What will your division or department be like in the future? What will it be doing? How will it be accomplishing its goals differently than now?
3. What will you need to do first, second, and third to get there? What are your goals in terms of sales or revenue, additional markets, new products or services, expansion of the geographical territory its serves, and so on?
4. Can you make a prediction of the share of the market, sales volume, and so forth that you might have at the end of the first year? Can you project those changes through the second, third, and even fifth year of your new department or internal venture's operation?
5. What are your plans for geographic expansion locally, nationally, and/or globally?
6. Will you use a graphic representation to show present and projected share of market, sales, and the like?

Summary

The inclusion of the title page, Table of Contents, and investment disclaimers; the treatment of graphics; and supplying supporting documents are not mere afterthoughts. These elements of a business plan are important and should never be taken lightly. Every plan you hand out should have a unique control or copy number on it to track the plan's distribution and inhibit people from copying it.

The Table of Contents lists the sections of your business plan, its major headings and subheadings, and their page numbers. The use of graphics, tables, charts, pictures, and other visuals are very effective in driving home your points.

If the purpose of your plan is to raise money from private investors, you should include a disclaimer and confidentiality statement in your plan. You might also need a nondisclosure agreement as a legal contract if you are seeking investment capital. You should also include all documents and materials that you feel support your business concept and its execution.

Your company mission statement and business objectives describe what your company stands for, what you believe in, and what you intend to achieve. A company's mission needs to answer three important questions: What does your company do? What customers does it serve? What makes you different from your competition? Your business objectives should take your company mission to the next step. It describes where you want the company to go in the near term and in the future in terms of sales or revenue, additional markets, new products or services, expansion of the geographical territory its serves, and so on.

The next chapter will explain how to prepare your company overview, its present situation, the company history, its strategic alliances, and how to identify potential funding sources.

Preparing Your Company Overview

4

In this chapter:

* Learn how to describe your company identity and current situation

* Learn how to identify funding sources and strategic alliances

* Learn how to identify and describe regulatory and legal issues affecting your business

* Write the company or division overview for your business plan

A business plan should provide the reader with a description of the company that plans to do the business. Too many plan writers confuse the company description with the business description. The *company description* describes what the company is and the *business description* details what the company does. You learn how to write the business description in Chapter 5, "Describing Your Product or Service."

Whether you're writing a business plan for a new or existing company, you should include a section that provides a company description and background. You also need to include this section in an internal business plan and use it to describe the division or department's role and responsibilities.

note All plan types include a company or division description, company history and/or present situation, regulatory and legal issues, potential funding sources, and strategic alliances.

So let's look at what goes into the company description section of your business plan.

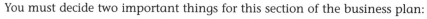

To do list

- ☐ Learn how to choose a legal form for your business
- ☐ Learn how to describe your business type
- ☐ Learn how to describe your company or division's history and present situation
- ☐ Learn how to identify regulatory and legal issues

Identifying Your Company

A business plan must provide basic information about a company or division that includes its name, the date it started, the legal form of organization, the type of business, and its location. If your company is an existing one, then a short history of your company or division is appropriate here.

You can see a sample of a company description in Appendix A, "Sample Business Plan." Included in the Company Overview section are examples of information about company ownership, history, location, and facilities.

Begin this section by listing the name of your company, the date it started, and its physical location. If this is a startup plan and the company doesn't exist yet, you can project a future date of operation that anticipates a startup after the business is funded or leave the startup date out. Next, describe the legal status of your company and the type of business you are in.

Here is an example of the first paragraph of an existing company description:

XYZ Company, founded in 1998, is a sole proprietorship located at 123 Main Street, Anytown, USA, that sells Hungarian fast food to the public.

If your company is a startup that is not yet established, your company description might read like this:

ABC Inc. is a C corporation that will sell customized billing software to medical offices and plans to commence operations after funding is established.

You must decide two important things for this section of the business plan:

1. The legal form of your company
2. The type of business you are in

Things You'll Need

- ☐ Current or proposed address of your company
- ☐ Access to advice and information on legal business entities
- ☐ Copies of your business license, if applicable

- ❑ Copies of a partnership agreement, if applicable
- ❑ Listing of important company milestones and successes (for existing businesses)
- ❑ Results of any tests or surveys of your business idea
- ❑ List of current business assets (where applicable)
- ❑ List of all regulations applicable to your business product, operation, or location

Choosing the Legal Form of Your Company

The legal structure of your company can take the form of three basic entities: The first is a sole proprietorship, the second is a partnership, and the third is some type of corporate identity. If you are a part of a larger company, you state what division or department you are and the relationship it has to the total company. If you're starting your own business, it pays to study these legal entities and look at the advantages and disadvantages of each.

Keep in mind that the choice of your company type does have tax consequences. So choose the one that best fits your personal situation.

If you're starting and running a business all by yourself, the simplest legal structure is the *sole proprietorship*. A sole proprietorship can also be referred to as *doing business as* (DBA). For example, a sole proprietorship could be called "John Doe, doing business as A-1 Résumé Writing Service."

The advantage of establishing a sole proprietorship is that it's cheap and relatively uncomplicated. No papers to sign or file with the government. Unless you incorporate your company, you create a sole proprietorship just by being in business.

As a sole proprietor, you and your business are legally inseparable. That means two things. Sole proprietors pay taxes on business income on their personal tax returns, and you are personally liable for what your business does—or doesn't do. If your business is sued for whatever reason (your employee strikes a pedestrian while delivering your flowers from your flower shop or you can't pay your suppliers for the flowers you bought), your personal assets—your savings, your house, your car—are not protected and are at risk in a suit.

Here's another thing to keep in mind. You personally pay all taxes on business income in the year the business earned it. That means whether you take the earnings out of the business or not, you are personally taxed on the income. Of course, you can deduct your business expenses

tip Since you are personally liable for what happens to your company if you are a sole proprietorship or partnership, you should consider liability insurance. In addition, both entities need a *succession plan*—a plan that describes what happens to the business if the sole proprietor dies or becomes incapable of running the business. In the case of the partnership, the succession plan should outline what happens if one of the partners dies, wants out of the business, or otherwise ceases her involvement.

on your personal tax returns. And if you're a sole proprietorship, you should include copies of your business license in the Supporting Documents section of your plan.

If you have a partner in your new business but don't want to incorporate, then the *partnership* form of business is the way to go. The advantage here is that it's simpler and less expensive to establish then setting up a corporation. You and your partner or partners still retain personal liability for the actions of your business and you are not shielded from a personal tax on the business earnings, although you can deduct your percentage of the business expenses. If your company is a partnership, you should include copies of your partnership agreement in the Supporting Documents section of your plan.

The last form of business entity is the corporation and it comes in three types:

- The C corporation
- The subchapter S corporation
- The limited liability corporation (LLC)

If personal liability and tax issues are of concern, then you should consider forming a corporation of some type. A corporation is considered a legal person. In the vernacular of the field, a corporation creates a veil between you and the company, protecting you personally from any of its legal activities. The word *legal* is important here. A corporation does not protect its members if the company performs an illegal, unethical, or irresponsible act. If that happens, the members and/or executive team of the corporation can be sued or taken to court—and jailed. The recent Enron debacle is a prime example.

Forming a *C corporation* does limit your personal liability for business debts and the earnings of the corporation do not pass directly into your personal tax return. Being a legal person, the corporation pays salaries and taxes and deducts expenses like any other person. The shareholders pay personal income tax only on money that's paid to them as salary, bonuses, or dividends. But running a corporation is not cheap and takes work. Meetings must be held, minutes recorded, tax forms filed, and so forth, all of which takes time from running your business.

A lighter version of the C corporation is the *subchapter S corporation*. The S corporation is a corporation and gives you the limited liability of a corporate shareholder. The difference is that as a corporate shareholder, you pay taxes on the same basis of a sole proprietor or a partner. Because the establishment of the LLC as an alternative corporate entity, the S corporation has lost a lot of its appeal and has been replaced in most cases by the LLC.

The *limited liability corporation*, or LLC, combines the best aspects of a corporation and partnership and fits somewhere between the partnership, sole proprietorship, and the corporation. It is desirable to companies because it includes limited personal liability but, like the owners of partnerships or sole proprietorships, the LLC is not a separate taxable entity like the corporation. Your tax situation is the same as a partner or sole proprietor and you must report your business earnings and losses on your personal income tax return.

Keep in mind that the business forms of partnerships and corporations incur set-up and ongoing professional costs and should be included in the pro forma section of your financial plan. To refresh your memory, a *pro forma* is your assumptions of your business's revenue, expenses, profits, and loss.

This book has too little space to go further into the forms of legal entities for companies. The Nolo website (www.nolo.com) is a great resource for information on the different forms of business entities and how to form them.

Identifying Your Business Type

What type of business you are in should also be added to your company description. There are basically four business types:

- A *retailer* buys ready-to-sell merchandise from suppliers and sells them directly to the consumer.
- A *wholesaler* or distributor buys merchandise from manufacturers or merchandise brokers and resells that merchandise to retailers.
- A *manufacturer* creates products from parts and components and sells those products to wholesalers and distributors. A manufacturer can also be a developer or producer that creates and finishes a salable commodity such as videos, music, software, or video games.
- A *service company* sells services to consumers, government, and other businesses.

Are there exceptions to these categories? Yes there are.

Take Dell or Hewlett Packard, for instance. They are both manufacturers and retailers. They manufacture their own computers and sell directly to consumers, bypassing the wholesalers. When writing your company description, you must mention what type of business you are so the reader understands the distribution strategy you detail later in your plan.

Describing Your Company or Division's History and Present Situation

Every journey has a starting point. And so does your company. Your company description should include some basic information about your company's past and present.

If your company or division has been around a while, here's your chance to toot your horn, so to speak. Tell the reader about your company's successes and perhaps some of the major milestones reached in the company's past. This is a chance to add some credibility to your company, which can be transferable to the success of your new endeavor.

If your company or division is new but in existence and looking for a new or first-time capital infusion, then your company description would include a description of your present situation. You might include the basic research done by the principle people of the company, the results of testing your business idea, or a description of your current business assets.

In either case, use the description of your company or division to give the reader a good background of where your company has come from and what your company has done.

Regulatory and Legal Issues

Some companies must consider if the business they are in is regulated by a government agency. And as you know, many government agencies today regulate to look after the safety and welfare of consumers.

If your business falls under the umbrella of one or more of these agencies, you should ask yourself, "Is what my company offers regulated or nonregulated? Will the regulatory authorities let me sell my product or offer my service?"

You must consider if the product you sell or the service you offer is legally feasible or if it carries some regulatory restrictions. It doesn't matter how good your business idea is if the government greatly restricts its sales or prevents it altogether.

RESEARCHING GOVERNMENT REGULATIONS

The list of regulatory agencies that oversee business in the United States includes an alphabet soup of government agencies and commissions, including the Federal Trade Commission (FTC), Securities and Exchange Commission (SEC), Federal Communications Commission (FCC), Federal Aviation Administration (FAA), Federal Election Commission (FEC), and Food and Drug Administration (FDA).

When looking for regulations that might apply to your business, check out these government sites:

- www.aallnet.org/sis/ripssis/federal.html
- www.gpoaccess.gov/cfr/
- www.regulations.gov/topical_guide.cfm
- cfr.law.cornell.edu/cfr/

Also, consider any and all local laws and/or zoning restrictions on where you will locate your company. You may need a permit of some sort to physically locate your place of business in a certain area of your community.

Identifying Current and Potential Funding Sources

In Tom Wolfe's novel, *The Right Stuff*, the refrain from NASA officials looking for government funding was "No bucks. No Buck Rogers." Same goes for your business. Without access to funds or company resources, your business plan remains just that—a plan!

If you are in need of funding or resource support for your plan, you should have some idea of where you plan to raise the necessary capital or company resources to implement your business plan. You must identify your sources of funding and how you are going to go about attaining them. How do you intend to fund your business? Debt financing (borrowing money from individuals or a bank)? Equity financing (selling a percentage of your company to investors)? Or some combination, such as debt instruments converting to equity sometime in the future?

In the Financial Plan section of your plan you describe what stage of development your company is in and what the funding will be used for. You also detail your exit strategy, or how your sources of funding are rewarded for the risk they are taking. You learn how to write this section of your plan in Chapter 13, "Detailing Capital Requirements."

Describing Strategic Alliances

The more credible the success of your business venture seems, the more support you gain for it. Forging strategic alliances is a good way to attain that credibility—and can help your business succeed.

> **tip**
> A strategic alliance can expand access to markets or to a broader geographic range—one currently beyond your reach. Such alliances may also provide advanced technology or quicker product development for your company.

A strategic alliance is an agreement between you and other companies, such as distributors or vendors of the products you sell, that can either be a formal or informal arrangement. The alliance can be as simple as a cost-sharing arrangement or as complex as a fully integrated merger of two companies. It could also mean you have acquired beneficial pricing from a vendor that allows you to sell more competitively, at the same time giving the vendor a way to sell more of their product. Or perhaps your strategic alliance represents a marketing agreement between you and a non-competing but complimentary company where you share marketing expenses, or maybe it's a joint venture between you and another company sharing the risks and the profits.

Any form of a formal or informal strategic alliance can lend credibility to the success of your business plan and increase your investor's or management's confidence.

But be careful not to form alliances for the purpose of controlling some segment of the marketplace. Some alliances can be seen as an attempt at a monopoly or even price fixing. This kind of activity is illegal and should be avoided.

To do list

- ☐ Research and identify your business type, form, legal history, and any regulatory issues
- ☐ Research and describe funding sources
- ☐ Define and describe strategic alliances
- ☐ Write the company or division overview for a startup, full, or internal business plan

Write the Plan!

Let's continue to write your plan. Answer the following questions as they apply to your type of plan to write this portion of your business plan—startup, full, or internal plan.

Startup Business Plan

Answer these questions to write your business plan's company description:

1. What is the name of your company?
2. When do you plan to open your company? Have you set a date or does it depend on when funding is attained?
3. Where is the company located? If you have a physical address for the company, what is it?
4. What does your business do?
5. What type of business are you in? Retail, wholesale, manufacturing, service company, or some combination?
6. What is the legal form of your company? Sole proprietorship, partnership, C corporation, subchapter S corporation, or LLC?

Answer these questions to describe your company history and/or present situation:

1. What basic research have you done on your product or service?
2. Do you have any results from testing your business idea?
3. What are your current nonfinancial company assets?

Answer these questions to describe the regulatory and legal issues applicable to your company:

1. Are there any regulatory issues that your company must face? Is what your company offers regulated or nonregulated? If so, what are those regulations?
2. Are there any local laws and/or zoning restrictions on where you will locate your company?

Answer these questions to describe your potential funding sources:

1. What are your present cash resources or liabilities?
2. What money are you and/or your associates investing in the company? What is the source of these funds?
3. How do you intend to fund your company? Debt financing? Equity financing? Some combination?

Answer these questions to describe your company's strategic alliances:

1. Do you have any strategic alliances? What are they?
2. How can they help your company succeed?

Full Business Plan

Answer these questions to write your business plan's company description:

1. What is the name of your company?
2. What date was it started?
3. Where is it located? What is the physical address of the place of business?
4. What does your company do?
5. What type of business are you in? Retail, wholesale, manufacturing, service company, or some combination?
6. What is the legal form of your company? Sole proprietorship, partnership, C corporation, subchapter S corporation, or LLC?

Answer these questions to complete the company history and/or present situation of the plan:

1. What is the history of your company and the factors that made it a success or retarded its progress? Be sure to list all important company milestones.
2. What is the present situation of your company?

Answer these questions to describe the regulatory and legal issues applicable to your company:

1. Are there any regulatory issues that your company must face? Is what your company offers regulated or nonregulated? If regulated, how?
2. Are there any local laws and/or zoning restrictions on where you will locate your business?

Answer these questions to describe your potential funding sources:

1. What are your present cash resources or liabilities?
2. What money are you and/or your associates investing in the company? What is the source of these funds?
3. How do you intend to fund your company? Debt financing? Equity financing? Some combination?

Answer these questions to describe your company's strategic alliances:

1. Do you have any strategic alliances? What are they?
2. How can they help your business succeed?

Internal Business Plan

Answer these questions to write your business plan's company description:

1. What is the name of your division or department?
2. Where is it located? What part of the company is it a part of?
3. What does your division or department do?

Answer these questions to describe your company history and/or present situation:

1. What is the history of your division or department and the factors that made it a success or retarded its progress?
2. What is the present situation of your division or department?

Answer these questions to describe the regulatory and legal issues applicable to your company:

1. Are there any regulatory issues that your division or department must face? Is what you're offering regulated or nonregulated? If regulated, how?

Answer these questions to describe your potential funding sources:

1. What is the present source of funding and/or resource support of your division or department?
2. What funding or resources is your division or department looking for?
3. What is the source of this potential funding or resource support?

Answer these questions to describe your company's strategic alliances:

1. Do you have any strategic alliances? What are they?
2. How can they help your business succeed?

Summary

A business plan should provide the reader with a description of the company planning to do the business. The company description describes what the company is and the business description details what the company does.

A business plan must provide basic information about a company or division that includes the name, the date it started (or, when applicable, when the business will start), the legal form of organization, the type of business, and its location.

Your company description should include some basic information about your company's past and present. Some companies must consider if the business they are in is regulated by a government agency. You must consider if the product you sell or the service you offer is legally feasible or if it carries some regulatory restrictions.

If you are in need of funding or resource support for your plan, you should have some idea of where you plan to raise the necessary capital or company resources to implement your business plan. The more credible the success of your business venture seems, the more support you gain for it. Forging strategic alliances is a good way to attain that credibility.

The next chapter will explain how to describe the product or service your company will sell and its production and delivery to the marketplace.

Describing Your Product or Service

5

The business of business is selling something. That something is the product or service you plan to offer to the marketplace. This description is the prime objective of your plan. You might say this is where the rubber meets the road in your business plan.

The reader of your plan wants to know not only what you plan to sell but also why consumers will buy it. Look at this section as your chance to clearly explain what you sell, its features, and its benefits. You should also use this section of the plan to discuss what needs or problems your product or service addresses in the marketplace.

Don't confuse this section with the Market Analysis section of your plan. Here, you want to focus on describing your product or service, explaining how you position your offering in the marketplace, and then supporting why someone wants to buy it. You have plenty of time to analyze your market more thoroughly in the Market Analysis section.

Let's first start by describing the product or service you sell.

To do list

- [ ] Learn how to describe your product or service's features and benefits
- [ ] Learn how your product or service can fill a human need
- [ ] Learn how to describe your product or service's full selling position
- [ ] Learn how to describe and protect your proprietary product or techniques

Showing What Your Business Sells

With the preliminaries of your company description and business objectives out of the way, you must turn to the task of describing the product or service you sell. Start by giving your reader a general overview of your offering before getting into the details. Provide a short explanation of how long your product or service type has been in the marketplace.

Be sure to read the section "Products and Services" in the sample plan in Appendix A, "Sample Business Plan," for an example of what goes into this section of the plan.

One important thing to remember is that your reader might not be familiar with your product or service type or the industry that you are in. That means you have to describe your product simply and in detail.

note Here's how the elements described in this chapter relate to each of the three plan types:

- Except for the confidentiality statement and the documentation on company patents, licenses, and copyrighted material, the internal plan answers the same questions and has the same parts as the full business plan.
- The startup plan does not answer the questions of existing contracts with potential customers and suppliers nor does it provide feedback from potential customers or third-party analysis about the viability of the product or service.

This section of your plan must include not only a description of the product or service you sell, but also what industry you sell within and the average cost of the product. Include a description of your product's *sourcing*, or where and how you obtain your product. Who do you buy it from? If you are writing an internal plan, this is an opportunity to review your sourcing strategy and whether you can earn a better profit by improving the sourcing of your product.

If you are creating a product, you must provide a detailed description of components or raw materials that go into the finished item and how much the components or raw materials cost. Also detail in your plan whether the product you sell requires any additional support and how you provide it.

If you're providing a service, tell the reader what the service is, why you can provide it, how it is provided, who does the work, and where the service is performed.

Professional services companies such as law or medical offices, consulting firms, accountants, and design companies provide services by employing people. A computer networking company offers access to the Internet, and a telephone company provides a service by owning and maintaining a network infrastructure.

> **tip**
> You should consider including pictures of the products you sell. Photos or graphics that illustrate your products are especially useful if they help the reader better understand your product's design or use.

These incur costs and should be explained as part of your service description.

Then again, you might be offering a combined product and service, such as selling merchandise and then providing the customer with a warranty service for the product.

Don't describe your product or service in language that is too technical with too many industry specific words or phrases, but don't describe your product or service in terms that are too broad, either. Describe your product in terms of size, color, height, weight, and function or processes.

If you can, be sure to back up your ability to sell your product or service by describing some market experience you or a listed partner have had to date. List any positive feedback you might have received from potential customers about your product or.service, and mention any contracts you might have with potential customers. It also helps to include any third-party evaluation or analysis of your product or service.

Finally, describe any spin-off or add-on opportunities you feel are possible with your product or service. For example, look back at Chapter 3, "Getting Started: Introducing Your Plan and Identifying Your Mission and Goals," under the subheading "Defining Your Company Objectives" and read the example from my concierge business on developmental objectives.

Things You'll Need

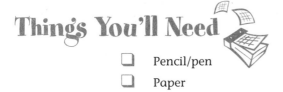

- ❑   Pencil/pen
- ❑   Paper

Portraying the Features and Benefits: Creating a Unique Selling Position

Customers are only interested in "What's in it for me?" Phrase your selling position in those terms and you go a long way toward creating an effective and successful unique selling position.

When creating your own *unique selling position*, make sure you clearly and simply describe what makes your product or service uniquely beneficial for your customers. Consider these fundamental characteristics of your product or service when creating your unique selling position. How many of them does your product or service meet?

1. Does it save time?
2. Does it reduce cost?
3. Does it offer large savings?
4. Is it exclusive?
5. Does it provide convenience?
6. Is it rugged?
7. Can you deliver it faster?
8. Do you provide better service?
9. Is it economical to use?
10. Is it easier or simpler to use?
11. Does it have a low operating cost?
12. Does it reduce upkeep or is it easy to upkeep?
13. Does it reduce waste?
14. Does it have long life?

Your unique selling position is not only used to describe your product or service, but it's also the key component of the marketing plan that you'll write later. If you don't know what your unique selling position is, you have a very hard time identifying the markets you want to sell into and the marketing vehicles you can use.

A common mistake made in business plans is the assumption that a product or service sells itself. Don't make the mistake of failing to identify for the customer the benefits of your product or service.

In the parlance of commerce this is called "selling the benefits—not the features." Or in other words, "sell the sizzle, not the steak." You must be able to define your product or service in terms of customer needs and benefits instead of thinking of your offering from your side of the equation. Think in terms of what customer need it fills and what it costs.

That's called *positioning* your product or service. And positioning comes in four flavors. They're called the four Ps.

- **Pricing**—If you're going to compete on price, don't just say you're the lowest—say why. For instance, perhaps you can sell at such a low price because of your ability to source product from the closeout industry, buying products at pennies on the dollar. Play up this uniqueness in your selling position.
- **Placement**—The Marines are looking for just a few good men—not all men, just a few. This is a great placement statement and makes their business unique and differentiates them among the armed forces. Look for a similar placement with your business.

- **Packaging**—Take a common product others sell and repackage it in a new way. For instance, take the iMac. It's just a computer, but look at the packaging. Not only did it sell, but it also had a positioning statement with it—get on the Internet in 20 minutes and think different. Another example is Starbucks coffee. It's just coffee that has been repackaged into a lifestyle.
- **Promotion**—Finally, look at the promotional possibilities of your product or service. Can you tie your product or service to a season or holiday where you can benefit from the promotional activities and mind-set that already exists at that time of year? Or perhaps there are other time-based connections, such as the birth of a child, birthdays, or anniversaries. The key here is to tie your product or service to activities, life events, and even particular demographic groups. You can then identify your selling position with those.

Do this. Put this book down, take out a pad and pencil, ask yourself these questions, and answer them as *simply* as you can. You're not creating a corporate mission statement here. Keep your responses simple.

- Why is my business special?
- Why would someone buy from me instead of my competition?
- What can my business provide a consumer that no one else can? What's the benefit to the consumer that I can deliver?

Don't omit the specific problem your product or service addresses and how that problem is solved.

Keep your answers specific and measurable; show a benefit to the buyer. Here's the hard part—answer these questions in just one sentence and make it so anyone can understand it. Test it on your spouse, family, friends, and neighbors and ask them what they think it means.

Above all else, remember that your unique selling position is not about you and it's not about your business—it's about your customer. To do that, you need to speak to the needs of the customer.

SELLING THE SIZZLE

When FedEx first got started, the business's founders were looking for a way to describe their company's unique selling position. Up until then, if you wanted to ship a small package across the country, you had to ship it on the bus and airline schedules. It might take up to several days to have your package delivered—and then *you* had to pick it up! FedEx had a new concept of delivering packages overnight and wanted to say its package delivery service was better than using the services of the buses and airlines. And they needed to say it in one simple phrase.

After much thought, they decided what differentiated FedEx from its competitors was that FedEx owned its own planes. This meant customers could ship products on *their* schedule and not the schedule of the airlines and buses.

So what did they come up with? This: "We have our own planes."

It didn't fly with the public. They didn't understand it. "So what?" they said. "What does that mean to me?"

FedEx went back to the drawing board and came up with this: "When you absolutely, positively have to have it overnight!" That worked. The public responded and the rest is commerce history. Consumers didn't care if FedEx had its own planes. They didn't care if their packages were delivered by Pony Express. The benefit to the consumers was that their package were delivered overnight right to their doors.

Another good example is Domino's Pizza. How do you differentiate one pizza service from another? Domino's did so by promising to deliver your pizza in "30 minutes or less—or the pizza is free!" Both FedEx and Domino's have had a measurable and beneficial unique selling position or USP. They're measurable— overnight and in 30 minutes—and have a unique benefit—delivered to your door and free if not delivered in time.

Expressing How Your Product or Service Fills Human Motivations and Needs

Another way to describe your product or service is in terms of the human motivations and needs it fulfills.

As you craft this description, you must understand what motivates a person to buy. What sorts of customers make purchases and why? As you learn in this section, all buying decisions are prompted by a central set of *human motivators*, including information, economic, entertainment, and social motivators. You then must understand what customer need can a product or service line such as yours fills. To describe your offering in terms of *human needs*, you need to call on the services of Dr. Abraham Maslow. Dr. Maslow was a twentieth century psychologist who spent a lot of time categorizing human needs. Maslow determined that all needs belong to the categories of physical, safety, belonging, and esteem. If he were alive today, I bet Maslow would have made a pretty effective business person. He could easily describe what human needs a product or service would be good at satisfying, just as you learn to do in this section.

With this understanding, you can list the customer need(s) you are trying to satisfy and why those needs exist.

Understanding Human Motivators

When preparing to write your product or service description, keep these important human motivators in mind:

- **Information**—Provide a ready source of information that meets a shopper's need and you can turn that shopper into a customer. Examples of products or services offering information motivators include news, financial data, insurance quotes, newsletters, books, and other types of media.

- **Economic**—A quality product, a nice selection, a secure and convenient way to buy—even a great deal—these and other economic benefits would entice a shopper to open his wallet and buy from your company. Examples include everyday products and services that people use.
- **Entertainment**—We all love to be entertained. We'll even pay for it if we feel the value is there. So think about ways of selling entertainment products and services to the consumer. Examples include sports and celebrity news, games, and puzzles.
- **Social**—Finally, human interaction, or the social aspects of being human, is a strong motivational force. The opportunity to hobnob with those of similar interests can be turned into a profitable business. Fill the human need to interact and you can build an effective business on it. Examples of products or services offering social motivators include community sites like iVillage.com and ePinions.com where a person can share his opinions and experiences with others.

Keep in mind that different shoppers are motivated by different things—even at different times.

WHY PEOPLE BUY

Every buyer has her own reasons for purchasing an item or service, but all purchases are driven by one or more central *buying motivations*. Consider these buying motivations and how they are fulfilled by your product or service when creating your unique selling position. How many buying motivations does your product or service meet?

1. Pride of appearance
2. Pride of ownership
3. Desire of prestige
4. Desire for recognition
5. Desire to imitate
6. Desire for variety
7. Desire for safety
8. Desire to create
9. Desire for security
10. Desire for convenience
11. Desire for uniqueness

Physical Needs

The basic physical human needs are food, shelter, and clothing. We all need to eat and drink. Your business might sell, for example, everyday, gourmet, natural, regional, or ethnic food and drink that certain customer segments would want to buy. Apparel also satisfies physical needs, meeting both the need to remain in fashion and to protect our bodies from the elements.

Physical needs can be serviced as well. You might have a product that provides information on how, what, and where to cook. People eat out frequently. A business that lists and categorizes restaurants and their reviews is another service your particular business might provide. Or your business can do double duty, providing information on where to hunt and fish and then how to cut and clean what you catch. Consider these examples when determining whether you can describe your product or service in terms of meeting physical needs.

Safety Needs

Feeling safe and secure is one of our strongest basic needs. Your product or service can help buyers protect themselves, their families, and homes. Health is another safety concern. Does your offering help consumers answer questions concerning health issues or products that can improve their health?

Maybe you sell products such as self-defense items and security devices to use when traveling or books and tapes on self-defense. Or perhaps you're offering child safety products such as baby seats and identification systems or home security products such as home safes and surveillance equipment. Do you sell first-aid equipment, home medical supplies, or products and services for people with disabilities?

Maybe you're going to offer a private investigative service, a directory of alarm services and their reviews, or an emergency alert service for the infirm and elderly. Any of these and many other products and services can be described in terms of meeting safety needs.

Belonging Needs

To be loved, to have friends, and to be part of a family fills our need to be a part of something greater than ourselves. You might be offering a product or service that helps people to express their appreciation for being part of something or to express affection for lovers, friends, and family by giving gifts. Other products that can fall into this category of needs fulfillment are the traditional flowers, cards, and candy.

Esteem Needs

We all like to be recognized and feel good about ourselves. How we feel about ourselves and how others perceive us is important to us. Recognition and vanity are strong personal needs we seek to fulfill.

Can you describe your product or service in terms of meeting esteem needs? You might be offering beauty and grooming items, such as perfume, bath and body lotions, cosmetics, cologne, razors, and electric shavers. Or perhaps you plan to sell jewelry, books and videos on personal care, dieting, or products to reverse the aging process.

As for services, you might be offering training and educational courses. Are you selling beauty tips or offering a jewelry appraisal service? Perhaps you can give advice on how to succeed in business or even—after reading this book—offer a course on how to set up your own business!

Describing Your Full Selling Position

There is one other way to describe your product or service. And that's in terms of your full selling position.

Your future customers also have expectations. They expect a fair price, a good selection, great service, buying convenience, and, especially if you plan to offer your product or service online, a secure and safe place to shop. In other words, they're looking for selection, price, service, convenience, and security.

Here's a closer look at the components of your *full selling position*:

- **Selection**—Do you sell a wide selection of products across multiple categories or do you sell a select, very focused selection of products? For example, if you sell books, CDs, or movies, do you sell a large selection of them but not a very deep one in the number of titles? Or perhaps your business focuses on one select area like science fiction, romance, non-fiction, rock and roll, classical, or rhythm and blues? You can describe your product or service in terms of the selection you offer.
- **Price**—What kind of pricing model does your business follow? Do you sell products or services at a discount? Do you want to be a low-cost leader in your market niche? Or are you a value-added reseller, adding additional value to products in the form of some kind of service that usually demands a higher price? Do you set the price of the products and services you sell—or does the consumer? Whatever pricing model you choose, you need to make it very clear to the reader of your plan.
- **Service**—A description of your full selling position must also include a description of the service you intend to offer. Is the way you service your customer part of your unique selling position? What makes the kind of service you offer unique? Perhaps you offer support 24 hours a day, 7 days a week, 365 days a year. Or maybe you offer some kind of guarantee or warranty on your product or service. Maybe it's a selling position that you use to gain a customer's confidence.
- **Convenience**—In today's hectic, fast-paced world, consumers are always looking for products or services that offer convenience. Can you describe your product or service in terms of providing convenience to the consumer?
- **Security**—This element applies if you plan to sell your product or service online. Online shoppers can be a very skeptical bunch. They've been trained

by the media to expect all kinds of online scams waiting to pick their pockets. If up to now you've given them a reason to buy from you, they have to trust you enough to hand you their money online. Shoppers are very concerned about using their credit cards to make purchases online, so you have to ensure you provide a secure way to take their credit card number off the Internet. You also have to prove that the personal information you collect from them is kept private and not shared with anyone else. I go into more detail later in Chapter 9, "Listing Your Distribution Channels."

Things You'll Need

- ❏ Computer
- ❏ Web access

Describing Your Company's Proprietary Products or Techniques

Your company might be taking the route of producing your own propriety product. If so, there are a few things you should have in your business plan, including a full description of those proprietary products or the techniques you use to produce them.

First, you should state in this section of your plan any proprietary rights you might hold on your product, including copyrights, patents, or trademarks. Make it obvious in your plan that you have or will have obtained the necessary documents or claims to protect your product or service. Include this documentation in the section on supporting documents.

Don't underestimate the importance of legally protecting your product. But on the other hand, don't be sidetracked by spending too much time and effort filing documents and having meetings with lawyers protecting your idea before you offer it. You can successfully sell a new product without first protecting it legally. You can spend the time later with lawyers and the patent office. The time and money spent to successfully protect your product idea can make you miss the market opportunity you know you can exploit.

> **tip** Remember, ideas are relatively easy to come up with. Their execution is quite another matter. Make sure you budget just as much time for executing your product idea as for protecting it.

Second, you should have already described in the first section of this chapter the proprietary product you sell—its size, shape, color, cost, design, quality, capabilities, and so on. In this section of the business plan, you should explain the technological lifespan of your new product. That is, will your product go out of style or be replaced by an improved product or better technology in the future? If so, you might have a plan to upgrade the product or add to it over time. Make mention of this fact and then give more detail in the Implementation Plan section you write later.

Third, if you're selling a product that is patented and the patent is held by someone else, make sure you mention this in your plan and provide evidence that you have permission to sell the product. Nothing can halt the progress of your business in its tracks faster than a lengthy lawsuit. Don't suppose it's all right to use a product just because it exists. If it does, you can be pretty certain someone holds a patent on it.

To find out if a product has a patent, contact the United States Patent and Trademark Office. They have a website at www.uspto.gov filled with information that can help. The site can tell you how to do a patent or trademark search and how to apply for a patent or trademark for your own product. If the product you want to use or create is covered under copyright laws, visit the website of the United States Copyright Office at www.copyright.gov to learn the ins and outs of copyright law and how to copyright your product.

Keep in mind that because your product is proprietary, you want to protect this sensitive information in your plan. Don't forget to record who receives copies of your plan. Also remember to include a confidentiality statement before the Table of Contents in your plan. Ask recipients to sign a nondisclosure statement and keep those on file.

To do list

- ☐ Learn to explain how your product is produced
- ☐ Understand what sourcing information your product description requires
- ☐ Learn to describe administrative and technology issues your business encounters, and your plan for addressing these issues

Outlining Production Processes

The reader of your plan knows you have the capability of creating the proprietary product you plan to sell. You demonstrate that capability in this section of your plan by describing these items and issues:

1. Production and sourcing
2. Technology issues
3. Administration

Let's take sourcing first. You should explain in this section of your plan how your product is produced. Don't get too technical; just explain as simply as you can the production process, the materials used, and the labor required.

If you're producing a product, you must note who your suppliers are and what parts, components, or materials of your product each supplies. List these suppliers and their contact information in a table in this section of your business plan. Also give a brief explanation of why you chose these suppliers—price, location, delivery time, and so on.

Include backup suppliers. Although you can order from one, two, or three main suppliers, suppose something goes awry and you can't get an important component or a piece of material to complete the production of your product. Show that you're prepared to deal with these issues by including the names and contact information of alternate suppliers.

Remember to add any sourcing documentation to the Appendix of your plan, including contracts with important suppliers, standard cost breakdowns, bills of materials, and other information.

note As for the sourcing of existing product from vendors or distributors, this is an opportunity, if you are writing an internal plan, to review your sourcing strategy and whether you can improve your product by changing the sourcing of your product.

You should also describe how you would deal with a sudden increase in orders. It has been known to happen. You might underestimate the popularity of your product with consumers. Or *USA Today* might have done a story on your product and you are swamped with orders. This happened to a company of mine. We were producing and selling our own brand of personal computer. Our tech department sent it into a very popular computer magazine for review against 20 or so other brands. To our surprise, not only did we get a good review but our computer was chosen as a top pick. Orders jumped immediately after the magazine hit the newsstands. We were lucky our suppliers could meet the sudden demand for parts.

Next to consider and describe in this section of your plan are any technology issues your business can be confronted with. Mention to the reader what types of technology are required to produce your product. Explain whether you have that technology in your company and/or whether it is readily available from somewhere else.

Finally, describe the inventory management requirements to produce your product. Fully explain and describe the technical and physical infrastructure you require to manage the production and storage of the product and the components or materials that go into producing it.

Things You'll Need

- ❏ List of vendors and suppliers
- ❏ Contracts, cost breakdowns, and other sourcing documentation

Write the Plan!

As you can see, the Product or Service Description section is a very important part of your plan. The bottom line is that you must sell the reader on your product as well as sell her on your plans and capability for selling it. As you write this section of your plan, think hard about the answers to the following questions, as they apply to your type of plan—startup, full, or internal plan.

Startup Business Plan

Answer these questions to describe what your business sells:

1. What is the name of your product or service?
2. Briefly describe the nature of your product or service in terms the average reader can understand.
3. How long has your type of product or service existed in the marketplace?
4. What is the target market for your product or service?
5. If you are providing a service, why can you provide it, how do you provide it, who does the work, and where is the service performed?
6. Are you providing a combined product and service? How do you do this? Who does each part?
7. What is new, exciting, or different about your product or service?
8. Can you supply any market experience with your product or service?
9. Do you have photos or graphics of your product you can include in your plan?
10. Does your product require any additional support after the sale? How do you provide it?
11. Do you see any spin-off or add-on opportunities?

Answer these questions to describe the features and benefits of your product or service:

1. What are the special features of your product or service?
2. What benefit to the consumer can you deliver?
3. What specific problem does your product or service address and how is that problem solved?
4. What makes your selling position unique?
5. Do you position your product or service on price, promotion, packaging, or placement?
6. What can your business provide a consumer that no one else can?
7. Why would a consumer buy your product or service rather than a competitor's? Does it save time, reduce cost, or offer large savings? Can you deliver it faster? Do you provide better service? Is it more economical, easier, or simpler to use?

Answer these questions to describe your customers' motivations to buy and how your product/service meets a human need:

1. What is the consumer motivation to purchase your product or service? The need for information? A quality product? A secure and convenient way to buy? A great deal? Entertainment? Filling a social need of human interaction?
2. What human need does your product or service fill? Can you describe your product in terms of physical, safety, belonging, or esteem needs?

3. Why does this human need or requirement exist?

4. Does your product or service appeal to the customer's pride of appearance or ownership; or the desire for prestige, recognition, safety, creativity, security, or uniqueness?

Answer these questions to describe your full selling position:

1. What is your full selling position? Can you describe your product or service in terms of price? Are you the lowest? How? Do you sell retail but add value? Do you sell at boutique prices?

2. Can you describe your product or service in terms of selection? Do you have a broad horizontal selection of products or services but not sell many varieties of any one kind? Or is your selling vertical, focused on selling many varieties of only a few types of products and services?

3. Can you describe your product or service in terms of providing convenience to the consumer?

4. Can you describe your product or service in terms of services, such as guarantees or warranties?

5. Can you describe your product or service in terms of security of your consumer's online purchases and the protection of his personal information?

Answer these questions to describe your company's proprietary products or techniques:

1. Do you have any patents, licenses, or proprietary rights not available to competitors? What are they?

2. Is your product copyrighted?

3. Describe your product in detail. What's its size, shape, color, cost, design, quality, capabilities, and so on?

4. Do you legally protect your proprietary product?

5. Do you have necessary permissions to use other another person's or company's patents or licenses? Do you show the necessary documentation in your plan? Are these patented or licensed products/processes available to competitors or do you have exclusive use?

6. Do you have a plan to upgrade the product or add to it over time?

7. Do you have a confidentiality statement before the Table of Contents of your plan?

Answer these questions to outline your production process:

1. If you're manufacturing a product, how do you do it? What processes do you use?

2. What components or materials do you need to produce your product?

3. Who are your primary suppliers?

4. Why did you choose them? Based on price, location, or delivery time?

5. Who are your backup suppliers if your primary suppliers fail to deliver?

6. What types of technology are required to produce your product? Do you have that technology in your company? If not, is it readily available from somewhere else?

Full Business Plan

Answer these questions to describe what your business sells:

1. What is the name of your product or service?
2. Briefly describe the nature of your product or service in terms the average reader can understand.
3. How long has your type of product or service existed in the marketplace?
4. What is the target market for your product or service?
5. If you are providing a service, why can you provide it, how is it provided, who does the work, and where is the service performed?
6. Are you providing a combined product and service? How do you do this? Who does each part?
7. What is new, exciting, or different about your product or service?
8. Can you supply any market experience with your product or service?
9. Do you have any positive feedback from potential customers about the viability of your product or service?
10. Do you have any existing contracts with potential customers and suppliers?
11. Do you have any third-party evaluation or analysis of your product or service?
12. Do you have photos or graphics of your product you can include in your plan?
13. Does your product require any additional support after the sale? How do you provide it?
14. Do you see any spin-off or add-on opportunities?

Answer these questions to describe the features and benefits of your product or service:

1. What are the special features of your product or service?
2. What's the benefit to the consumer that you can deliver?
3. What specific problem does your product or service address and how is that problem solved?
4. What makes your selling position unique?
5. Do you position your product or service on price, promotion, packaging, or placement?
6. What can your business provide a consumer that no one else can?

7. Why would a consumer buy your product or service rather than a competitor's? Does it save time, reduce cost, or offer large savings? Can you deliver it faster? Do you provide better service? Is it more economical, easier, or simpler to use?

Answer these questions to describe your customers' motivations to buy and how your product/service meets a human need:

1. What is the consumer motivation to purchase your product or service? The need for information? A quality product? A secure and convenient way to buy? A great deal? Entertainment? Filling a social need of human interaction?

2. What human need does your product or service fill? Can you describe your product in terms of physical, safety, belonging, or esteem needs?

3. Why does this human need or requirement exist?

4. Does your product or service appeal to the customers' pride of appearance or ownership; or the desire for prestige, recognition, safety, creativity, security, or uniqueness?

Answer these questions to describe your full selling position:

1. What is your full selling position? Can you describe your product or service in terms of price? Are you the lowest? How? Do you sell retail but add value? Do you sell at boutique prices?

2. Can you describe your product or service in terms of selection? Do you have a broad horizontal selection of products or services but not sell many varieties of any one kind? Or is your selling vertical, focused on selling many varieties of only a few types of products and services?

3. Can you describe your product or service in terms of providing convenience to the consumer?

4. Can you describe your product or service in terms of services, such as guarantees or warranties?

5. Can you describe your product or service in terms of security of your consumer's online purchase and the protection of his personal information?

Answer these questions to describe your company's proprietary products or techniques:

1. Do you have any patents, licenses, or proprietary rights not available to competitors? What are they?

2. Is your product copyrighted?

3. Do you show the necessary documentation in your plan?

4. Describe your product in detail. What's its size, shape, color, cost, design, quality, capabilities, and so on?

5. Do you legally protect your proprietary product?

6. Do you have necessary permissions to use another person's or company's patents or licenses? Do you show the necessary documentation in your plan? Are these patented or licensed products/services available to competitors or do you have exclusive use?

7. Do you have a plan to upgrade the product or add to it over time?

8. Do you have a confidentiality statement before the Table of Contents of your plan?

Answer these questions to outline your production process:

1. If you're manufacturing a product, how do you do it? What processes do you use?

2. How much does it cost? Break down the costs in terms of components or materials and assembly or production.

3. What components or materials do you need to produce your product?

4. Who are your primary suppliers?

5. Why did you choose them? Based on price, location, or delivery time?

6. Who are your backup suppliers if your primary suppliers fail to deliver?

7. Do you have contracts with suppliers? Add them to your plan.

8. How do you deal with sudden increases in orders?

9. What types of technology are required to produce your product? Do you have that technology in your company? If not, is it readily available from somewhere else?

10. What are the inventory management requirements to produce your product?

11. What are the technical and physical infrastructure needs to manage the production and storage of the product and to manage the components or materials that go into producing it?

Internal Business Plan

Answer these questions to describe what your business sells:

1. What is the name of your product or service?

2. Briefly describe the nature of your product or service in terms the average manager can understand.

3. How long has your type of product or service existed in the marketplace?

4. What is the target market for your product or service?

5. If you are providing a service, why can you provide it, how is it provided, who does the work, and where is the service performed?

6. Are you providing a combined product and service? How do you do this? Who does each part?

7. What is new, exciting, or different about your product or service?

8. Can you supply any market experience with your product or service?

9. Do you have any positive feedback from potential customers about the viability of your product or service?

10. Do you have any existing contracts with potential customers and suppliers?

11. Do you have any third-party evaluation or analysis of your product or service?

12. Do you have photos or graphics of your product you can include in your plan?

13. Does your product require any additional support after the sale? How do you provide it?

14. Do you see any spin-off or add-on opportunities?

Answer these questions to describe the features and benefits of your product or service:

1. What are the special features of your product or service?

2. What's the benefit to the consumer that you can deliver?

3. What specific problem does your product or service address and how is that problem solved?

4. What makes your selling position unique?

5. Do you position your product or service on price, promotion, packaging, or placement?

6. What can your business provide a consumer that no one else can?

7. Why would a consumer buy your product or service rather than a competitor's? Does it save time, reduce cost, or offer large savings? Can you deliver it faster? Do you provide better service? Is it more economical, easier, or simpler to use?

Answer these questions to describe your customers' motivations to buy and how your product/service meets a human need:

1. What is the consumer motivation to purchase your product or service? The need for information? A quality product? A secure and convenient way to buy? A great deal? Entertainment? Filling a social need of human interaction?

2. What human need does your product or service fill? Can you describe your product in terms of physical, safety, belonging, or esteem needs?

3. Why does this human need or requirement exist?

4. Does your product or service appeal to the customers' pride of appearance or ownership; or the desire for prestige, recognition, safety, creativity, security, or uniqueness?

Answer these questions to describe your full selling position:

1. What is your full selling position? Can you describe your product or service in terms of price? Are you the lowest? How? Do you sell retail but add value? Do you sell at boutique prices?

2. Can you describe your product or service in terms of selection? Do you have a broad horizontal selection of products or services but not sell many varieties of any one kind? Or is your selling vertical, focused on selling many varieties of only a few types of products and services?

3. Can you describe your product or service in terms of providing convenience to the consumer?

4. Can you describe your product or service in terms of services, such as guarantees or warranties?

5. Can you describe your product or service in terms of security of your consumer's online purchase and the protection of her personal information?

Answer these questions to describe your company's proprietary products or techniques:

1. Do you have any patents, licenses, or proprietary rights not available to competitors? What are they?

2. Is your product copyrighted?

3. Describe your product in detail. What's its size, shape, color, cost, design, quality, capabilities, and so on?

4. Do you legally protect your proprietary product?

5. Do you have necessary permissions to use another person's or company's patents or licenses? Do you show the necessary documentation in your plan? Are these patented or licensed products/services available to competitors or do you have exclusive use?

6. Do you have a plan to upgrade the product or add to it over time?

Answer these questions to outline your production process:

1. If you're manufacturing a product, how do you do it? What processes do you use?

2. How much does it cost? Break down the costs in terms of components or materials and assembly or production.

3. What components or materials do you need to produce your product?

4. Who are your primary suppliers?

5. Why did you choose them? Based on price, location, or delivery time?

6. Who are your backup suppliers if your primary suppliers fail to deliver?

7. Do you have contracts with suppliers? Add them to your plan.

8. How do you deal with sudden increases in orders?

9. What types of technology are required to produce your product? Do you have that technology in your company? If not, is it readily available from somewhere else?

10. What are the inventory management requirements to produce your product?

11. What are the technical and physical infrastructure needs to manage the production and storage of the product and the components or materials that go into producing it?

Summary

As you've learned in this chapter, the reader of your plan wants to know not only what you plan to sell, but also why consumers will buy it. The Product or Service Description section of your plan must also explain to readers where and how you source your products and what resources you need to provide your service.

Don't describe your product or service in language that is too technical with too many industry-specific words or phrases. If you are creating a product, you must provide a detailed description of components or raw materials that go into the finished item and how much the components or raw materials cost. Let the reader of your plan know you have the capability of creating the proprietary product you plan to sell.

Your unique selling position is not only used to describe your product or service but it's also the key component of the marketing plan that you'll write later. In this section of the plan, you define your product or service in terms of customer needs and benefits instead of thinking of your offering from your side of the equation.

Keep in mind that different shoppers are motivated by different things, even at different times. Positioning comes in four types: price, promotion, packaging, and placement. You can describe your product or service in terms of fulfilling human physical, safety, belonging, and esteem needs. Another way to describe your product or service is in terms of your full selling position of price, selection, service, convenience, and security.

The next chapter will explain how to introduce your management team and key personnel to the reader of your plan and the value they bring to your plan for executing and running your new venture.

Presenting Your Organizational Structure and Management Team

I t's not just what you do in your business that counts to potential investors; they also want to know who is going to do the business of your business. The readers of your plan want to know your *organizational structure*—who does what in your company and what responsibilities and tasks are assigned to each member. The readers of your plan also want to know how many of your team are executives, managers, and key personnel.

You can see a sample of what a management plan looks like in Appendix A, "Sample Business Plan."

Your management and personnel team are the human resources of your company, and you describe this team in the Organizational Structure section of your business plan. This section tells the reader what types of human resources your business requires in the short and near term, the specific skill sets required to successfully launch and/or maintain your business, the names of the people slotted for these roles, and their relevant background and expertise.

In this chapter:

* Describe the organizational structure of your business
* Learn to prepare a narrative description and organizational chart
* Write the Organizational Structure and Management Team section of your startup, full, or internal business plan

Your organizational structure will become the basis from which to project your personnel cost in your financial plan. That's why your organizational structure must be well defined and based on realistic operational needs.

In this chapter, you learn how to form an organizational structure that matches your business. You also learn how to describe each element of that structure within your business plan, along with some specific techniques for creating a narrative description and organizational chart that will present the structure accurately and clearly to the readers of your plan.

note Here's how the information in this chapter relates to the three plan types.
- The questions for both the startup and full business plans are very much the same except that in the startup plan, the questions on vice presidents and their needs are not necessary.
- The questions on a board of directors, a board of advisors, and an executive team are not necessary in the internal plan.

To do list

- ☐ Learn how to describe the organizational structure of your business, based on the form your business takes
- ☐ Understand the elements of a management team, and learn to describe those that apply to your business
- ☐ Identify and describe any employee benefits you want to offer

Describing Your Organizational Structure

How you describe your organizational structure and what you include in the description depends on a number of factors, including these two major issues:

- The organizational form of your business
- The types of people who make up your team

The *organizational form* of your business affects your organizational structure and the human resource requirements of your company. The organizational form also impacts the numbers and types of personnel who make up your management team. You learn more about how to describe each of these important areas in the sections that follow.

Matching Your Description to Your Organizational Form

The way you describe your personnel team is determined by whether your company is a sole proprietorship, partnership, or corporation. If you're a sole proprietorship, *you* are the management team. So, this section describes the abilities and expertise you bring to the new business, the areas in which you will need help, and how you'll get that help.

Don't present to the reader a one-man-team approach to management. A knowledgeable reader or investor knows it's hard for one person to wear many hats and successfully run and grow a company.

For example, if you're lacking in marketing experience, you might bring on a consultant to help you with your advertising plan. Or perhaps you'll take a course or two in marketing. In this section, you also want to explain whether you will hire a bookkeeper or use an outside accounting service to keep your books, and whether you will store and ship your products or use a third-party fulfillment service.

These decisions will impact your financial plan and should be well thought out.

As I said before, you might find gaps in your organizational structure—especially key management. You should mention these gaps in management and key personnel that still need to be filled.

For example, if you're a startup company, you should list personnel gaps and describe how you intend to fill them. It is better to detail these gaps and identify holes in your organizational structure than to pretend they don't exist. An educated reader will see these gaps and wonder how you will fill them. Tell the reader how these weaknesses will be corrected and how they will be filled.

On the other hand, if your business is a partnership, be prepared to discuss who the partners are and what experience and skills they bring to the company. You should explain how the different abilities of the partners compliment each other and add to the success of the company.

If your business form is a corporation, you should list the officers of the corporation—president, vice president, secretary/treasurer—and the board of directors. In the directors' short bios, describe who they are, their areas of expertise, why they were chosen, and what they will contribute to the company.

When describing your organizational structure, keep these tips in mind:

- First, list all the tasks that need to be done in your company. Keep their description as broad as possible; for example, administration, sales, marketing, operations, customer service, public relations, production, research and development, and so on.
- Second, organize these tasks into departments.
- Third, detail the roles and responsibilities of each of these departments.
- Fourth, include the names of those who fill these positions, or if unavailable, describe the positions' responsibilities and the type of expertise and experience necessary for the people who will fill those positions.

When seeking investment capital for your company, fill as many key positions in your company as possible before you seek funding. Investors, especially venture capitalists, invest more in people than they do in the business idea. They want to know you have a team in place that can execute the business plan you have proposed. So make sure you show a well-rounded team of professionals in every important and critical aspect of your company.

Describing Your Organizational Team

The organizational form of the company affects the kinds of management and personnel team you describe in this section of your plan. Each business is different and the organizational structure must reflect the business operation and objectives. A business might include the following in the Management Team section and others might not. They are

- Board of directors
- Board of advisors
- Executive team
- Management team
- Administration and key personnel

The following sections talk about these management groups in more detail.

Board of Directors

If your business is incorporated, you will have, and need, a *board of directors*. A board of directors is made up of people elected by the shareholders to govern a corporation; typically this group hires or appoints the company's executive team. If your business is a corporation, you will have a board of directors. List these directors in your management plan. Give the name and a brief, one-page bio for each board member and outline that member's contribution to your company. Include the board members' résumés in the Supporting Documents section of your business plan.

Board of Advisors

If you're not incorporated and your business is a sole proprietorship or partnership, include a *board of advisors*. The board of advisors is a less formal group than a board of directors and does not have authority over the company or executive team. If you have a corporation, you should consider using a board of advisors for these reasons:

- It shows the reader you have a small group of people on board who can advise you on business matters and who have expertise and experience you might lack.
- It tells the reader you are aware of your shortcomings in certain areas and have taken the necessary steps to fill in those gaps. This is particularly important when seeking outside investment.

tip **Plan to Succeed** Your board of directors or board of advisors can supply you with necessary professional services you would normally have to pay for. For example, if you have a lawyer, an accountant, a publicist, and so forth on your board, they could supply you with their professional advice free of charge, thus saving you an expense. This is of particular value if you're a small company just starting out and need to keep expenses down.

An experienced board of advisors can add much credibility in the eyes of an investor. For each member of this board, list the name, experience, and ways in which the individual is expected to contribute to the success of your company.

Executive Team

If you are creating a large company and seeking millions of dollars in investment, you should plan on having an executive team and describing it in your management plan. The *executive team* of your company will include the chief officers, vice presidents, and key managers responsible for overseeing the various company functions and divisions. This team could include, for example, a chief operating officer, company president, chief financial officer, and chief technology officer. The executive team could also include a number of vice presidents that oversee the different company operations, such as marketing, operations, sales, public relations, information technology, research and development, and so on. You should also include the key managers who will report to the vice presidents of their divisions.

caution

Don't make the mistake of placing unqualified friends or family in key management positions. You're running a professional company and your management team should reflect that professionalism.

Management Team

Small- or medium-sized companies normally do not need an executive team. If you're a smaller or startup company, your *management team* would consist of a president/CEO and managers instead of vice presidents. The members of the management team have titles such as operations manager, sales manager, marketing manager, production manager, and so on. If you are a small company, figure out the three or four most important tasks that must be performed in your company and fill these slots first. Try to limit your management team to three to five people—those involved in the day-to-day operations of your company and responsible for its eventual success.

As you compile your management team, don't cut corners on the sales and marketing personnel. These are the bread and butter of your business and are responsible for bringing in revenue.

Administrative and Key Personnel

Finally, your organizational structure—especially if your company is small—includes *administration* and *key personnel* that are neither executives nor managers. Examples of these are a bookkeeper, a customer service supervisor, a sales supervisor, a marketing assistant, an office manager, and so on. You would also include the number of sales, warehouse, and order processing personnel.

If you are using consultants in your business, list them among this group. Accountants, lawyers, and technology advisors (such as web developers and information technology professionals) are examples of such consultants. For each member—both in-house and consultants—remember to describe the individual's expertise and what kind of service she is performing for your company.

A word to the wise: Given a choice between a good business idea with second-rate managers and a mediocre business idea with first-rate managers, investors and venture capitalists prefer the latter.

Describing Employee Benefits

Besides salaries and wages, you must also describe for investors the employee benefits you intend to offer. *Employee benefits* are defined as an indirect form of compensation in addition to salaries and wages. Some employee benefits are mandated by law. These include social security, unemployment, and workers' compensation. Other employee benefits, such as healthcare, life insurance, and retirement plans (such as 401K plans or employee stock options), are sponsored voluntarily by employers.

If you plan to offer such benefits in addition to salaries and wages, list them here in this section and give a brief explanation of them. Keep in mind that health benefits or life insurance premiums will add to your personnel expenses and will be included in your financial plan.

To do list

- ❑ Write a narrative description for each management position within your company
- ❑ Draw up an organizational chart showing the management and reporting structure of your company

Writing Your Description and Creating an Organizational Chart

You should describe your organizational structure using both a narrative description and an organizational chart.

You should construct a narrative description—no more than a few paragraphs—of each person on your team and include

- His position title within the company
- The roles, duties, and responsibilities of that position—what he will be doing, whom he will be overseeing, and to whom he will report
- Describe any previous experience or expertise that relates directly to the position the individual fills in your company—what he did, how long he did it, for whom he did it
- Any previous successes in the area he will be working in or responsible for within your company
- The individual's education or training experience

Each individual's narrative description should be no longer than a page. Include his full résumé in the Supporting Documents section of your plan.

Another way to present the organizational structure of your company is by including an org chart, or organization chart, in this section of your plan. An *organization chart* is a simple diagram showing the various jobs and functions found in a company and their relationships to one another. It graphically shows how the main company functions are divided, and gives the reader a clear definition of the roles and responsibilities of the management team and key personnel of your company.

Here's a sample organization chart for a small retail business:

Retail Catalog House

PRESIDENT

Marketing	Sales	Operations	Administration
Marketing Manager	Sales Manager	Operations Manager	Office Manager
PR Person	Salesperson 1	Customer Service Rep	Bookkeeper
Administrative Assistant	Salesperson 2	Shipping and Receiving Clerk	

Many good charting programs for org charts are on the World Wide Web. You can download a free charting program at www.smartdraw.com/specials/orgchart.asp.

When assigning roles and duties to your management team and key personnel, don't make the mistake of assigning responsibility without authority. Your manager or supervisor must have both. Assigning responsibility without authority is a recipe for failure in your organization.

CONSIDER HAVING AN EMPLOYEE NONCOMPETE AGREEMENT

One fear a company has is the possibility of an employee leaving the company and taking valuable trade secrets with them to a competitor. A *noncompete agreement* can protect a company against such a possibility and you should consider having employees sign one. When an employee signs a noncompete agreement, he promises not to use the company's sensitive information for personal gain, work for a direct competitor, or disclose confidential information to competitors. A noncompete agreement must be reasonable. It cannot last too long (a reasonable agreement lasts for six months to two years after the employee leaves the company), cover too wide a geographic area, or prohibit an employee from engaging in too wide a selection of businesses.

You can buy noncompete agreements at www.nolo.com.

Things You'll Need

- ❑ Your business plan draft
- ❑ Résumés and other supporting documentation

Write the Plan!

Answer thefollowing questions to write the organizational structure and management team section of your business plan. Use the questions listed for your type of plan—startup, full, or internal plan.

Startup Business Plan

Answer these questions to create your organizational structure:

1. Why are you and your team best suited to start this business idea?
2. What are the major tasks or functions that must take place within your organization? Briefly describe your organizational structure in terms of these tasks. Organize these tasks into departments, such as sales, marketing, operations, administration, research and development, customer service, public relations, production, and management.
3. What are the roles and responsibilities of each of these departments?
4. Who will fill your executive, management, and staff positions?
5. If certain critical positions are not filled, describe the positions' responsibilities and the type of expertise and experience required of the people who will fill those positions.

6. If you are inundated with orders for your product or for items to be serviced, do you have a plan for increasing personnel?

7. What is the organizational form of your business?

8. If you're a sole proprietorship, what are the abilities and expertise you bring to the new business? What are the areas in which you will need help? How will you get that help?

9. If your business is a partnership, who are the partners? What experience and skills do they bring to the business?

10. If your business is a corporation, who are the officers of the corporation—president, vice president, secretary/treasurer? Who are on your board of directors?

Answer these questions to describe your board of directors:

1. Who are they? List their names and include a short bio.

2. Why are they qualified? How will they be chosen?

3. What's their expertise?

4. What role will they play in the business?

5. What will they contribute to the business?

6. Have you included their résumés in the Supporting Documents section of your business plan?

Answer these questions to describe your board of advisors:

1. Who are they? List their names and include a short bio.

2. Why are they qualified? How will they be chosen?

3. What role will they play in the business?

4. What special advice or expertise will they be contributing to the company?

5. Have you included their résumés in the Supporting Documents section of your business plan?

Answer these questions to describe your executive team:

1. Who are they? List their names and include a short bio.

2. Will you have a chief operating officer, company president, chief financial officer, and chief technology officer?

3. Why are they qualified? How will they be hired?

4. What's their expertise?

5. What are their wages?

6. What will they be doing? Outline the duties and job descriptions.

7. Will you offer them any employee benefits? What are they? Health insurance? Life insurance? Disability insurance? Retirement plan? Stock options?

Answer these questions to describe your management team:

1. Who are they? List their names and include a short bio.
2. What are the three or four most important tasks that must be performed in your company?
3. Will you have a chief operating officer, operations manager, sales manager, marketing manager, and production manager? Have you limited your management team to three to five people—those involved in the day-to-day operations of your company and responsible for its eventual success?
4. Why are they qualified? How will they be hired?
5. What's their expertise?
6. What are their wages?
7. What will they be doing? Outline the duties and job descriptions.
8. Will you offer them any employee benefits? What are they? Health insurance? Life insurance? Disability insurance? Retirement plan? Stock options?

Answer these questions to describe your administrative and key personnel:

1. Who are they? List their names.
2. How will they be hired?
3. What are their wages?
4. What will they be doing? Outline the duties and job descriptions. Will you have a bookkeeper, a customer service supervisor, a sales supervisor, an administrative assistant, a receptionist, a marketing assistant, and an office manager?
5. List the number of sales, warehouse, and order processing personnel.
6. Will you offer them any employee benefits? What are they? Health insurance? Life insurance? Disability insurance? Retirement plan? Stock options?
7. Are you using consultants? What are their names and their companies' descriptions?
8. What kind of service will they be performing for your company?

Within a narrative description for each position, answer these questions to describe your organizational structure:

1. What is the title of the position?
2. What are the roles, duties, and responsibilities of each position? What will these individuals be doing? Whom will they be overseeing? Whom do they report to?
3. What previous experience or expertise do they have that relates directly to the position? What did they do in previous positions? How long did they do it? For whom did they do it?
4. What are the previous successes in the area of the company they will be responsible for?
5. What is their education or training experience?

Finally, create an organizational chart that shows the various jobs and functions found in your company and their relationship to one another.

The Full Business Plan

Answer these questions to create your organizational structure:

1. Why are you and your team best suited to start this business idea?
2. What are the major tasks or functions that must take place within your organization? Briefly describe your organizational structure in terms of these tasks. Organize these tasks into departments, such as sales, marketing, operations, administration, research and development, customer service, public relations, production, and management.
3. What are the roles and responsibilities of each of these departments?
4. Who fills your executive, management, and staff positions?
5. If certain critical positions are not filled, describe the positions' responsibilities and the type of expertise and experience required of the people who will fill those positions.
6. If you are inundated with orders for your product or for items to be serviced, do you have a plan for increasing personnel?
7. What is the organizational form of your business?
8. If you're a sole proprietorship, what are the abilities and expertise you bring to the new company? What are the areas in which you need help? How will you get that help?
9. If your business is a partnership, who are the partners? What experience and skills do they bring to the company?
10. If your business is a corporation, who are the officers of the corporation— president, vice president, secretary/treasurer? Who are on your board of directors?

Answer these questions to describe your board of directors:

1. Who are they? List their names and include a short bio.
2. Why are they qualified? How are they chosen?
3. What's their expertise?
4. What roles will they play in the company?
5. What will they contribute to the company?
6. Have you included their résumés in the Supporting Documents section of your business plan?

Answer these questions to describe your board of advisors:

1. Who are they? List their names and include a short bio.
2. Why are they qualified? How are they chosen?
3. What roles will they play in the company?

4. What special advice or expertise will they be contributing to the company?

5. Have you included their résumés in the Supporting Documents section of your business plan?

Answer these questions to describe your executive team:

1. Who are they? List their names and include a short bio.

2. Do you have a chief operating officer, company president, chief financial officer, and chief technology officer?

3. Do you have a number of vice presidents that oversee the different aspects of your company operation, such as marketing, operations, sales, public relations, information technology, and research and development?

4. Why are they qualified? How are they hired?

5. What's their expertise?

6. What are their wages?

7. What will they be doing? Outline the duties and job descriptions.

8. Will you offer them any employee benefits? What are they? Health insurance? Life insurance? Disability insurance? Retirement plan? Stock options?

Answer these questions to describe your management team:

1. Who are they? List their names and include a short bio.

2. What are the three or four most important tasks that must be performed in your company?

3. Do you have a chief operating officer, operations manager, sales manager, marketing manager, and production manager? Have you limited your management team to three to five people—those involved in the day-to-day operations of your company and responsible for its eventual success?

4. Why are they qualified? How are they hired?

5. What's their expertise?

6. What are their wages?

7. What will they be doing? Outline the duties and job descriptions.

8. Will you offer them any employee benefits? What are they? Health insurance? Life insurance? Disability insurance? Retirement plan? Stock options?

Answer these questions to describe your administrative and key personnel:

1. Who are they? List their names.

2. How are they hired?

3. What are their wages?

4. What will they be doing? Outline the duties and job descriptions. Do you have a bookkeeper, a customer service supervisor, a sales supervisor, an administrative assistant, a receptionist, a marketing assistant, and an office manager?

5. List the number of sales, warehouse, and order processing personnel.

6. Will you offer them any employee benefits? What are they? Health insurance? Life insurance? Disability insurance? Retirement plan? Stock options?

7. Are you using consultants? What are their names and companies' descriptions?

8. What kind of service will they be performing for your company?

Within a narrative description for each position, answer these questions to describe your organizational structure:

1. What is the title of the position?

2. What are the roles, duties, and responsibilities of each position? What are these individuals doing? Whom will they be overseeing? Whom will they report to?

3. What previous experience or expertise do they have that relates directly to the position? What did they do in previous positions? How long did they do it? For whom did they do it?

4. What are the previous successes in the area of the company they will be responsible for?

5. What is their education or training experience?

Finally, create an organizational chart that shows the various jobs and functions found in your company and their relationship to one another.

The Internal Business Plan

Answer these questions to create your organization structure:

1. Why are you and your team best suited to start this business idea?

2. What are the major tasks or functions that must take place within your department or internal organization? What are the roles and responsibilities of those doing these tasks?

3. Who fills your executive, management, and staff positions?

4. If you are inundated with orders for your product or for items to be serviced, do you have a plan for increasing personnel?

Answer these questions to describe your management team:

1. What are the three or four most important tasks that must be performed in your division? Who fills them? List their names and include a short bio.

2. Why are they qualified? How are they hired?

3. What's their expertise?

4. What are their wages?

5. What will they be doing? Outline the duties and job descriptions.

Answer these questions to describe your administrative and key personnel:

1. Who are they? List their names.

2. How are they hired?

3. What are their wages?
4. What will they be doing? Outline the duties and job descriptions.
5. Are you using consultants? What are their names and their companies' descriptions?
6. What kind of service will they be performing for your division?

Within a narrative description for each position, answer these questions to describe your organizational structure:

1. What is the title of the position?
2. Describe the roles, duties, and responsibilities of each position. What will she be doing? Whom will she be overseeing? Whom will she report to?
3. What previous experience or expertise does she have that relates directly to the position? What did she do? How long did she do it? For whom did she do it?
4. What are the previous successes in the area of the company she will be responsible for?
5. What is her education or training experience?
6. Create an organizational chart that shows the various jobs and functions found in your company and their relationship to one another.

Summary

The readers of your plan want to know your organizational structure—who does what in your company, the various responsibilities each person has, the tasks assigned to each of them, the tasks given to each division of your company, and how many of your team are executives, managers, and key personnel. Your management and personnel team are the human resources of your company.

Your organizational structure will become the basis from which to project your personnel cost in your financial plan. Don't make the mistake of placing unqualified friends or family in key management positions. You may find gaps in your organizational structure. You should mention these gaps in management and key personnel that still need to be filled.

How you describe your organizational structure and what you include in that description depends on the organizational form of your business and the types of people who make up your team. You should describe your organizational structure by using a narrative description and an org chart.

The next chapter will show you how to describe the marketplace your company will operate within and identify the types of customers who will purchase your products or services.

Part III

Where and How?

Describing Your Marketplace

A businessman once lamented that "50% of my marketing does not work. But I don't know which 50%." If he knew his market, he would have been able to decipher the difference.

A *market analysis* is not only important when creating a marketing plan, but also necessary to communicate to the reader of your plan that you have researched and analyzed the market you sell within. In describing your marketplace, this section of your plan deals with an analysis—evaluation and expectations—of your market.

The Marketplace section of your business plan is written in a manner that gives readers a good understanding of your marketplace, its present situation, and its future based on known patterns and trends. You write this section to explain why you chose this market and to support your decisions with objective data.

You can see a sample of a market analysis in the sample business plan in Appendix A, "Sample Business Plan."

Now, you don't have to create a market analysis worthy of a Ph.D., but you do want to keep your analysis clear and concise. The content of your marketing analysis also depends upon the type of plan you are writing. If you're writing an internal plan, your market analysis can be fairly brief because your company knows your market pretty well and only requires an analysis of factors within your business. On the other hand, if you're writing a plan for an entirely new market segment for your existing business or division or for a new company, your analysis has to be more detailed in its explanation and requires research from outside your business. And yes, if you are looking for investment, you should show the reader you have a grasp of the marketplace you plan to sell into.

 note Here's how the information in this chapter relates to the three plan types:

- The questions to be answered for both the startup and full business plan are the same.
- The questions on analyzing industry participants are not needed in the internal plan, nor are the questions on patterns and trends in the industry and the industry statistics needed because management would be aware of them.

 But don't overdo it. This is a business plan, not a thesis. Planning your business is not a test of your knowledge but of your understanding of the product or service you're selling, its market-place, and the customer you serve. Also, don't try to attack too many markets at once—particularly if you are a startup or early-stage company.

Things You'll Need

- ❑ Trade publications related to your industry
- ❑ Computer and Internet access
- ❑ Merchant directory

Doing the Research

 Don't assume everyone is a buyer of your product or service. You need to do the proper research to determine who is your target customer. So, where do you begin your research on your market? Here are a few places to start.

First, check out the industry publications for your marketplace. Industry magazines, trade journals, and websites are a good source for descriptions of the current state of your industry segment and for data that supports the growth potential of your chosen market. Second, use the Internet. The Web is a prime source for business analyses, financial statistics, demographics, trade associations, and just about everything you need for a complete business plan.

 Many businesses offer online guidance for compiling information useful for market analyses. Rhodes-Blakeman Associates (RBA), for example, is an organization that provides training and advice on the use of technology for accessing information. The RBA website has some key starting points for market and industry research and can be found at www.rba.co.uk/sources/mr.htm. This website lists a wide selection of information resources where you can find market research content aggregators, market research publishers, internet surveys, and government sources. Another excellent source is Findex at www.findexonline.com. This company publishes a worldwide directory of market research reports that is a guide to 10,000+ off-the-shelf report titles from more than 350 market research publishers. The Wall Street Executive Library at www.executivelibrary.com/Research.asp is another directory of the best information sources on the Internet.

Using statistics and data compiled by others can provide secondary research data. If you have the time and the money, however, you can gather your own data. Customer surveys and focus groups can provide you with first-hand knowledge of your target market. Or you can hire a telemarketing firm to call and survey a cross section of your target market to get its reaction to your product or service offering. If you're selling to businesses, you can contact these businesses directly, explain what kind of product or service you are offering, and get their reactions to your offering. You can also consider contracting a market research firm to do the research for you.

Even a simple friendly conversation with a representative cross-section of people from within your target market could be very enlightening. You could have these friendly conversations at selected neighborhood merchants. Introduce yourself and see if people will answer a few quick questions.

In summary, your Market Analysis section should describe the target customer segment you sell to, a summary of the existing market, and projections of anticipated market growth. Another reason market analysis is so important is that it helps determine where marketing dollars will be spent. You may not have access to a comprehensive databank of this information but you should seek to include enough data to provide the reader with a working knowledge of your marketplace—especially if you are looking for investors.

APPROACHING MARKET RESEARCH

The success of your product or service depends on your knowledge of the market you plan to sell within. So market research becomes a very important factor in your company's success. You should use both primary and secondary research in your market analysis.

Primary research includes activities such as face-to-face and phone interviews, focus groups and surveys. This is the kind of information that you collect yourself. Secondary research involves investigating research that already exists, such as that in books, periodicals, industry research reports, and company annual reports. This kind of information can be found at your local library, or even better, on the Internet.

The Internet is a gold mine of market research information. Go to www.google.com and type in keywords of the industry you plan to do business in and you'll be surprised at the amount of research data you can find. The Internet is also a great tool for conducting competitive research. This is an important part of your market research and should not be ignored. Seeing what your proposed competition is doing will help you better understand your market and how to position your company against the competition.

To do list

- ❑ Define your customer types
- ❑ Describe your customer demographics
- ❑ State your market's geographical location
- ❑ List your customers' motivations

Defining Your Market Segment—Targeting the Customer

A *target market* is defined as a group of potential customers with a set of common characteristics that are distinguishable from other types of customers. Your job is to describe in your plan these common characteristics and why you make those potential customers your own.

For example, let's say your target customers all own automobiles. Better yet, older automobiles, perhaps 30 years old or older. Because parts are not readily available for older cars, you decide to open a business that services and repairs these older vehicles. By choosing to sell products and services to car owners with vehicles 30 years old or older, you've segmented the automobile repair and service market. Your research should determine how many of these older automobiles are owned in the geographical area of your repair shop. That is to say, you need to determine how big the market is for this type of business. You might be able to find this information in U.S. census data or from database marketers who get their information from the motor vehicle department of your state. Once you've identified these potential customers, state in your plan how you feel you can service this market. Do you have the strengths, resources, and unique selling position to service these customers?

Defining and Segmenting Your Target Customer Group

You might have more than one target customer. For instance, you might be an accountant that has both business and individual clients. Or perhaps you manufacture computers for the home, business, and educational markets. You need to identify and describe each group of target customers in the same way.

tip

Keep this in mind: Don't explain *why* your target market needs you. Explain *how* you plan to meet your target market's needs.

If done properly, this part of your market analysis clearly identifies the current and prospective buyers of your company's products or services. This research is not only important to clearly define your target customers, but it also helps when you create the sales and marketing strategies to reach them.

Another example of segmenting and targeting a market could be an electronics retailer selling televisions. Are you selling high-end plasma high definition TVs or the run-of-the-mill standard televisions? By defining the type of TV you sell, you are also defining the target audience you sell to. You can even make this target market segmentation more precise. Let's consider this example; if you are proposing a restaurant, you might refine your product and target market by establishing a fast-food restaurant. But even within that targeted segment, you might further target your market by selling food to families with young children as opposed to offering more adult fare.

Another market strategy is to divide your market into categories. Apple Computer did this and was very successful at it. They divided the computer market into home, education, small business, large business, and government. Each of these markets had a different focus, targeting a different type of customer with a certain kind of computer use.

Describing Your Target Market and Customers

The key to good targeting is to define your customer base as tightly as possible, and to be very clear in describing the characteristics of your target customers. Do this by defining your target customer both *quantitatively* and *qualitatively*. Age, income, product type, geography, buying patterns, customer needs, and so on all effect how you segment and classify your target market. Consider these types of characteristics when describing your target market:

- Customer types
- Customer demographics
- Market geographical location
- Customer motivations

The following sections discuss these customer characteristics in more detail, and explain how you can use these characteristics to categorize and describe your target market.

Customer Types

The type of customer you sell to, especially if you plan to sell online, is one way to categorize your target market. Here are some of the customer types you might describe in your own target market:

- **Convenience shoppers**—These are customers who are looking for convenience, want to save time, and are primarily impulse shoppers. These customers prize convenience over price. These customers are at the heart of the target market for convenience stores such as 7-Eleven and Circle K.
- **Window shoppers**—These customers are willing to take their time when making a purchase. They like to have as much information as possible before making a purchase.

- **Brand name shoppers**—Another type of customer is drawn only to brand names and are very brand conscious when shopping.
- **Bargain shoppers**—These customers are only interested in a good deal. They either are looking to buy products and services at a discount, or they are keen comparison shoppers looking for the lowest price.

Customer Demographics

You can describe customer demographics in terms of business customers and consumer customers. The demographic traits you provide depend on the type of customer to which you are most likely to market your product or service. If your demographic focus is the private consumer, you need to describe demographic traits such as personal income, gender, occupation, marital status, ethnicity, and education. You also need to point out to your business plan's reader how much disposable income your target consumers have to spend on your product or service.

If your focus is on the business customer, the demographic traits you should describe include the type of industry you sell to, the kind of product or service you offer, the revenue of your target business, the number of employees, and whether it's a private or public organization.

Market Geographical Location

You can also describe your target market in terms of where your target customers are located. Stating the geographical location of your customers is not only necessary for defining your target market, but also helps when you devise your sales and marketing budget needed to capture market share.

And although Internet technology has greatly enlarged the potential universe of customers, you still need to physically describe your target market in terms of where they live, work, or play—the place where you intend to find customers and offer your product or service.

Customer Motivations

Finally, describing the buying motivations of your customer is another way to define your target market.

First among these motivations, of course, is the product or service motivator—the need you can satisfy with merchandise and services. The unique selling position you described Chapter 6, "Presenting Your Organizational Structure and Management Team," is designed to meet a specific product or service motivational need. Second is the information motivation—the need to know. Your target market might be

note For an online business, one other motivation is met by your service—community or the need to connect with others. The Internet is well suited for meeting this motivational need and many companies have developed along those lines. One example is iVillage, at www.ivillage.com, a website for women. Another is ePinions, at www.epinions.com, which is a consumer opinion site on products and services from A to Z.

those customers who are information addicts. These customers are motivated by their need to know the latest financial, celebrity, or sports news. And third is the entertainment motivator—customers' need to be entertained.

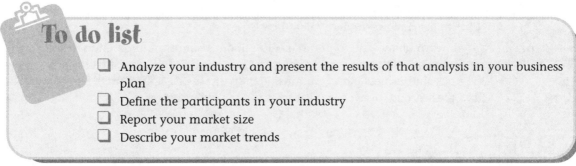

To do list

- ☐ Analyze your industry and present the results of that analysis in your business plan
- ☐ Define the participants in your industry
- ☐ Report your market size
- ☐ Describe your market trends

Analyzing Your Industry, Its Participants, Your Market, and Market Trends

The better you know your industry, the more likely you are to succeed in your business venture.

You must demonstrate to the reader of your plan that you have a solid understanding of how your industry functions. And the more you know about your industry, the better you can market and sell within it.

Whether you're a retailer, service company, manufacturer, or any other type of business that sells to either companies or consumers, your business plan's industry analysis must explain the general state of your industry and the participants within it. You also need to know this information later on when you describe and write the Competition section of your plan.

Your industry analysis should also include information on principal distribution channels and sales cycles. For example, you should explain whether you plan to create your own sales force to sell a product you have manufactured or you plan to use already established sales representatives in the industry.

> **tip**
> An added bonus of using an established sales and marketing channel instead of creating your own is that your business idea and its success increases the credibility of your business in the eyes of investors and bankers.

Your decisions about distribution channels affect your financial plan. In the preceding example, if you are going to market and sell your manufactured product to distributors or retailers, you have to budget into your financial plan the cost of hiring, training, and paying a sales force. You also have to create a more extensive marketing plan to reach the distributors and retailers you target. However, if you contract out to a sales representative company, your cost for sales and marketing is far less.

Every product or service has a sales cycle, and your industry's sales cycle affects the revenue of your business. You should identify the sales cycle in your plan. Some companies experience seasonal lulls, as will yours if its products or services are tied to specific times of year. An accounting service, for example, experiences a spike in business during tax time, but may drop off during the rest of the year. Other examples of companies with seasonal sales cycles include those that sell items related to Christmas, Halloween, and Valentine's Day.

You'll learn about writing in more detail about your distribution and sales strategies in Chapter 9, "Listing Your Distribution Channels." But in this Industry Analysis section of your business plan, you must identify those principal distribution channels and the seasonal or event driven sales cycles of your business.

Things You'll Need

- ❑ List of participants in your industry
- ❑ Data on the size of your market
- ❑ Information on your market trends
- ❑ Computer and Internet access

Conducting and Presenting an Industry Analysis

It's not enough to know your own business and to accurately describe it in your business plan. You must also show the reader you have a good grasp of the industry your business is a part of. You must understand and describe the forces, trends, and market potential of your industry and the projected growth that supports your company in meeting its business objectives. Demonstrating to the reader, investor, or banker that you understand the patterns and trends of your industry helps build a case for your company's success.

When approaching your industry analysis, first think of similar companies that provide products and services like yours. Also include in your analysis companies selling complementary or supplementary products or services. Look at the value chain of your product or service. A *value chain* is described as a series of linked business processes creating value in both products and services delivered to the customer.

For example, any business participating in the production or presentation of your product or service, from the gathering of raw materials through distribution and sales of the product to the end user or consumer, is part of your industry value chain. All of these businesses must be considered when doing your industry analysis.

When you do your analysis, consider these factors and describe them in the presentation of your findings:

- The size of your industry in both revenue and number of companies
- Your industry's growth now and in the past and its trends into the future
- The factors influencing the growth of your industry

- Government regulations affecting your industry
- The distribution and sales channels of your industry, and how difficult or easy it is to gain entrance to them

STEPS TO A USABLE INDUSTRY ANALYSIS

Many business people are stumped on where to begin an industry analysis. Here's the process, all laid out in a few simple steps:

1. Formally identify your industry. Find your industry *standard industrial classi-fication (SIC)* code. These codes are created by the Federal Office of Management and Budget, and they define and name the different indus-tries that exist in our economy. SIC codes are used as identifiers in reports such as industry census data and financial reports. By knowing the SIC code, you can use these reports to help you analyze the activities in your industry and in many other types of market research.

   You can find a list and explanation of the SIC codes at http://www.listsareus.com/business-sic-codes-a.htm#codes or http://www.osha.gov/pls/imis/sic_manual.html.

2. Look for general industry information. A good government site for busi-ness statistics is FedStats at http://www.fedstats.gov/. It's a portal to statistics from more than 100 government agencies.

3. Identify trade organizations and publications. Trade associations are a gold mine of information about industries and their participants. Online databases of associations can be found at http://www.ipl.org/div/aon.

4. Determine your market size. The easiest and least expensive way is to do this is to use your local library's magazine directories to find out how many magazines service a particular market. The number of magazines and each of their circulations are good indicators of the size of their market. Three of the best directories are

   ❋ *Bacon's Magazine Directory*

   ❋ *Oxbridge Communications Directory of Periodicals*

   ❋ *SRDS Magazine Media Source*

5. Finally, research the market trends in your industry. You can keep abreast of the latest trends in your industry by using the resource links at http://marketing.about.com/od/markettrends/.

Describing Industry Participants

Who sells in your industry is as important as what is sold. You can't fully describe the nature of your industry without describing the nature of its participants. For example, a big difference exists between the cable television industry and the retail food industry. While there are hundreds of thousands of food companies in this country, there are only a handful of cable TV companies. Even within the food industry itself, segmentation affects the number of participants.

For example, formal, sit-down restaurants form an industry made up of a large number of many small- to medium-size participants; the fast-food business, on the other hand, is dominated by a few national brands in thousands of national sites. The auto industry is similar to the fast-food industry. A small handful of auto-makers dominate the manufacturing wing of the auto industry, with thousands of smaller dealerships selling their cars. In computer manufacturing, there are a few large firms whose names are well known, and thousands of smaller firms.

You must describe in your plan the participants in your industry and how your company will function as one of them.

Defining and Describing Market Size

You should know the size of the market you plan to sell into. How large is your target market? Are there a large number of buyers ready to purchase your product? For example, is there a food store that sells products which are consumed frequently or have to be replenished constantly? Or are there a small handful of very large-spending target customers, such as those who purchase pianos or high-end sports cars?

If you're seeking funding, investors want to know how big the potential market is for your product or service, as well as the percentage of the market you will take—your market penetration. *Market penetration* is defined as the market percentage a product captures. A strategy for increasing sales of current products in current markets can affect your market penetration.

If you're creating either an internal plan or a new company, be prepared to explain in this section whether your current market share is growing, holding steady, or declining. You should also describe how you attract, hold, or increase your market share.

Finally, you don't have to have a large target market. A smaller well-defined target market you can properly serve can be just as beneficial to your company—and just as persuasive to the readers of your business plan.

Analyzing and Describing Market Trends

Describing the trends in your industry helps support your business idea in the eyes of your reader. You should consider the factors that might be changing your market and thus provide support for your business concept. Depending upon the type of business you're in, market trends could be changes in demographics, consumer taste, or consumer needs. By understanding the factors affecting market trends in your industry, you better explain the need for and possible success of your business concept.

An example of a market trend could be the current interest in nostalgia. The nostalgia trend is seen today in automobiles, furniture, clothing, and so forth. Your company might plan to take advantage of this trend and sell into this market. Or perhaps your product takes advantage of the growing demographic of the aging baby boom population and the increasing possibility of selling products and services into that marketplace. American tastes in food and drink are also changing. The boom in low-carbohydrate foods is a good example of a trend many companies have jumped on and are now supplying all types of low-carb food and drink.

Identify the trends in your industry, describe them in your plan, and detail how your business takes advantage of them.

Things You'll Need

- ❑ Draft business plan
- ❑ Market research information/results

Write the Plan!

Answer the following questions to write this portion of your business plan as they apply to your type of plan—startup, full, or internal plan.

The Startup Business Plan

Answer these questions to define your market segment:

1. How and when did your market originate? What other brief historical information would be helpful in informing readers about your market?
2. What need or demand does your company fill?
3. What are the different categories of your market? Can you segment your target market into different categories, such as business, consumer, education, non-profit, government, and so on?
4. Who are the current and prospective buyers of your company's products or services?
5. Are they brand-conscious buyers, impulse buyers, window shoppers, or bargain shoppers? What motivates your customer to buy? The need to satisfy with merchandise or services, the need for information, the need to be entertained, or the need to participate in community?
6. What about their demographic profile? What are your typical consumer's personal income, gender, occupation, marital status, ethnicity, and education level? If businesses are your target, describe the type of industry you sell to, the kind of product or service you offer, the revenue of your target business, the number of employees, and whether it's a private or public organization.

7. Where is your target market located? What are the physical limitations of your target market? State in terms of where they live, work, or play.

8. Are there unusual opportunities for additional differentiation of your product or service through technology, positioning, or segmentation?

Answer these questions to provide an analysis of your industry:

1. What are the forces, trends, and market potential of your industry that supports your company in meeting its business objectives? Ideally cite experts such as a market expert, market research firm, trade association, or credible journalist.

2. What are the significant statistics for your industry? Revenue size, number of firms, units sold, and employment figures?

3. What are the principle distribution and sales channels for your products or service in your industry? Do you use existing channels or create your own?

4. Where does your business fit into the value chain of your industry? Describe how you can meet a window of opportunity.

5. Is it difficult to gain distribution access to your industry?

6. What are the barriers of entry into your industry?

7. What government regulations affect your industry and your company? Is your industry highly regulated or does it fall below the government's radar?

8. What similar companies are providing products and services like yours? How many people or businesses are currently using a competitor's product that is the same as or similar to the one you are offering or planning to offer?

9. What companies are selling complementary or supplementary products or services?

10. Describe how your product or service can be more successful than the competition's. Cite some achievements of your team in similar or related fields.

Answer these questions to provide an analysis of the participants within your industry:

1. What is the nature of the participants in your industry? Is your industry dominated by a few large companies or are there thousands of little companies vying for the same target market?

2. How do you participate in this industry?

3. How many companies are expected to enter your industry in the future?

Answer these questions to describe the size of your market:

1. How large is the potential target market for your product or service?

2. Do you have a primary and secondary market for your product or service?

3. Are there a large number of buyers ready to purchase your product or a small handful of very large-spending target customers?

4. Do you have a large target market or a smaller, well-defined target market?

5. What is the probable range of market share attainable, given the competitive status and customer demand? What percentage of the market does your company take or can you increase sales of current products in current markets?

6. What is the range of profitable revenue potential, based on a reasonable market penetration or market share?

7. How do you attract, hold, or increase your market share?

Answer these questions to describe market trends within your industry:

1. What are the patterns and trends of your industry? Is the industry growing, flattening, or shrinking?

2. What factors are influencing growth or decline in your industry?

3. What have been the trends in previous years?

4. What trends are expected in coming years?

5. What are the changes in demographics, consumer taste, or needs for your industry?

The Full Business Plan

Answer these questions to define your market segment:

1. Discuss a little history of your market. How and when did it originate?

2. What need or demand does your company fill?

3. What are the different categories of your market? Can you segment your target market into different categories, such as business, consumer, education, non-profit, government, and so forth?

4. Who are the current and prospective buyers of your company's products or services?

5. Are they brand-conscious buyers, impulse buyers, window shoppers, or bargain shoppers? What motivates your customer to buy? The need to satisfy with merchandise or service, the need for information, the need to be entertained, or the need to participate in community?

6. What about their demographic profile? What are your typical consumer's personal income, gender, occupation, marital status, ethnicity, and education level? If businesses are your target, describe the type of industry you sell to, the kind of product or service you offer, the revenue of your target business, the number of employees, and whether it's a private or public organization.

7. Where is your target market located? What are the physical limitations of your target market? State in terms of where they live, work, or play.

8. Are there unusual opportunities for additional differentiation of your product or service through technology, positioning, or segmentation?

Answer these questions to present an analysis of your industry:

1. What are the forces, trends, and market potential of your industry that supports your company in meeting its business objectives? Ideally cite experts such as a market expert, market research firm, trade association, or credible journalist.
2. What are the significant statistics for your industry? Revenue size, number of firms, units sold, and employment figures?
3. What are the principle distribution and sales channels for your product or service in your industry? Do you use existing channels or create your own?
4. Where does your business fit into the value chain of your industry? Describe how you can meet a window of opportunity.
5. Is it difficult to gain distribution access to your industry?
6. What are the sales cycles in your industry? Are they seasonal? What are the sales peaks and valleys?
7. What are the barriers of entry into your industry?
8. What government regulations affect your industry and your company? Is your industry highly regulated or does it fall below the government's radar?
9. What similar companies are providing products and services like yours? How many people or businesses are currently using a competitor's product that is the same as or similar to the one you are offering or planning to offer?
10. What companies are selling complementary or supplementary products or services?
11. Describe how your product or service can be more profitable than the competition's?

Answer these questions to present an analysis of the participants in your industry:

1. What is the nature of the participants in your industry? Is it dominated by a few large companies or are there thousands of little companies vying for the same target market? Or are the numbers of participants somewhere in between?
2. How do you participate in this industry?
3. How many companies are expected to enter your industry in the future?

Answer these questions to describe the size of your market:

1. How large is the potential target market?
2. Do you have a primary and secondary market for your product or service?
3. Are there a large number of buyers ready to purchase your product or a small handful of very large-spending target customers?
4. Do you have a large target market or a smaller, well-defined target market?
5. What is the probable range of market share attainable, given the competitive status and customer demand? What percentage of the market does your company take or can you increase sales of current products in current markets?

6. What is the range of profitable revenue potential, based on a reasonable market penetration or market share?
7. How do you attract, hold, or increase your market share?

Answer these questions to describe market trends within your industry:

1. What are the patterns and trends of your industry? Is the industry growing, flattening, or shrinking?
2. What factors are influencing growth or decline in your industry?
3. If you're creating an internal plan, is your current market share growing, holding steady, or declining?
4. What have been the trends in previous years?
5. What trends are expected in coming years?
6. What are the changes in demographics, consumer taste, or needs for your industry?

The Internal Business Plan

Answer these questions to define your market segment:

1. Who are the current and prospective buyers of your company's products or services?
2. Are they brand-conscious buyers, impulse buyers, window shoppers, or bargain shoppers? What motivates your customer to buy? The need to satisfy with merchandise or services, the need for information, the need to be entertained, or the need to participate in community?
3. What about their demographic profile? What are your typical consumer's personal income, gender, occupation, marital status, ethnicity, and education level? If businesses are your target, describe the type of industry you sell to, the kind of product or service you offer, the revenue of your target business, the number of employees, and whether it's a private or public organization.
4. Where is your target market located? What are the physical limitations of your target market? State in terms of where they live, work, or play.
5. Are there unusual opportunities for additional differentiation of your product or service through technology, positioning, or segmentation?

Answer these questions to provide an analysis of your industry:

1. What are the forces, trends, and market potential of your industry that supports your division in meeting its business objectives? Ideally cite experts such as a market expert, market research firm, trade association, or credible journalist.
2. What are the principle distribution and sales channels for your products or service in your industry? Do you use existing channels or create your own?
3. Where does your business fit into the value chain of your industry? Describe how you can meet a window of opportunity.
4. Is it difficult to gain distribution access to your industry?

5. What are the sales cycles in your industry? Are they seasonal? What are the sales peaks and valleys?

6. What are the barriers of entry into your industry?

7. What government regulations affect your industry and your company? Is your industry highly regulated or does it fall below the government's radar?

8. What similar companies are providing products and services like yours? How many people or businesses are currently using a competitor's product that is the same as or similar to the one you are offering or planning to offer?

9. What companies are selling complementary or supplementary products or services?

10. Describe how your product or service can be more successful than the competition's.

Answer these questions to describe the size of your market:

1. How large is the potential target market?

2. Do you have a primary and secondary market for your product or service?

3. Are there a large number of buyers ready to purchase your product or a small handful of very large-spending target customers?

4. Do you have a large target market or a smaller, well-defined target market?

5. What is the probable range of market share attainable, given the competitive status and customer demand? What percentage of the market does your company take or can you increase sales of current products in current markets?

6. What is the range of profitable revenue potential, based on a reasonable market penetration or market share?

7. How do you attract, hold, or increase your market share?

Summary

A market analysis deals with an evaluation of your market and the expectations for your own company associated with the results of that evaluation. A market analysis is not only important when creating a marketing plan, but also necessary to communicate to the reader of your plan that you have researched and analyzed the market you sell within. You don't have to create a market analysis worthy of a Ph.D. but you do want to keep your analysis clear and concise. In summary, your Market Analysis section should describe the target customer segment you sell to, a summary of the existing market, and projections of anticipated market growth.

In this chapter, you learned that it's not enough to know your own business and to accurately describe it in your business plan. You must also show the reader you have a good grasp of the industry your business is a part of. Who sells in your industry is as important as what is sold. You also must know the size of the market you plan to sell into. Describing the trends in your industry helps support your business idea in the eyes of your reader. The next chapter will show you how to craft your marketing strategy and how to reach and communicate with your target market.

Crafting Your Marketing Strategy

8

The universe of marketing can sometimes resemble what William James called a world of "blooming, buzzing confusion." For both offline and online, you have a wide variety of advertising, promotion, publicity, media relations, and public relations marketing vehicles to use. In the offline world, you have magazines, newspapers, brochures, catalogs, television and radio ads, promotional fliers, telemarketing, direct mail, billboards, and press releases. In the online world you have a choice of search engine submittals; purchasing top placement in the search engines; key word purchases; promotional emails; text, HTML, and rich media newsletters, and much, much more.

But this almost infinite variety of tools can all work together in concert under four basic marketing platforms to achieve a company's business goals and objectives. I call these four marketing platforms P.A.R.M.: The first is *positioning*, which rests on the second of *acquiring*, which rests on *retaining*, which rests on *monetizing*. In addition, these platforms rest on others beneath them—the wide variety of the actual marketing tactics available for your marketing plan. In this chapter, you learn how to reflect an understanding and savvy use of each of these marketing platforms within the Marketing Strategy section of your business plan.

To do list

- ☐ Learn the components of a successful marketing strategy
- ☐ Discover how to position your company online

Creating a Marketing Strategy

You have done your homework on your industry, defined your market segment, identified a consumer need, and targeted your potential customers, but all is for naught if you can't reach and convince anyone to buy your great product or service. How well you market your business ultimately determines the success or failure of your company.

In other words, what you need is a marketing strategy.

You can see a sample of a marketing strategy in Appendix A, "Sample Business Plan."

Your *marketing strategy* is your marketing plan. Marketing is sometimes believed to mean advertising and sales promotion. But it's more than that. *Marketing* includes everything from company positioning, market research, new product or business development, advertising, promotion, public relations, and even the sales function itself. A *marketing plan* details what, to whom, when, and how a business sells. One addition to a company's marketing strategy is the *sales plan*. A sales plan describes how sales are made and to whom.

It's time now to create a marketing strategy to reach target customers with your unique selling position by describing a position that enhances, supports, and promotes your product or service as meeting their needs.

note Here's how the information in this chapter relates to the three plan types:

- Time and resources are usually less in a startup company, so this type of plan typically doesn't consider an extensive use of an integrated digital strategy, trade show events, seminars and workshops, search engine marketing, customer loyalty programs, selling complementary products or services, sending industry newsletters, and so on. It is assumed that in a startup plan, only one person, or very few, do the selling or use manufacturer's reps.

- Internal plans assume a company already has a digital presence and the company positioning on the Internet has been done. Existing companies already have a relationship with an advertising agency, have a customer loyalty program, do not sell complementary products or services, and do not place community elements on their website. The public relations policies are already set by the existing company and not the new division, as are relationships with trade associations.

Things You'll Need

- ❏ Internet access
- ❏ Website for your company

Choosing the Tools for Your Marketing Strategy

A well-thought-out marketing strategy describes how you intend to reach your target customer. The Marketing Strategy section of your plan should outline the necessary steps to reach prospects and convert them into paying customers. You must be able to identify the different avenues of advertising and promotion you use to effectively sell your product or service and how you use them.

Your marketing strategy should encompass as many marketing tools as your budget allows to communicate with your target customers and promote your offering.

Do not make the mistake of not specifically identifying the media outlets you use to advertise and promote your product or service. Don't omit important details such as when, where, why, and how you reach your target customer, along with costs.

These media outlets include advertising (ads in print, TV, radio, and the Internet), public relations (a list of media that are approached as well as a schedule of planned events), sales promotions (a description of collateral marketing material as well as a schedule of planned promotional activities, such as special sales, coupons, contests, and premium awards), and sales strategy (including pricing procedures, returns and adjustment rules, sales presentation methods, lead generation, customer service policies, salesperson compensation, and market responsibilities).

Positioning Your Company Online

Following the directions in the previous chapters, you should have a good start in successfully positioning your product in your marketplace. That is to say, you have described the first part of P.A.R.M.

But there are other marketing platforms that stack up under positioning in the online world. And these should be considered in your marketing plan, too.

How do you position your company in the digital marketplace? First, look at your collateral and communications material, including your letterhead, business cards, brochures, and advertising copy (print, radio, and TV). Make sure all are integrated into your digital strategy solution. For example, all of your offline collateral materials and activities should include, at the very least, an email address and a reference to the URL of your website. You might mention in your plan that you offer readers, viewers, and listeners the ability to sign up for your online or offline newsletter for further information on your company. If you have a printed catalog, describe how you integrate it to work in concert with your website.

Positioning also includes submitting your website to the major search engines. List these engines in your plan.

The communication process you have with site visitors is also important. How do you communicate to potential customers in the online world? In fact, how do you communicate to any visitor that communicates with you through your digital presence? I like the term *digital presence* better than website because websites as they are today are only one way to access a company over the Internet. In your marketing plan, think about how you are communicating to potential customers through Internet-enabled devices, such as handheld computers, PDAs, cell phones, TVs, cars, refrigerators, and microwave ovens.

As in other parts of your plan, keep your writing simple. Too much jargon in both technical and business terms can turn off the reader.

note Search engines are one of the Web's major resources for driving qualified traffic. Being listed in the top search engines on the Internet is very important if you want your website to be found. Most people use search engines when looking for products, information, or services on the Internet. Here are some of the top search engines you should submit your website to:

- **Yahoo!**—http://www.yahoo.com
- **Google**—http://www.google.com
- **MSN**—http://search.msn.com
- **AOL Search**—http://search.aol.com
- **AltaVista**—http://www.altavista.com
- **Ask Jeeves**—http://www.askjeeves.com
- **Open Directory**—http://dmoz.org
- **LookSmart**—http://www.looksmart.com
- **Lycos**—http://www.lycos.com

To do list

- ❑ Describe your advertising vehicles
- ❑ Decide whether you'll use an advertising agency
- ❑ Consider direct response and telemarketing
- ❑ Plan to acquire customers online
- ❑ Create a media buy schedule

Acquiring Customers

The second platform, in your marketing strategy is *acquisition*. The objective of every company, of course, is to acquire customers. When describing your acquisition plan, first choose the marketing vehicles and then explain how best they can enable you to reach your target market. Make sure you describe the phases of your advertising plan. For example, is your budget heavier in the first few months of the year and later tapers off, or do you have a consistent acquisition campaign running for many months?

Don't make the mistake of being too general in your description ("I will buy ads on local newspapers and radio") or too unrealistic ("I will spend no money on advertising because I will trade my product or service for ad space") in your marketing plan.

Describing Your Advertising Placements

When describing your advertising vehicles, be specific in their size, frequency, and type. If you plan to run print ads, you need to state the size of the ads and if they are black and white or in color. If you plan to buy radio or TV ads, state how long the spot is (30 seconds, one minute) and its frequency (once a day, twice a day, and so on).

Trade shows are another type of acquisition strategy, if it applies to your business. Trade shows can offer you good exposure to clients or customers in your market. List in your plan the names and dates of the trade shows you plan to attend or display products or services. If you offer any show specials, describe them in your plan. And if you plan to advertise in the show directory, state this also.

The expected results of your marketing effort should be realistically based upon the proposed marketing budget in your financial plan. State where you will put your advertising dollars, why you chose those methods, how your message will reach your target market, when your advertising campaign will begin, how much your plan will cost (including both placement cost and production of your ads) and what format your advertising will take. Mention if you will be using co-op dollars to help fund your advertising plan. If so, detail how much will bee paid cooperatively with by vendors or distributors and by whom. Back up your decisions and include copies of your promotional materials, such as brochures, direct mail advertisements, and flyers, in the Supporting Documents section of your plan.

Be sure to give a line item description in your financial plan of each advertising method you use to market your business. You should outline the proposed mix of your advertising media, use of publicity, and/or other promotional programs. Are you doing a saturation advertising campaign, a direct response promotion, telemarketing, distributing brochures or catalogs, or buying leads? The cost of these must be reflected in your financial plan.

tip A good advertising campaign relies on message repetition. Say the same message in one or two media types over and over again.

As for the number of people you would like to reach, if you are on a limited budget, it might be better to reach fewer, more likely prospects more often, than too many people occasionally. And don't make the mistake of attacking an entire market instead of a narrow niche.

When you plan to reach your target customers is as important as how. You should state in your marketing strategy when you plan to initiate your advertising and promotional campaign and detail how long it will run. You should describe the frequency of your advertising and tell the reader how often you run ads and use other types of promotional vehicles, such as events, seminars, and workshops.

In any advertising campaign, to acquire customers you must develop short, effective copy that clearly identifies your unique selling position. Turn your unique selling position into a one- or two-line catchy phrase or slogan describing your unique selling position to your target audience and put it in this section of your plan.

Hiring an Ad Agency

You might decide to use an advertising agency to handle your advertising and promotion. An *advertising agency* is a company specializing in the planning, producing, and placing of advertising on behalf of its clients for a fee.

The agency spends your advertising budget and typically retains 15% as compensation for its efforts. If you use an ad agency, make sure you list their fees as a line item in your financial plan.

A good place to find a directory of ad agencies is Adweek at http://www.adweek. com/aw/directories/index.jsp. The cost of their directory is several hundred dollars a year but you get searchable databases with comprehensive information on all agencies. A directory of ad agency directories can be found at http://directory. google.com/Top/Business/Marketing_and_Advertising/Advertising/Directories.

Using Direct Response and Telemarketing

Finally, you might consider adding to your plan two other types of customer acquisition tools—direct response and telemarketing.

Direct response promotions include direct mailers to your target market with an incentive to act. You might offer some kind of inducement for the recipient of your direct response promotion, such as an incentive to make a purchase (20% off or free gift with purchase), visit your store (free trial membership), or visit your website (download of a trial software product). Any direct response vehicles you use should be described in this section of your business plan. *Telemarketing* is defined as the use of the telephone to market your products or services directly to prospective customers and/or to receive orders and inquiries generated from other advertising and promotions you might use for acquiring customers.

Acquiring Customers Online

A company's online acquisition strategy is different from the traditional ways of advertising and promotion. The Internet has its own forms of advertising and promotion that should be integrated into your marketing strategy.

Your first consideration here is the actual design of your digital presence. Having a website or a presence on an Internet-enabled device is not enough. It has to be designed to attract prospective customers as well. This means making your digital presence user friendly and useful to visitors. I discuss the creation and use of a digital presence later in Chapter 9, "Listing Your Distribution Channels."

Creating a list of partners you can crosslink to and/or exchange banner ads with is one way to acquire new customers. *Banner ads* are the small graphic ads you see at many websites. Clicking on a banner ad takes you to another site where you can learn more about the product or service being advertised.

> **tip**
>
> Online advertising can be an alphabet soup of possibilities. There's CPM, CPC, and CPA, to name the most popular used. Here's what they mean:
> - **Cost per thousand impressions (CPM)**—The number of times a banner is viewed on a web page
> - **Cost per click (CPC)**—The amount of times a person clicks on a banner ad
> - **Cost per action (CPA)**—The number of times an action, such as a sale, registration, or download, is performed by someone clicking through to the banner ad's website

Choosing an Online Acquisition Strategy

Another online acquisition strategy is to create an *opt-in mailing list* on your digital presence where visitors can sign up for special promotions, an informative newsletter, and even a preferred customers club. This allows you to build an in-house database of prospects and customers to market to later. Mention in your plan how you build an opt-in mailing list, or *house list*, you use for your ongoing marketing campaigns.

GRASSROOTS MARKETING ONLINE

Before you open your checkbook and spend money marketing online, you should use the resources of the Internet to market for free. This strategy also goes over well if you're seeking money from investors. By showing them you have thought through the many uses of free Internet advertising, it enhances your credibility with them. Here's how:

- **Reciprocal links**—Exchange website links with complimentary product or service companies online.
- **Banner exchanges**—Swap advertising banners with compatible websites.

Start your free swapping by finding out who already links to you. Do that by going to the Google search engine at http://www.google.com and type in the search box, **link:***your site name* with the appropriate **.com, .net, .org**, and the like after it.

Another way to acquire customers is to anonymously post to different discussion boards and forums on the Internet, informing readers that you've found a great place to buy your product or use your service. This is not exactly kosher, but it can work if you don't overdo it. And besides, it's free. You can find a directory of newsgroups and discussion boards at http://lists.topica.com.

Purchasing ads in newsletters and e-zines catering to your target audience is an efficient and inexpensive way to acquire new customers, as is renting opt-in lists to use in an outward bound email campaign. Mention these in your plan and where you will advertise.

Renting email lists is another way of marketing on the Internet and could be a possible customer acquisition strategy for your business plan.

A *double opt-in list* means not only must the user take an action to add himself to a list, but he then receives a confirmation of his subscription. He must reply to be added to the list. This is the best way to avoid your business being branded as a spammer, which is not good for your company reputation on or off the Internet.

caution But you must be careful when renting a list. Don't fall for the spam email promotions you may receive in your inbox promising to sell you 10 million email addresses for $29.95. Make sure the list you buy is a double opt-in list.

You may also consider using the power of free as an acquisition strategy. Consumers love that little word, so you might offer the following to entice customers to your business:

- Free shipping
- Free gift with purchase
- Free coupons
- Free samples
- Free sweepstakes

Mention how you use the power of free in your marketing plan.

Using Search Engine Marketing

Finally there's *search engine marketing (SEM)*. Where search engine optimization (SEO) is a programming function, SEM is a marketing function. There are two types of SEM:

- **Paid inclusion**—You buy the top-ranking position in the search results for a particular search term.
- **Paid placement**—You bid on and buy a small pay-per-click ad on search engines, such as google.com and overture.com, and only pay when someone clicks on your ad.

Obviously, the paid inclusion strategy guarantees you top placement in the search results as long as you pay the monthly fee. The paid placement strategy only guarantees your ad appears in the top positions on the sponsored websites if your bid for those positions is higher than your competitor's bids.

Whichever search engine marketing strategy you choose, make sure this expense appears in your financial plan.

If you plan to use SEM paid placement as an acquisition tool in your marketing plan, you should list the search terms or keywords you will bid on. Your search terms or keywords should focus on specific terms pertinent and specific to your market and not broad-based terms. For example, if you're selling apparel, don't choose the word *apparel*. Use more specific terms for the product you sell, such as *women's high-heel boots*.

> **note** Relevancy of the keywords you choose is also very important. Do *not* mislead visitors to your site with a bait and switch ad listing that promises one thing with your keyword or search term, and the web page you direct them to shows a product or service that is entirely different. This goes for any type of advertisement you place on the Internet.

There are two very good resources to use that help you choose keywords for your SEM campaign. They are at http://inventory.overture.com/d/searchinventory/suggestion and http://www.goodkeywords.com.

Creating a Media Buy Schedule

The largest portion of your market budget will be the money you spend on all types of *media buys* in magazines, newspapers, billboards, radio, and TV spots. Your media plan outlines what money is to be spent where and when.

To help the reader get a clearer picture of the costs and benefits of these varied types of ads and their placement, you should provide in your plan a proposed media buy schedule. You should, at the very least, provide a one-year media buy schedule in your plan. A media buy schedule consists of

- Name of the media outlets
- Circulation of the media type
- Audience or readership profile of the media type
- Your budget for media
- Ad description of the media placements
- Date of the media placements

In your plan, create a table with these headings and include the necessary information.

Your first column should list the names of the media outlets you plan to advertise in and include newspapers and magazines (including electronic versions), TV spots, radio ads, billboards, and website banner ads and sponsorships. The second column includes the circulation of the media outlet—how many potential readers or viewers that media outlet reaches.

The third column should contain your budget for that media outlet, or how much an individual ad costs. The fourth column includes a brief description of the ad for each media outlet. For example, a 1/4-page four-color magazine ad, a 60-second radio or TV spot, or the size of the banner ad on a website. If a banner ad, tell how many page views or actions are performed by the viewer you are paying for.

The fifth column describes the dates of the ad placement or insertions and the sixth column provides a brief readership profile of the media outlet and the target audience of the ad.

Here's an example.

Periodical or Electronic Media	Circulation	Budget	Ad Description	Insertion Dates
The Daily Star	150,000	$6,000	1/2-page B/W	May 2005 3× week
Wired Magazine	300,000	$12,000	1/2-page Full color	June 2005
KTXX - Radio	250,000	$2,500	30-second spot	June 1st to 15th 3× drive time

The media buy schedule outlines your course of action for your advertising and promotion campaign and should be included as a table in this section of your business plan.

Retaining Customers

It's well known that it costs up to ten times more to acquire a new customer than to retain the ones you have. So, retention becomes a very important objective of your marketing program.

That's why creating a house list, whether for online or offline use, becomes very important. A *house list* is an opt-in mailing list of previous customers who have voluntarily given you their contact information. You can use your house list of previous customers and prospects to market to them periodically, offering special deals to existing customers and other types of incentives to prospects to get them to buy.

Other ideas for retaining customers you might list in your marketing plan include a loyalty or preferred customer program, periodic catalogs to existing customers, an ongoing customer newsletter, and a number of online retention strategies. Any and all of these retention strategies should be described in this section of your business plan.

Using Customer Programs and Catalogs

Offering a loyalty or preferred customer program to your customers is one way to keep them as customers. Provide a program offering customers discounts when they buy in the future, special deals such as free add-on products or services, or perhaps a point program where they can earn cash rebates on future purchases. Examples of these types of customer loyalty programs are the ones credit card companies use to entice you to use their credit card. You can earn air miles, for example, using Capital One's credit card, earn discounts on new General Motors automobiles with a GM card, or cash rebates using a Discover card. There are programs where a customer can earn points each time they purchase from a merchant that they can convert into products or services in the future.

You can either create a customer loyalty program yourself or have companies who offer and manage programs do it for you. One such company is Elliance, at http://www.elliance.com/Services/loyalty-programs.asp.

Catalogues are not only an acquisition tool but also an effective retention device. Though they cost money, they are an excellent idea to keep your products or services in the mind of your customers and prospects. Even a small two- or four-page printed newsletter mailed out to your house list every so often performs the task of keeping your products or service in front of the eyes of customers and prospects.

Retaining Customers Online

The strategies and procedures for retaining customers online are different from those of offline. To begin with, marketing to existing customers without their permission can harm your business.

If you send any kind of electronic marketing vehicle to customers without first getting their permission, you can be branded as a spammer. And being accused of sending spam, as I said before, can and will hurt your company and its reputation.

So, in this section of your business plan, you should describe the types of electronic retention devices you use and inform the reader briefly how you get permission from your house list of customers and prospects. If you want to send a periodic electronic newsletter or promotional email, state that you include an easy way for the recipient to unsubscribe at any time, either in the electronic communication itself or by directing them to a website where they can unsubscribe.

Describe in your plan how you will use your opt-in house list for promotional and/or informative emails and other contact on a consistent, periodic basis. Remember to make a distinction between promotional and informative emails. Send promotional emails, such as sales and specials, to those who signed up for them, and informative email newsletters to those who signed up for information about your product or market niche. Don't do a bait and switch on your subscribers. If you do, you'll find your opt-in house list shrinks considerably when your subscribers hit the unsubscribe button.

Another retention strategy is to create a discussion board on your website for your customers and visitors to interact with each other. If you maintain a good discussion board or forum and participate in them yourself, these can be a valuable customer retention tool. In addition, you acquire some great feedback on your product or service and how your business is perceived by customers and visitors to your site. Along these lines, you might even consider providing some special knowledge about the product or service niche you serve by establishing an "ask the expert" board where customers and visitors alike can ask specific questions of your expert staff on your products, service, and industry and receive answers.

To do list

- [ ] Establish and explain your pricing structure
- [ ] Describe your plan for making money from online customers

Monetizing Customers

The goal of your business is obviously to make sales. How you plan to make those sales must be described in your business plan. This information must include your pricing structure and your plan for making money from online sales. If you plan to sell through your digital presence, you need to describe how you monetize the traffic coming to your website.

Establishing and Describing Your Pricing Structure

The first thing you need to decide is at what price you can sell your product or service. You must describe your unit of sale. The *unit of sale* is the discrete product or service you sell. For example, if it's a product, the unit of sale might be one computer monitor, one computer system, one camera, one bicycle, or even one screw or nail. If you are selling a service, your unit of sale might be one hour of work or a fixed price per project.

Your pricing structure is critical to the success of your business. The price you sell your product or service at must be high enough to cover all your expenses and the cost of goods sold, if any, and earn a profit. You should have a good idea of what you can charge for your product or service from the market research you have already done. One way to set your price is to price your products or service between the price ceiling and the price floor.

The *price ceiling* is determined by the market you sell within. It is the highest price a consumer will pay for your particular product or service. This price is determined by the consumer and is based on the perceived value of your offering. Based on your market research, you know what your competitors are charging for the product or service you sell.

Don't make the assumption that offering a lower price leads to increased sales. Consumers are looking not only for the best price but the best value.

For example, the best value could include the following, all of which will affect the price you must charge to meet that desired value:

- Warranties on the product or service
- Guaranteed satisfaction and no hassle returns on the product or service
- Free shipping
- Free service after the sale
- Cash rebates
- Credits on future purchases
- Selection
- Convenience
- Customer service
- Product reviews

Consumers buy from your *full selling position*, which is another way of saying your unique selling position. When you create your pricing structure, think in terms of supply value, not just a low price.

The *price floor* is the minimum price you can sell at and still cover all your expenses and show a profit. The profitable business operates between the price ceiling and the price floor.

So how do you price your product or service? Consider these strategies as they apply to your type of business:

- **Markup pricing**—If you plan to be a retailer, markup pricing is calculated by adding your desired profit to the cost of the product.
- **Cost-plus pricing**—If you're in the business of manufacturing a product, cost-plus pricing assures all costs, both fixed and variable, are covered and the desired profit percentage is attained.

Monetizing Customers Online

Although monetizing in the offline world is pretty straightforward—you sell directly to consumers or other businesses and organizations through a physical presence—making money from traffic to your website offers additional opportunities not easily executable in the offline world.

It goes without saying that any company selling online must have a robust and user-friendly shopping cart on their website. But there are other ways to make a buck off your site visitors.

First, your customers and visitors are of value to other business who might sell complementary products or services. If you sell luggage or products used for travel, for example, a travel agency website would be interested in presenting travel offers to your site visitors. If so, you can sign them up as sponsors of certain areas of your website and have them pay your company for the sponsorship.

Another way to monetize your site visitors is to join affiliate programs of noncompeting companies on the Internet and get paid for selling their products or services.

For example, if you sell camping equipment, you can sign up for one of the affiliate programs of the online bookstores and sell outdoor and camping books.

Creating a Public Relations Plan

It has been said that a jungle is a rain forest with poor PR and a squirrel is a rat with good PR. Pubic relations is an often ignored but important part of your marketing strategy.

Editorial coverage in the media outlets your target market is exposed to is a good way of getting visibility for your business without spending money. If your product or service is unique for your industry, trade publications might be willing to give your company some valuable exposure at no cost. Send out press releases periodically to them and to any other media outlets that target your market. In addition, if you are paying for space in a printed medium, you should negotiate some editorial coverage to accompany any paid advertising.

Your press releases should be sent as part of your comprehensive promotional program. These activities should be covered in your business plan.

tip Your press releases should contain genuine news—not fluff. You must make your releases newsworthy by pinpointing a problem solved or a need filled for the readers or viewers of a particular media outlet.

PRESS RELEASE DO'S AND DON'TS

DO make your press releases short and to the point.

DO include all necessary contact information.

DO spell check your release. And do it twice just to make sure!

DO keep typefaces large, legible, and readable for both email and faxes.

DO write a clear and meaningful subject line. The subject line should reflect the contents of your release.

DON'T write unclear press releases. If it doesn't make sense to the reader, news outlets won't use it.

DON'T send a release to a publication without knowing the audience or what the publication is all about.

DON'T send attached files. Don't send a word processing document or a zipped file that the contact needs to download, unzip, load into his word processor, determine the compatibility, print, review, and so on.

You should also convey in your business plan your public relations policies, practices, and anticipated projects. Carving out your place in your community and how you help it should be described in your marketing plan. Note the different community and business organizations and associations you plan to affiliate with, such as the Chamber of Commerce, the Better Business Bureau, or the United Way Fund.

Your active participation in trade associations is another way to participate in your community for visibility.

Describe how you maintain a high profile in your local and business community. Convey to your plan's reader how you use a printed and electronic newsletter sent to selected vendors, distributors, dealers, sales reps, trade editorial staff, and other professionals following your business. Include a sample mock-up of your newsletter in the Supporting Documents section of your business plan.

All of these public relations strategies can offer high visibility and prestige for your company and should be outlined in your plan.

Describing Your Sales Strategy

Your sales strategy needs to be in sync with your marketing strategy. You need to describe to the reader how you plan to sell your product or service. Will you rely on an inside sales or an outside sales force to sell the wares and services of your company? If you're a startup company, it is easier to rely on wholesalers or commissioned sales representatives, who already have an established presence and reputation in the marketplace, than to create a sales force from scratch to sell your product or service. If you will be using manufacturer's reps, tell the reader how the rep firms are selected, the criteria you will use, how their qualifications improve your sales penetration strategies, and the territories they will cover.

Another area to consider is the type of product or service you sell.

If it's highly technical, complicated, or offers a range of customized options, you want to consider the expense of training and supporting these kinds of sales people in your financial plan. Your sales force, in this case, must be highly knowledgeable, in addition to being personable.

If you're considering a paid inside sales force, describe in your plan how customer contacts will be made and maintained. What kind of background, experience, and skills should they have and how will they be recruited?

Consider telephone contact and direct mailings, and detail the specifics of your sales plan. If you're considering using a paid inside or outside sales force, describe the salary range, commissions (cost per sale), benefits, and incentives you plan to offer. You should also detail the expected productivity of your sales people, in terms of calls per day, sales days per month, and repeat orders. This kind of information helps you when creating your financial plan.

If you're developing an internal plan, describe who will sell the product or service and how will the process differ from the company's present method of operation.

In the case of your sales force, you should describe to the reader any specific territories assigned to the sales people in your sales force, as well as the size and nature of those territories and the degree of exclusivity each has.

If you are a startup and plan on being your own chief salesperson, you should refer to your expertise of selling in this area. State any previous sales experience with the product or service you are selling.

A solid sales strategy is as important as a strong marketing strategy and should be carefully explained in your business plan.

Write the Plan!

Answer the following questions to write this portion of your business plan as they apply to your type of plan—startup, full, or internal plan.

The Startup Business Plan

Answer these questions to describe your company positioning:

1. How will you convey your digital presence in your collateral material? Will you include your URL, email address, newsletter information, and the like on your letterhead, business cards, brochures, and advertising copy (print, radio, or TV)?
2. What Internet search engines and web directories will you submit your digital presence to?

Answer these questions to describe your customer acquisition strategy:

1. When will your advertising campaign begin? How long will it run? What are the phases of your advertising plan? Will you budget heavier in the first few months of the year and then taper off, or will you have a consistent acquisition campaign that runs for many months? Explain.
2. Where will you place your advertising dollars? What format does your advertising take—print, radio, TV, or billboards? Why did you choose these methods over others? What are the sizes, frequencies, and types of the advertising vehicles you will use? What is their circulation or number of listeners or viewers? Who will create these marketing messages? How much will they cost?
3. How will your message reach your target market? How much will your plan cost (including both placement cost and production of your ads)?
4. Are you using co-op dollars to help fund your advertising plan? List your vendor and distributor names and explain how much you will be reimbursed by them for your co-op advertising expense.
5. Do you use direct response promotion, telemarketing, the distribution of brochures or catalogs, or buying leads? What sources of leads will you use? How much do they cost?
6. How can you describe to your target audience your unique selling position in a one- or two-line catchy phrase or slogan? Does it describe what your company does?

7. Are you using an advertising agency to handle your ad placements? Who are they? Why did you choose them? What specific services of the agency will you use?

8. Will you be exchanging banner ads and/or links with other online websites? Which sites? What kind of free exchanges will you participate in? Detail.

9. Will you be buying banner ads or sponsorships on other websites? Will you be buying CPM, CPC, or CPA? From whom? How many of each will you buy? How much does it cost?

10. Will you purchase ads in online newsletters or e-zines? From which sources? How much do the ads cost? What is the circulation of the outlets' sites?

11. Will you create an opt-in mailing list? How? What will you offer prospects for their contact information?

12. Will you rent email lists? From whom? How much does it cost?

13. Will you be offering anything free to entice prospects and customers to buy from your business? What is your offer?

14. Will you use some kind of customer referral system? Describe how you would get referrals.

Answer these questions to create your media buy schedule:

1. How much money will you dedicate to advertising and promotion in the first, second, and third year?

2. What type of media ads will you use? A printed ad; a radio or TV spot; a banner ad; paid inclusion or paid placement; or a direct response outlet, such as direct mail or telemarketing?

3. What is the circulation of each of the media outlets you've chosen?

4. What is the audience or readership of each of the media outlets?

5. How much do you plan to spend for advertising in each type of media?

6. What is the cost of the media placement per prospect?

7. What is the description of the media placement?

8. What are the dates of the media placement?

Answer these questions to describe your customer retention strategy:

1. Will you be sending out periodic catalogs? How often?

2. Will you have a printed and/or email newsletter? What will it contain? How often will you send it out? What will it cost to produce?

3. Will you have a discussion board on your website? Describe its purpose and how it will work.

4. Will you have an "ask the expert" section on your website?

Answer these questions to describe your monetization strategy:

1. What is your unit of sale? What is the selling price of your unit of sale?

2. What is the price ceiling for your product or service in the marketplace?

3. What is the price floor for your product or service in the marketplace?

4. Will you be selling on price, selection, convenience, service, or a combination of them?

5. What is the perceived value to the customer of your product or service?

6. Is your perceived value or full selling position based on warranties on the product or service? Guaranteed satisfaction and no hassle returns? Free shipping? Free service after the sale? Cash rebates? Credits on future purchases? Selection? Convenience? Customer service? Product reviews? Personalization services, such as personal shoppers?

7. How will you set your price? Will you use markup pricing or cost-plus pricing when determining the price of your product or service? Describe why.

Answer these questions to describe your public relations plan:

1. What is your public relations plan? What media outlets will you target for your press releases? Will you be using press releases to announce your grand opening?

2. What are your public relations policies? What are the community and business organizations and associations you plan to affiliate with?

3. What trade associations will you be a member of?

Answer these questions to describe your sales strategy:

1. If you'll be using manufacturer's reps, how are the rep firms selected, what criteria will you use, what are their qualifications to improve your sales penetration strategies, and what territories will they cover? Will they also rep complementary products that are of interest to the same buyers of your product or service?

2. If you are a startup and plan on being your own chief salesperson, what is your expertise of selling in this area? State any previous sales experience with the product or service you will be selling.

The Full Business Plan

Answer these questions to describe your company positioning:

1. How will you convey your digital presence in your collateral material? Will you include your URL, email address, newsletter information, and the like on your letterhead, business cards, brochures, and advertising copy (print, radio, or TV)?

2. How will your digital presence be integrated into your digital strategy solution?

3. How can readers, listeners, and viewers subscribe to your online and/or offline newsletter?

4. What Internet search engines and web directories do you submit your digital presence to?

5. Will your digital presence include more than just a website? Will customers and prospects be able to reach you on cell phones, PDAs, or TV? Explain.

Answer these questions to describe your customer acquisition strategy:

1. When will your advertising campaign begin? How long will it run? What are the phases of your advertising plan? Will you budget heavier in the first few months of the year and then taper off, or will you have a consistent acquisition campaign that runs for many months? Explain.

2. Where will you place your advertising dollars? What format will your advertising take—print, radio, TV, or billboards? Why did you choose these methods over others? What are the sizes, frequencies, and types of the advertising vehicles you will use? What is their circulation or number of listeners or viewers? Who will create these marketing messages? How much do they cost?

3. How will your message reach your target market? How much will your plan cost (including both placement cost and production of your ads)?

4. Do you plan on attending and/or displaying at trade shows? What are the names and dates of the trade shows you will attend or display product or services? Will you offer any show specials? Explain.

5. Are you using co-op dollars to help fund your advertising plan? List your vendor and distributor names and explain how much you will be reimbursed by them for your co-op advertising expense?

6. Will you use direct response promotion, telemarketing, distribution of brochures or catalogs, or buying leads? Who will you use? How much does it cost?

7. Will you use other types of promotional vehicles, such as events, seminars, and workshops?

8. How can you describe to your target audience your unique selling position in a one- or two-line catchy phrase or slogan? Does it describe what your company does?

9. Will you be using an advertising agency to handle your ad placements? What agency? Why did you choose it? What specific services of the agency will you use?

10. Will you be exchanging banner ads and/or links with other online websites? Which sites? What kind of free exchanges will you participate in? Detail.

11. Will you be buying banner ads or sponsorships on other websites? Will you be buying CPM, CPC, or CPA? From whom? How many of each will you buy? How much does it cost?

12. Will you purchase ads in online newsletters or e-zines? From which sources? How much do the ads cost? What is the circulation?

13. Will you create an opt-in mailing list? How? What will you offer prospects for their contact information?

14. Will you be renting email lists? From whom? How much does it cost?

15. Will you be offering anything free to entice prospects and customers to buy from your business? What will you offer?

16. Will you use a search engine marketing strategy, such as paid placement or paid inclusion? If you use paid placement, where will you purchase the placement and how much does it cost? If using paid inclusion, what key-words will you use? Where will you buy them from? How much does it cost?

17. Will you use some kind of customer referral system? Describe how you get referrals.

Answer these questions to create your media buy schedule:

1. How much money will you dedicate to advertising and promotion in the first, second, and third year?

2. What type of media ads will you use? A printed ad; a radio or TV spot; a banner ad; paid inclusion or paid placement; or a direct response outlet, such as direct mail or telemarketing?

3. What is the circulation of each media type?

4. What is the audience or readership of each media type?

5. How much do you plan to spend on each media type?

6. What is the cost of the media placement per prospect?

7. What is the description of the media placement?

8. What are the dates of the media placement?

Answer these questions to describe your customer retention strategy:

1. Will you have a loyalty or preferred customer program? How will it work? What will be offered? Free add-on products or services, or perhaps a point program where they can earn cash rebates on future purchases?

2. Will you be sending out periodic catalogs? How often?

3. Will you have a printed and/or email newsletter? What will it contain? How often will you send it out? What does it cost to produce?

4. Will you have a discussion board on your website? Describe its purpose and how it will work.

5. Will you have an "ask the expert" section on your website?

Answer these questions to describe your monetization strategy:

1. What is your unit of sale? Describe. What is the selling price of your unit of sale?

2. What is the price ceiling for your product or service in the marketplace?

3. What is the price floor for your product or service in the marketplace?

4. Will you be selling on price, selection, convenience, service, or a combination of them?

5. What is the perceived value to the customer of your product or service?

6. Is your perceived value or full selling position based on warranties on the product or service? Guaranteed satisfaction and no hassle returns? Free shipping? Free service after the sale? Cash rebates? Credits on future purchases? Selection? Convenience? Customer service? Product reviews? Personalization services, such as personal shoppers?

7. How will you set your price? Will you use markup pricing or cost-plus pricing when determining the price of your product or service? Describe why.

8. Will you be selling complementary products or services from non-competing websites? Which ones? What is the agreement you have with the websites?

9. Will you be joining other companies' affiliate programs? Which ones? What products or services do they sell?

Answer these questions to describe your public relations plan:

1. What is your public relations plan? What media outlets will you target for your press releases? Will you be using press releases to announce your grand opening, expansion, new facilities, or new divisions?

2. What are your public relations policies? What are the community and business organizations and associations you plan to affiliate with?

3. What trade associations will you be a member of?

4. Will you be sending an industry newsletter to selected vendors, distributors, dealers, sales reps, trade editorial staff, and other professionals that follow your business? What will it consist of? To whom will you send it?

Answer these questions to describe your sales strategy:

1. Will you use an inside or an outside sales force to sell the wares and services of your company?

2. If you'll be using manufacturer's reps, how are the rep firms selected, what criteria will you use, what are their qualifications to improve your sales penetration strategies, and what territories will they cover? Will they also rep complementary products of interest to the same buyers of your product or service?

3. Is your product or service highly technical and complicated, or does it offer a range of customized options? If so, how will you select and train your sales people?

4. If you're considering a paid inside sales force, elaborate in your plan how customer contacts will be made and maintained. What kind of background, experience, and skills should they have and how will they be recruited?

5. If you're considering using a paid inside or outside sales force, what is the salary range, commissions (cost per sale), draw against commissions, benefits, and incentives you plan to offer? Do you have any specific territories assigned to your sales people? Include the size, nature, and degree of exclusivity of the territories.

6. What is the expected productivity of your sales people, in terms of calls per day, sales days per month, and repeat orders?

The Internal Business Plan

Answer these questions to describe your customer acquisition strategy:

1. When will your advertising campaign begin? How long will it run? What are the phases of your advertising plan? Will you budget heavier in the first few months of the year and then taper off, or will you have a consistent acquisition campaign that runs for many months? Explain.

2. Where will you place your advertising dollars? What format will your advertising take—print, radio, TV, or billboards? Why did you choose these methods over others? What are the sizes, frequencies, and types of the advertising vehicles you will use? What is their circulation or number of listeners or viewers? Who will create these marketing messages? How much do they cost?

3. How will your message reach your target market? How much does your plan cost (including both placement cost and production of your ads)?

4. Do you plan on attending and/or displaying at trade shows? What are the names and dates of the trade shows you plan to attend or display product or services? Will you offer any show specials? Explain.

5. Are you using co-op dollars to help fund your advertising plan? How much are you reimbursed for your advertising expense by your vendors or distributors?

6. Will you use direct response promotion, telemarketing, the distribution of brochures or catalogs, or buying leads? Who will you use? How much does it cost?

7. Will you use other types of promotional vehicles, such as events, seminars, and workshops?

8. How can you describe to your target audience your unique selling position in a one- or two-line catchy phrase or slogan? Does it describe what your company does?

9. Will you be exchanging banner ads and/or links with other online websites? With whom? What kind of free exchanges? Detail.

10. Will you be buying banner ads or sponsorships on other websites? Will you be buying CPM, CPC, or CPA? From whom? How many? How much does it cost?

11. Will you purchase ads in online newsletters or e-zines? From whom? How much does it cost? What is the circulation?

12. Will you create an opt-in mailing list? How? What will you offer a prospect for his contact information?

13. Will you be renting email lists? From whom? How much does it cost?

14. Will you be offering anything free to entice prospects and customers to buy from your business? What will you offer?

15. Will you use a search engine marketing strategy, such as paid placement or paid inclusion? If you use paid placement, where will you purchase the

placement and how much will it cost? If using paid inclusion, what keywords will you use? Where will you buy them from? How much does it cost?

16. Will you use some kind of customer referral system? Describe how you get referrals.

Answer these questions to create your media buy schedule:

1. How much money will you dedicate to advertising and promotion in the first, second, and third year?
2. What type of media ads will you use? A printed ad; a radio or TV spot; a banner ad; paid inclusion or paid placement; or a direct response outlet, such as direct mail or telemarketing?
3. What is the circulation of each media type?
4. What is the audience or readership of each media type?
5. How much do you plan to spend on each media type?
6. What is the cost of the media placement per prospect?
7. What is the description of the media placement?
8. What are the dates of the media placement?

Answer these questions to describe your customer retention strategy:

1. Will you be sending out periodic catalogs? How often?
2. Will you have a printed and/or email newsletter? What will it contain? How often will you send it out? What does it cost to produce?

Answer these questions to describe your monetization strategy:

1. What is your unit of sale? Describe. What is the selling price of your unit of sale?
2. What is the price ceiling for your product or service in the marketplace?
3. What is the price floor for your product or service in the marketplace?
4. Will you be selling on price, selection, convenience, service, or a combination of them?
5. What is the perceived value to the customer of your product or service?
6. Is your perceived value or full selling position based on warranties on the product or service? Guaranteed satisfaction and no hassle returns? Free shipping? Free service after the sale? Cash rebates? Credits on future purchases? Selection? Convenience? Customer service? Product reviews? Personalization services, such as personal shoppers?
7. How will you set your price? Will you use markup pricing or cost-plus pricing when determining the price of your product or service? Describe why.

Answer these questions to describe your public relations plan:

1. What is your company's current public relations plan? What media outlets will you target for your press releases? Will you be using press releases to announce your grand opening, expansion, new facilities, or new divisions?

2. Will you be sending an industry newsletter to selected vendors, distributors, dealers, sales reps, trade editorial staff, and other professionals that follow your business? What does it consist of? To whom?

Answer these questions to describe your sales strategy:

1. Will you use an inside or an outside sales force to sell the wares and services of your new venture or division?

2. If you'll be using manufacturer's reps, how are the rep firms selected, what criteria will you use, what are their qualifications to improve your sales penetration strategies, and what territories will they cover? Will they also rep complementary products of interest to the same buyers of your product or service?

3. Is your product or service highly technical and complicated, or does it offer a range of customized options? If so, how will you select and train your sales people?

4. If you're considering a paid inside sales force, elaborate in your plan how customer contacts will be made and maintained. What kind of background, experience, and skills should they have and how will they be recruited?

5. If you're considering using a paid inside or outside sales force, what is the salary range, commissions (cost per sale), draw against commissions, benefits, and incentives you plan to offer? Do you have any specific territories assigned to your sales people? Include the size, nature, and degree of exclusivity for these territories.

7. What is the expected productivity of your sales people, in terms of calls per day, sales days per month, and repeat orders?

Summary

How well you market your business ultimately determines the success or failure of your company. Your business plan should describe in detail your marketing strategy. A marketing strategy is the marketing plan for your business. Marketing includes company positioning, market research, new product or business development, advertising, promotion, public relations, and even the sales function itself. A marketing plan details what a business sells, to whom, when, and how. In this chapter, you've learned how to describe each of those elements by creating a marketing strategy, describing how you acquire and retain customers, explaining your plan for making money from those customers, and making a sound public relations plan that includes an outline of your sales strategy.

The next chapter will show you how to describe the distribution channels you plan to use to sell your product or service.

Listing Your Distribution Channels

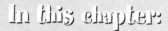

U p to a mere decade ago, delivering your product or service to market was a fairly simple affair. Your distribution options were few. If you made a product, you found a distributor to sell it into the retail or wholesale marketplace. If you sold third-party products, you bought them from a distributor and offered them in your retail storefront. If you provided a service, you offered it directly to the consumer.

With the dawning of the Internet, all that has changed. Now you have a wide variety of ways to distribute your product or service and place it in the hands of your target customer. Today's distribution options include selling through a physical storefront, wholesale channels, catalogs, magazines, online storefronts, or a combination of both online and offline channels (known as *clicks and bricks*). A full and effective selling strategy must consider all of these as possible distribution channels for your product or service. The channels you choose must be described in this section of your business plan.

You can see a sample of a distribution strategy in Appendix A, "Sample Business Plan."

In this chapter:

* Describe your real-world presence and distribution channels

* Portray your digital presence and distribution channels

* Write the section describing your distribution channels for your startup, full, or internal business plan

To do list

- ☐ Describe your physical plant and location
- ☐ Choose your distribution channels
- ☐ Think about channel conflict

Describing Your Real-World Presence and Distribution Channels

Distribution is defined by the Small Business Development Center as "the manner in which products are physically transported to the consumer or the way services are made available to the customer" (see the SBDC's Bear Paw Development Corporation, "Business Plan Outline"). The type of distribution network you choose depends upon the industry you're in and the size of your market. It is important that you clearly outline in your plan the process by which you manufacture, distribute, and sell your product or service.

If you manufacture your own product, distribution includes the entire process of moving the product from the factory to the end user. If you purchase and sell other companies' products, distribution includes the process of buying from wholesalers or distributors and selling product to the end user. If you are offering a service, your distribution process is simple. You offer it from an office or storefront directly to your target customer.

One of the first things about your distribution plan you must convey to your readers is where and how you set up your physical plant.

note Here's how the information you learn in this chapter relates to the three plan types:
- The questions to be answered for the startup business plan are very similar to those of the full business plan, excluding the questions on long-term facility needs, disaster recovery plans, and worst-case distribution scenarios. These issues needn't be addressed in a startup plan.
- Many questions regarding the distribution channel do not apply to internal plans because the current company has some of the distribution mechanisms in place. The internal plan need not include descriptions of the physical plant, office equipment, buy or lease arrangements, inventory storage and control, insurance, long-term equipment needs, and disaster recovery plan because these elements are typically handled by the current company.

tip Look at your competition and see what channels of distribution they're using. Ask yourself if you should use the same channels, or whether an alternative channel gives you more of a competitive advantage.

Describing Your Physical Plant

If you're looking to fund a new venture or an extension of an existing company, an investor or executive wants to see your physical plant described in your plan. Your description must include the type and layout of the building you operate from, the area where the building is located, the major equipment you need to run the business, and your plan for obtaining and storing materials and finished goods.

First, describe in your plan whether your new company will operate from a storefront, warehouse, office, manufacturing facility, or some combination of these. Perhaps your new company or venture will do business out of an office environment with little or no walk-in traffic. Maybe you plan on selling from a retail storefront or distributing products from warehouse facilities. No matter what type of physical plant you plan to do business from, you should describe where it will be located, how much space you will need and whether you plan to rent or buy your physical operating space. You should also describe any advantages to your choice of location.

Be sure to specify the square footage you require. It's important that you know ahead of time the size and type of space required for your business because the cost of the space is included in your financial plan. Give some thought in your plan as to future expansion needs. If your financial plan calls for a small space to start with, explain when you expect to need a large space and how much it will cost.

Second, you should describe the significant equipment you will need to run your business and its cost. This description includes general office equipment, such as copy, postage, and fax machines; telephones; computers; printers; point-of-sale equipment; and so on. Specify any plans for increasing the number of office machines as your business grows. If you require company vehicles, include a description of those, too. State in your plan whether you will purchase or lease your equipment and the reasons for your decision. Also convey to the reader where you plan to buy or lease your equipment.

If you require some specialized equipment, explain its purpose and function. If the equipment is for manufacturing your product, explain all the pieces needed, how they function, and how much each piece of equipment can produce.

Third, if you are manufacturing your product, convey to the reader the process of manufacturing your product from raw material through finished product and describe where you will obtain and store materials. Describe where your finished goods will be stored and the cost of storage.

Finally, provide a layout of your facility in the Supporting Documents section of your business plan, especially if you plan to manufacture your product. Don't skimp on information in this document. Make sure your layout includes a floor plan and identifies all machinery and equipment needed to produce your product. The layout should also demonstrate applicable workflow processes and the material handling procedures.

PLANNING FOR DISASTER

As a business owner, it's enough of a challenge to deal with competitor and supplier issues; but you also must create a plan for minimizing and recovering from manmade and natural disasters. This plan must detail how you will cope with threats to your company's physical plant and the materials and records you keep within it. Though a company cannot predict the future, it can prepare for the risks that might lie ahead; those plans should be described in your business plan.

Planning for disaster is a two-step process:

* **Step one**—Assess your company exposure to various risks.

* **Step two**—Implement strategies to prevent, lessen, or recover from those risks, and prepare and maintain a disaster recovery plan.

In addressing these steps, you should plan against these threats:

* Physical threats from natural and manmade disasters, such as fire, theft, floods, arson, and sabotage

* Threats to your sensitive computer system and files, such as hacker break-ins, malicious code attacks (for example, viruses), data loss or corruption, software or computer failure, and telecommunications and computer system outages

* People- and personnel-related threats linked to civil unrest, disgruntled employees, terrorism, and even industrial espionage

Here are some implementation strategies for your disaster recovery plan:

* Describe how you will train your staff in use of the disaster recovery plan.

* Outline your plan to protect and back up your computer files. Include a description of backup procedures you will implement, how often the backups will be done, and where backups will be stored.

* Detail the size and type of insurance you will purchase against fire, natural disaster, deliberate sabotage, and even business interruption.

Choosing and Describing Your Distribution Channels

Your choice of distribution channels depends largely on the type of business you have and the target customer you want to reach. The reader of your plan needs to know which channels you use and how you use them. Here are some of the most common distribution channels used by companies today:

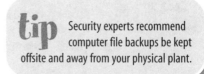

tip
Security experts recommend computer file backups be kept offsite and away from your physical plant.

* **Direct sales**—This is a very cost-effective channel for selling directly to the end user. Dell, Inc. is an excellent example of this type of selling. Dell manufactures its own computer equipment and sells directly to the consumer through the Internet, catalogs, TV spots, and printed advertisements. You can command a higher gross profit margin using this distribution channel

because you are not selling through a middleman, such as a wholesale distributor. If you have a service business, the direct sales method is preferred. If you choose the direct sales approach to distribution, you should describe how you will do it in your plan. Will you sell direct to consumers via mail-order, catalogs, or the Internet?

- **Original equipment manufacturer (OEM)**—When you sell your product as an OEM, the products you manufacture and sell are incorporated into the finished product of some other company. Intel, which manufactures the microprocessors that go into today's personal computers, PDAs, cell phones, other consumer electronic equipment, automobiles, and home appliances, is a good example of an OEM.

  If you choose the OEM approach to distribution, describe what any other company products your products will be in. List the potential or actual companies who will purchase your products for inclusion in their equipment or merchandise.

- **Manufacturer's representatives**—Manufacturer's reps operate out of agencies that handle an assortment of complementary products and divide their selling time among them; they target different types of customers. This is a very effective distribution and sales channel for those companies that don't want or need an in-house sales force.

  If you choose the manufacturer's representatives approach to distribution, give the reader some potential names of the companies you will be working with and the kinds of products they represent.

- **Wholesale distributors**—Using the wholesale distributor's channel, a manufacturer sells to a wholesaler, who in turn sells the product to a retailer or other agent for further distribution through the channel until it reaches the end user. This is the most common way for a company to distribute its products into the sales channel. The book distributor Ingram Book Group is a good example of this type of distribution channel.

- **Retail storefront**—The most common way to reach the end user if you're selling third-party products or services from other companies is the retail storefront. These companies buy directly from the distributor or wholesaler and sell to end users. This is the distribution channel of choice if the end user is the general consuming public.

- **Direct mail**—One of the newer forms of distribution is direct mail, where a retailer or manufacturer sells to the end user using a direct mail campaign. This is one of the most successful channels for selling products and services. The first direct mail catalog was created by Sears and Roebuck, and it started the catalog and direct mail boom we see today. Hundreds of millions of catalogs and direct mail pieces are sent out every year.

- **Internet sales**—Finally, there's the new kid on the block. This new distribution channel, often called *e-commerce*, is only a decade old but is growing in leaps and bounds. In 2003, more than 18 billion dollars were spent online by consumers, and projections call for a 10%–20% increase year after year. Your use of this new distribution channel should be described in some fashion in your business plan. I cover this new form of selling in the later section, "Describing Your Digital Presence and Distribution Channel."

Considering Channel Conflict

Simply put, *channel conflict* occurs when a company sells products or services to the same set of customers through a variety of distribution channels. If your distribution strategy poses this risk, you must describe in your plan what the channel conflicts might be and how you will handle them if they arise.

A perfect example of channel conflict occurred in the early computer industry. A decade ago, it was foolhardy for a computer manufacturer, such as IBM, Apple, or Hewlett-Packard, to sell its computer products direct to the end user. If computer manufacturers sold their wares directly, retailers—the source of another important distribution channel—saw the computer companies as direct competitors. Those manufacturers who sold directly to end users risked losing the retailers who bought their product for retail storefront distribution. Further, manufacturers didn't want to create a nationwide sales force to sell directly to individual consumers on a local level.

But then the Internet stepped in and companies saw the potential of e-commerce. Whereas before, a manufacturer or distributor would find it difficult to sell direct to consumers in existing distribution channels, the Internet made it easier to market and sell its products direct to the consumer. Today, manufacturers have the opportunity to sell direct to consumers using the Internet and many have dealt successfully with channel conflict issues.

To do list

- ❏ List the types of e-shoppers you plan to sell to
- ❏ Register a domain name
- ❏ Demonstrate an understanding of the e-commerce host essentials
- ❏ Describe the design of your online storefront
- ❏ Learn the legal issues of e-commerce

Describing Your Digital Presence and Distribution Channel

In today's business environment, every company should have a digital strategy, and investors and management are expecting to see one in your business plan. A business plan needs to explain how you expect to use online technology in your business. If your business plan calls for selling products or services online, you should describe in your plan whether your business will be a pure play or a clicks and bricks type of Internet business.

A *pure play* Internet business is one that sells only online. Amazon.com is an example of a pure play online business. It does not sell from a retail storefront, office, or any other physical presence. It is what is called an *e-tailer*. Wal-Mart, on the other hand, sells both online and through their physical storefronts around the world. They are an example of a clicks and bricks company. Catalog companies, such as L.L. Bean and Victoria's Secret, have a combined distribution strategy. They started as a direct mail cataloger, went to the Internet, and then to storefronts. The Discovery Channel on cable TV has a similar strategy and went from old media to new storefronts.

There are many types of distribution channels to choose from on the Internet. The most popular are business-to-consumer (B2C) and business-to-business (B2B). These parallel the distribution and sales channels in the offline world. Other distribution channels include business-to-government (B2G), consumer-to-government (C2G), consumer-to-consumer (C2C), and business-to-employee (B2E). Revenue generated from these distribution channels includes that from advertising sales, subscription-based sales, and transaction-based sales.

Describing the Types of e-Shoppers You'll Target

The online consumers your digital strategy can serve come in several forms and each of these *e-shoppers* has a distinct reason for buying from your company. These online customer types are not categorized by basic human needs as we did when you created your unique selling position. If you plan to sell online, you need to understand the e-shopper's buying motivations and explain to the reader of your plan why your product or service will attract their business. These shoppers can be categorized into four main types:

- **Impulse buyers** are impatient but lucrative online shoppers. They account for nearly half of all e-commerce transactions and enjoy the convenience of online shopping. You can get their attention by proving that buying from you saves them time. If this is the e-shopper type you plan to target, explain the convenience factors you provide on your e-commerce website. Or perhaps you use the technology of Internet-ready appliances, such as cell phones and PDAs, to have consumers easily and conveniently place orders with your company anytime and anywhere.

- **Surfers** are, in the offline world, window shoppers because they look at four times more web pages than other types of e-shoppers. They are drawn to new features and content on your digital presence, so you can get their attention by constantly updating your product or service offering. If these types of e-shoppers are your target, describe how you update your product or service offering to keep them coming back to your digital presence and what marketing strategy you use to continuously attract them to your website.

- **Connectors** are new to the Internet and are less likely to shop. But they are very brand conscious. They enjoy connecting with others online because community is big with them. You can get their attention by emphasizing affiliations with strong brand names and providing chat rooms, email discussion lists, and free electronic greeting cards on your website. This type of shopper can be easily attracted to your digital presence by adding community elements to your storefront.
- **Bargain shoppers**—the name says it all. If you want to sell to these e-shopper types, be prepared to compete on price. To attract them, you need to offer price comparisons, auctions, and classified ads on your website. You can get their attention by offering low prices and involving them in the community of your storefront to exchange shopping tips and advice with other bargain shoppers.

But remember, when you sell on price, you need to state to the consumer *why* you can sell at the best price. Is it because you buy direct from the manufacturer? Have very low overhead and sell at a very small gross profit margin? Or perhaps you make your own product? You must make it clear to the consumer and the reader of your plan.

You should choose your targeted e-shopper or e-shoppers and describe them in this section of your plan.

Registering a Domain Name

Every website has what is called a *uniform resource locator (URL)*—the World Wide Web address of a website on the Internet. For example, the URL for the consumer electronics megastore chain, Best Buy, is *http://www.bestbuy.com*. When you set up shop on the World Wide Web, you need to select and purchase a domain name for your storefront.

So where do you start when finding and registering a domain name for your company? First, find out whether the domain name you want is available. Head over to Network Solutions, at http://www.networksolutions.com, or Register.com, at http://www.register.com, and see if it's available.

Because you are setting up a business on the Internet, your domain name uses a **.com** extension, so when you search, make sure the **.com** choice is in the drop-down window. (There is a new extension called **.biz** that's gaining popularity with businesses but consumers still look for the **.com** extension.) If the domain name you want is not available, they suggest other names that might fit your original request.

Registering a domain name is not free. You have to pay an annual fee to maintain it. Be sure to include this cost in your budget.

SOME DOMAIN NAME TIPS

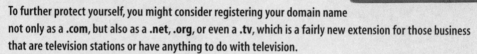

If you need help creating a valid domain name, here's a very useful site to help you choose one. Just enter a few words that represent your domain name and E-gineer's Domainator creates a valid domain name from those words. Try it at http://www.e-gineer.com/domainator/index.phtml.

When you register your domain name, you are asked to name both an administrative and technical contact. It is very important that you name yourself, not an employee, as the administrative contact. The administrative contact is the *only* one who can make changes to your domain registration. Don't be caught having to chase down someone who no longer works for your company to make future changes to your registration.

To further protect yourself, you might consider registering your domain name not only as a **.com**, but also as a **.net**, **.org**, or even a **.tv**, which is a fairly new extension for those business that are television stations or have anything to do with television.

Finally, why lose potential customers because they misspelled your URL? Register the obvious misspellings of your domain name and redirect them back to your site.

Describing e-Commerce Host Essentials

After you have secured your domain name, it's time to consider finding a home for your storefront. This is called finding a host. A *host* is a computer or server on which you place your website. The host's server is connected to the Internet 24 hours a day, seven days a week. This is how your customers find you and shop at your online store. No matter where you host your storefront, you need to consider some e-commerce host essentials and describe in your plan how you address those essentials.

A lot of thought should go into choosing a home for your online business. Your website is your business and you should expect that wherever you host it, the basic essential services are available. You should describe in your plan what your storefront hosting will require.

Determine these factors and describe them in your plan:

- **Bandwidth or connection speed**—You want to ensure your website loads quickly onto a shopper's computer. E-shoppers are an impatient lot and if your storefront doesn't load within 10 seconds, they're off to your competitor's storefront with a click of their mouse. You have only a few seconds to catch their attention. You should find out the bandwidth/connection speed from the hosting service. You may find out that they may offer high connection speed for higher prices.

- **Security**—Taking an order online is the reason why you have a storefront, so make sure the hosting service you choose offers data encryption for credit card transactions. Online shoppers are very concerned about using their credit cards online. Make sure the hosting service transactions are secure; if you plan to host the storefront yourself, make sure you describe in your business plan the techniques you use to secure transactions.

> **note** Also ascertain what kind of disaster recovery provisions the hosting service offers. They should have the ability to back up your website.

- **Tech support**—Make sure you or your hosting service has the ability to provide technical support 24 hours a day, every day of the week. Every minute your storefront doesn't function or is unavailable for viewing is lost sales to your business.
- **Cost**—Finally, consider the cost. In this section of your financial plan, make note of the cost of hosting your storefront.

The requirements you choose affect your financial plan because a hosting service costs money. If you decide to host your storefront yourself, there are the expenses of buying and servicing a web server or servers to host your digital presence.

Describing Your Storefront Design

If you're serious about selling online, you need to have a professionally designed and programmed storefront. The reader of your plan wants to see you have some basic understanding of what an e-commerce site should have, and how it should look and function. Before you even begin to design your e-commerce site, you should look for and work with an e-commerce developer.

Don't be confused with someone who is an ordinary web developer or programmer. These types of professionals are fine for other kinds of websites but not for an e-commerce site. You need to hire a developer who understands the necessary parts of an e-commerce site and can program them into your web store.

Your plan should describe, to some extent, the architecture of the web store you plan to use. The storefront should have a robust and easy-to-use shopping cart program to take and process online orders. A good e-commerce developer knows how to integrate shopping, order processing, and fulfillment elements into your web store. At a minimum, the basic storefront should contain the following types of web pages:

- A *home page* that starts selling when a visitor hits your storefront
- An *about us* page describing your company and how you are unique in your marketplace
- Your *product or services* pages, describing what you sell
- A *contact* page with all necessary contact information for your company, including customer service information

- A *privacy policy* page informing the shopper of the kind of personal information you collect and how you plan to use it
- A *frequently asked questions (FAQ)* page answering the most frequently asked questions a shopper might have about your company, its products or services, and how he can place an order

Another expense you should consider in this section is your ability to process credit cards online. You need to sign up your company with a payment gateway service. A *payment gateway* on the Internet verifies and authorizes a credit card purchase from your shopper, and then sends this information to your merchant bank. Your understanding and choice of a payment gateway needs to be stated in this section of your business plan.

STOREFRONT ESSENTIALS

Keep these tips in mind when designing your web store:

- First, make your storefront reflect your business. If you're a seller of low-cost products or services, or you offer a warehouse-like discount line, make your storefront reflect this image. The same goes for selling high-end products or services. Put some extra time and design in showing the visitor that your higher prices are reflected in high design. In either case, keep the look and feel of your web store professional.

- Keep the number of images to a minimum. Nothing slows down the downloading of a website like a multitude of large graphic images. On your product pages, use thumbnails next to product descriptions, and then give the shopper a choice to enlarge the image on the page.

- Finally, write your copy for the Web. Shoppers browse pages rather than read them. Keep your text to a minimum on each page, and don't confuse shoppers with a lot of verbiage that presents too much gray type on a page.

Staying Legal

The Internet is a great medium for commerce. With it, you can create new marketing methods, tap new markets, and target potential customers with electronic ease. And it also can get you sued by millions of consumers for violating their privacy!

Consumer privacy issues and concerns can have a drastic effect on your ability to market to, connect with, and create an ongoing relationship with your customers—critical to your e-business's success in the future. A lot of thought should be given to your privacy policy and how you communicate it to visitors and customers to your site. Make your privacy policy accessible right from your home page and describe it thoroughly in your business plan. Be sure your privacy policy clearly states the following:

- What information is collected when shoppers buy from you
- How you use this information
- What you intend to do with it

Finally, be aware of the Children's Online Privacy Protection Act (COPPA). COPPA bars the online collection and use of personally identifiable information from children under the age of 13, unless verifiable parental consent is provided. If you plan to sell to children online, be aware of this law and convey to the reader how you abide by it in your business plan.

Write the Plan!

Answer the following questions to write this portion of your business plan as they apply to your type of plan—startup, full, or internal plan.

The Startup Business Plan

Answer these questions to describe your business's real-world presence:

1. What is the physical location of your business? What kind of facility will you use? A storefront, an office, a warehouse, a manufacturing facility, or a combination?
2. What square footage will you require? What is the layout of your facility?
3. What office equipment will you need?
4. Do you plan to buy or lease your building and/or equipment? Why? If leasing, from where and why?
5. Do you require any specialized equipment? What is its purpose? What does it cost?
6. How does each piece of equipment function, and how much can each piece of equipment produce?
7. If you are manufacturing your product, explain the manufacturing process from raw material through finished product, and describe where you will obtain and store materials.
8. What is the layout of your manufacturing plant?
9. What are your future expansion needs?
10. Where will your product or service be available to the customer?
11. How does it get there?
12. Where is your inventory stored?
13. How much does it cost to warehouse or store your inventory?
14. How will you keep track of inventory? Provide specific procedures and equipment used.
15. What type of insurance does your business need?

Answer these questions to describe your distribution channels:

1. What are the pros and cons of the various methods of distribution you will choose? Why did you make these choices? Do your customers purchase through a retail store, by direct sales, through manufacturer's representatives, through the mail, through wholesale distributors, online, or through catalogs? Will you use a combination of some or all?

2. Are you an OEM? Are the products you produce incorporated into another manufacturer's finished product?

Answer these questions when describing your plan for avoiding channel conflict:

1. Will you be combining conflicting channels of distribution? Will you be selling to both end users and retailers, or to both retailers and wholesalers?

2. How will you minimize channel conflicts?

Answer these questions when describing your digital presence:

1. Do you have an Internet sales and distribution strategy?

2. Will you be a pure play or clicks and bricks company?

3. Is your distribution channel business-to-consumer (B2C), business-to-business (B2B), business-to-government (B2G), consumer-to-government (C2G), consumer-to-consumer (C2C), or business-to-employee (B2E)? Some combination of channels?

4. Will you generate revenue from sources other than sales, such as ads on your website from other companies or charging subscriptions?

5. What types of e-shoppers do you want to attract? Impulse buyers, surfers, connectors, or bargain shoppers? How will you attract them?

6. What domain name can you use and register?

7. Where will you host your online storefront? At your company? With a third-party hosting service? Why? How much does it cost?

8. Will you use the services of an e-commerce developer to design your storefront? Who will it be and how much does it cost?

Answer these questions when describing how you will address e-commerce legal issues:

1. What is your privacy policy for information you will collect from site visitors and customers? What information is collected when shoppers buy from you? How will you use this information?

2. Does your business comply with COPPA?

The Full Business Plan

Answer these questions to describe your business's real-world presence:

1. What is the physical location of your company or storefront? What kind of facility will you use? An office, a warehouse, a manufacturing facility, or a combination?

2. What square footage will you require? What is the layout of your facility?

3. What office equipment will you need?

4. Do you plan to buy or lease your building and/or equipment? Why? If leasing, from where and why?

5. Do you require any specialized equipment? What is its purpose? What does it cost?

6. How does each piece of equipment function, and how much can each piece of equipment produce?

7. If you are manufacturing your product, explain the manufacturing process from raw material through finished product, and describe where you will obtain and store materials.

8. What is the layout of your manufacturing plant?

9. What are your future expansion needs?

10. Where will your the product or service be available to the customer?

11. How does it get there?

12. Where is your inventory stored?

13. How much does it cost to warehouse or store your inventory?

14. How will you keep track of inventory? Provide specific procedures and equipment used.

15. What type of insurance does your business need?

16. What are your long-term facility and equipment needs?

17. Describe your disaster recovery plan. What risks to business operations are there and how do you plan against them?

Answer these questions to describe your distribution channels:

1. What are the pros and cons of the various methods of distribution you will choose? Why did you make these choices? Do your customers purchase through a retail store, by direct sales, through manufacturer's representatives, through the mail, through wholesale distributors, online, or through catalogs? Will you use a combination of some or all?

2. Are you an OEM? Are the products you produce incorporated into another manufacturer's finished product?

3. What are some of the worst-case scenarios that can happen to prevent the distribution of your product or service, such as a shipper strike, vehicle breakdown, or loss of Internet connection? What are your contingency plans?

Answer these questions when describing your plan for avoiding channel conflict:

1. Will you be combining conflicting channels of distribution? Are you selling to both end users and retailers, or to both retailers and wholesalers?
2. How will you minimize channel conflicts?

Answer these questions when describing your digital presence:

1. Do you have an Internet sales and distribution strategy?
2. Will you be a pure play or clicks and bricks company?
3. Is your distribution channel business-to-consumer (B2C), business-to-business (B2B), business-to-government (B2G), consumer-to-government (C2G), consumer-to-consumer (C2C), or business-to-employee (B2E)? Some combination of channels?
4. Will you generate revenue from sources other than sales, such as ads on your website from other companies or charging subscriptions?
5. What types of e-shoppers do you want to attract? Impulse buyers, surfers, connectors, or bargain shoppers? How will you attract them?
6. What domain name can you use and register?
7. Where will you host your online storefront? At your company? With a third-party hosting service? Why? How much will it cost?
8. Will you use the services of an e-commerce developer to design your store-front? Who will it be and how much does it cost?

Answer these questions when describing how you will address e-commerce legal issues:

1. What is your privacy policy for information you will collect from site visitors and customers? What information is collected when shoppers buy from you? How will you use this information?
2. Does your business comply with COPPA?

The Internal Business Plan

Answer these questions to describe your business's real-world presence:

1. Do you require any specialized equipment? What is its purpose? What does it cost?
2. How does each piece of equipment function, and how much can each piece of equipment produce?
3. If you are manufacturing your product, explain the manufacturing process from raw material through finished product, and describe where you obtain and store materials.
4. What is the layout of your manufacturing plant?
5. What are your future expansion needs?
6. Where will your product or service be available to the customer?
7. How does it get there?

Answer these questions to describe your distribution channels:

1. What are the pros and cons of the various methods of distribution you will choose? Why did you make these choices? Do your customers purchase through a retail store, by direct sales, through manufacturer's representatives, through the mail, through wholesale distributors, online, or through catalogs? Will you use a combination of some or all?

2. If you are involved in a service business, will you provide in-shop service? Will you make service calls, and, if so, how will mileage costs be handled? What is your planned response time to fill your customers' needs?

Answer these questions when describing your plan for avoiding channel conflict:

1. Will you be combining conflicting channels of distribution? Will you be selling to both end users and retailers, or to both retailers and wholesalers?

2. How will you minimize channel conflicts?

Answer these questions when describing your digital presence:

1. Do you have an Internet sales and distribution strategy?

2. Will you be a pure play or clicks and bricks company?

3. Is your distribution channel business-to-consumer (B2C), business-to-business (B2B), business-to-government (B2G), consumer-to-government (C2G), consumer-to-consumer (C2C), or business-to-employee (B2E)? Some combination of channels?

4. Will you generate revenue from sources other than sales, such as ads on your website from other companies or charging subscriptions?

5. What domain name can you use and register?

6. Where will you host your online storefront? At your company? With a third-party hosting service? Why? How much does it cost?

7. Will you use the services of an e-commerce developer to design your storefront? Who will it be and how much does it cost?

Answer these questions when describing how you address e-commerce legal issues:

1. What is your privacy policy for information you will collect from site visitors and customers? What information is collected when shoppers buy from you? How will you use this information?

2. Does your business comply with COPPA?

Summary

This chapter has described how a full and effective selling strategy must consider all possible distribution channels for your product or service, and how the channels you choose must be described in the Distribution Channels section of your business plan.

If you purchase and sell other companies' products, distribution includes the process of buying from wholesalers or distributors and selling to the end user. If you are offering a service, your distribution process is simple. You offer it from an office or storefront directly to your target customer. As you've learned in this chapter, your plan must not only describe the distribution channels you'll use, but also describe how you'll avoid channel conflicts. This chapter also explained how to describe in your business plan how you expect to use online technology in your business. The next chapter will show you how to identify and describe your competition.

Describing Your Competition

10

There's no escaping competition in life. That goes double for business. The business environment is very competitive, more so now than ever before. We saw in the preceding chapter the many different ways a company can distribute and sell into the hands of the customer—and the variety of ways a competitor can compete with your business.

A reader of your plan wants to know who your competitors are, how they compete with you, and how your business is positioned to compete with them. This information outlines your competitive advantage. You are well prepared to defend and describe your business's competitive advantages because many of the previous chapters have helped you define your unique selling position and identify the distribution channels necessary for success in your marketplace. In this chapter, you learn how to draw upon that information and research to write the Competitive Analysis section of your business plan.

You can see an example of a competitive analysis in Appendix A, "Sample Business Plan."

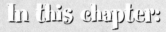

In this chapter:

* Learn how to describe your competitors
* Understand and describe your competitive environment

To do list

- ☐ Identify your direct and indirect competitors
- ☐ Describe your company's barriers to competition

Describing the Competitive Environment

The important thing to do when preparing this section of your plan is to first do a little homework. If you're an existing company or division, you are pretty familiar with your competition. But if you are a new company or entering a new market niche, you need to do a bit of research to fully describe the competitors your new venture faces.

Pick a dozen or so of your nearest competitors and start a file on them. Find examples of their advertising and promotional materials and their pricing strategy, and toss them into a file folder. Check current and back issues of the Yellow Pages to see if your competitors are increasing, decreasing, or maintaining their promotional exposure.

Don't forget to be thorough in your competitive research. Remember that through today's distribution opportunities, your competitors might be around the corner but also around the world.

Keep in mind that direct competitors are not the only competition you have. You will most likely have indirect competitors. A *direct competitor* is a business offering the same product or service to the same market as you. An *indirect competitor* is a company with the same product or service but with a different target market than your market.

> **note** Except for the questions on the impact of a division's venture on an existing company in the internal business plan, the questions and techniques you learn in this chapter apply to all plans.

> **tip** Don't forget to check your competitors' websites, too. Often, you find valuable information on company websites about current and past promotions, plans for expansion, and new product or service plans. A good way to find your competitors online is to enter the keywords that describe your business, product, or service into a search engine like Google.com.

One of the best examples of an indirect competitor is Amazon.com. When Amazon.com opened for business, the major bookstores ignored the company, thinking it didn't represent a direct competitor because it sold on a fledgling and unproven distribution channel called the Internet. If anything, most booksellers considered Amazon.com an indirect competitor. The bookstores were sorely wrong.

Other examples of indirect competition are companies like Hewlett-Packard and IBM. Retailers never dreamed these computer manufacturers would ever sell directly to the end user and compete for their retail business. But these computer manufacturers did begin selling directly to the public, and continue to do so today. You should give some serious thought to who might be direct or indirect competition now and in the foreseeable future, and convey this information to the reader of your plan.

Things You'll Need

❑ Research you've compiled on competition

❑ Advertising and promotional materials supplied by your competitors

❑ Yellow Pages or other business directory

❑ Computer and Internet access for conducting supplemental research

❑ Paper or electronic files for filing information on your competitors

Identifying Your Competition

When you're ready to write this section of your plan, pull out your file folder on the competition you have created and follow these steps to compile a competitive analysis on each of them:

1. First, list the names and locations of each competitor—direct and indirect.

2. Describe the way your competitors position and sell their products and services. Study how competitors sell and uniquely position their products or services, and how they promote them through their advertising and marketing materials. Study what they wrote and, even more important, *how* they wrote it. Do they have a slogan? If so, how do they use it? Is their copy well written? Is the quality of their products or services well presented? Does it catch your attention? Does it get their message across? Can you use the same copy techniques in your business? Once you've done this, look at your business model and see how you can position your business against these competitors. What makes your product or service unique? What can your business provide that your competitors can't? And if your product or service is close to what your competitors are offering, why should a consumer buy from you?

3. Describe the competition's methods of distribution. Describe how they sell into your marketplace, whether as wholesalers, retailers, through personal selling, corporate sales, or so forth. How will your method of distribution differ? Will it give you a competitive advantage?

4. Describe your competitors' images. What part of the market are they trying to appeal to? Can you appeal to the same market in a better way? Or does you company image differ in a substantial way. If not, can you find an untapped market for what you offer?

5. Analyze each competitor's pricing strategy and how it compares to your pricing strategy. If its prices are lower, how does your unique selling position compete? Based on your research, describe how your competitors operate their businesses compared to how you operate yours.

6. You should also describe the nature of your competitor's business performance. Is it steady, increasing, or decreasing? Take into account what and how much it sells (in units and sales dollars), the number of years it has been in business, and its specific market niche.

7. Add a pie chart in this section of your plan showing what share of the market each of your competitors has and the share your company plans to take. Review the section on Determining Market Share in Chapter 7, "Describing Your Marketplace."

8. Describe each of your competitor's strengths, weaknesses, and any distinct differences in the products or services it sells compared to your products and services. Does this give your business a market advantage in some way? Are there specific competitive advantages you hold over your competition? Also, describe your competitors' possible or likely response to the entry of your business in the marketplace, and list businesses that might compete with you after you enter the market.

COMPETITIVE RESEARCH RESOURCES

The Internet is filled with resources that can help you find your competition and provide you with the necessary information to evaluate them. Here are just a few of the media sources, web directories, and competitive intelligence services you can draw on:

* The U.S. Web100 (http://metamoney.com/usIndustryListIndex.html)

  This site lists the top 100 companies in the United States, organized in industry categories.

* Hoover's, Inc. (http://www.hoovers.com/free/)

  A directory of more than 15,000 business-related websites, divided into seven major categories.

* CI Seek (http://www.bidigital.com/ci/)

  This site offers the Competitive Intelligence Resource Index, a search engine and categorical listing of sites relating to competitive intelligence.

* Business.com (http://www.business.com)

  This business search engine and directory includes company and industry profiles, news, financials, statistics, and, most importantly, competitive analysis.

* And the granddaddy of all company information—Dun & Bradstreet (http://www.dnb.com/us/)

  For many decades, Dun & Bradstreet has provided detailed information on business that can be a valuable source for researching your competition. But this information does not come cheap. Be prepared to pay for the information they provide.

If you fail to present your competitors or claim you have no competition, an investor or executive manager might assume a market doesn't exist for your product or service. Claiming you don't have any competition is a red flag to anyone investing in your company or loaning you money. Every business has competition of some sort and it must be described in your business plan.

Describing Your Company's Barriers to Competition

No successful business can keep competitors from copying its approaches, offerings, and techniques, but you should explain how you plan to keep one step ahead of the competition during the first three to five years of your company. Part of this information is included in your implementation plan that you write in Chapter 12, "Creating Your Implementation Plan". In the Competitive Analysis section of the business plan, however, you must describe for your reader what barriers to market entry by potential competitors exist for your business.

Several ways exist to create barriers to competition. Perhaps your company owns intellectual property rights, such as copyrights or patents. For example, in technology-based businesses, intellectual property (IP) protection via patents is usually central to a competitive strategy.

Or maybe you've built into your business a high *switching cost*. That is, your customers would experience a high level of inconvenience or cost if they left you and went to a competitor. An example is the old cell phone industry, before you could take your cell phone number with you. Today, that barrier to competition is gone and consumers can easily switch from one carrier to another without having to get a new cell phone number.

You might have a service business that relies heavily on expert knowledge and the ability to have barriers to competition because the expertise you have is rare or unique. Whatever your barrier is, you need to convey what it is to the reader of your plan.

caution This is not the place in your plan to toot your own horn. In other words, describe your competition from an objective and *unbiased* perspective. In addition, don't underestimate the power and strength of your competitors.

caution Creating a barrier to competition is much harder today than a decade ago. The Internet and the realities of e-business have permanently changed the barriers to competition. Now anyone with a good idea, a plan for strong execution, and ample venture funding can pose a competitive challenge to even the most established businesses today.

Write the Plan!

Answer the following questions as they apply to the type of plan you're writing. Startup and full business plans use an identical set of questions. The internal business plan uses all of these questions, plus a few others, as outlined in the sections below.

The Startup and Full Business Plans

Answer the following questions to describe your competitive environment:

1. Who is your primary competition?
2. Who is your indirect competition?
3. Has your competition fallen short in satisfying your target customer's needs?

Answer these questions to identify and describe your competition:

1. What are the names and locations of your direct and indirect competitors? Are they local, geographical, national, international, or on the Internet?
2. What is each competitor's unique selling position? How does it promote that position through its advertising and marketing materials? How does your unique selling position differ from those of your competitors?
3. Do your competitors have slogans? If so, how do they use them?
4. Is their promotion and ad copy well written? Is the quality of their product or service well presented? Does it catch your attention? Does it get their message across? Can you use the same copy techniques in your business?
5. How does the competition sell into your marketplace? Are competitors represented as wholesalers, retailers, personal sellers, or corporate sellers?
6. What business image do your competitors have? What part of the market are they trying to appeal to? Can you appeal to the same market in a better way? Or can you find an untapped market?
7. What is the competition's pricing strategy? What is their values proposition?
8. From your research, how would you describe how competitors operate their businesses as compared to the way you operate your business?
9. Is the competition's business steady, increasing, or decreasing? What and how much do they sell (in units and sales dollars), how many years have they been in business, and what's their specific market niche?
10. How would you describe in a pie chart the various market shares of your competitors and what share of the market you plan to capture?
11. What are your competitors' strengths, weakness, and distinct differences in the products or services they sell compared to your products or services? Does this give your business a market advantage in some way? Are there specific competitive advantages you hold over your competition?
12. What are your competitors' possible or likely responses to the entry of your business in the marketplace? What businesses might compete with you after you enter the market?

Answer these questions to describe your barriers to competition:

1. What are your barriers to competition? What are the barriers to market entry by potential competitors?
2. Do you have intellectual property rights, such as copyrights or patents?
3. Did you build into your business a high switching cost?
4. Is your business expertise rare or unique?

The Internal Business Plan

In addition to all of the previous questions in all categories, answer the following question as you describe your competitive environment within the internal business plan:

1. How will your current business or company help your new venture succeed?
2. If the new business venture succeeds, will it hurt your company somewhere else? What is the potential significance and impact for this venture on the existing company offering?

Summary

The people who read your plan want to know who your competitors are, how they compete with you, and how your business is positioned to compete with them. In this chapter you've learned that the important thing to do when preparing the Competitive Analysis section of your plan is to first do a little homework. Pick a dozen or so of your nearest competitors and start a file on them. You've also learned to include both direct and indirect competitors in your research, and to remember you're competing in a global market.

In addition to describing your competition, this chapter has also discussed how you should describe the barriers to competition in place for your business. No successful business can keep competitors from copying it, but readers want to know how you plan to keep one step ahead of the competition during the first three to five years of your business.

The next chapter will show you how to list and describe your business risks and opportunities.

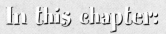

Describing Your Business Risks

I t's hard starting and running a successful business, and it involves taking risks. These risks cannot be eliminated entirely, but they can be reduced to a manageable level, so they don't impede the success of a new venture.

The reader of your plan who needs to make a decision on whether to support your business idea with money or resources is looking for an explanation of the risks your business idea will face, and how you will manage them.

The trick, of course, is to present your risks without scaring away your investors. No investor expects a business plan to paint a risk-free picture. Your ability to identify, discuss, and mitigate the risks to your business demonstrates your skills as a manager and increases your credibility with potential investors or management. In this chapter, you learn how to write the Risk section of your business plan by including an accurate assessment of the risks you'll face and a plan for managing them.

You can see a sample of a Risks section in Appendix B, "Sample Elements."

11

In this chapter:

* Identify and describe the risks your business idea faces

* Describe your strategy for dealing with risks

To do list

- ☐ Identify your business risks
- ☐ Categorize relevant risks
- ☐ Determine appropriate risk-management measures

Listing Your Business Risks

We've already discussed some of the risks to a new business in prior chapters. There are risks from competition and imitation, losing primary suppliers, natural causes, and human malice. This is a good place in your plan to summarize the risks stated in prior sections and add some others.

note All of the questions you read in this chapter should be answered in all three types of business plans.

Your plan should address several kinds of risks, but you don't need to address every kind of risk to your business. Pick the risk categories most relevant to your company and include a paragraph or two about each one.

The most common risks to consider are

- Competitive risks
- Marketing and promotional risks
- Distribution risks

Here's an example for describing these risks in this section of your plan.

Let's say you are opening a business that sells original homemade sugar cookies. Your sugar cookies are unique in your geographical area because they contain imported almonds. No one else at this time offers cookies like these in your area. Besides the normal risks from fire, theft, and so on, your business faces some unique risks. Here's how they could be described:

- You face the risk of losing your competitive advantage if another company in your area begins marketing similar cookies.
- You risk rejection by the marketplace; maybe no one wants to buy your new cookie.
- You risk losing access to the supplies that make your product unique because there's only one supplier of your special imported almonds in the area.
- You risk failing in your unique marketing strategy of creating a Cookies and Milk Day, and delivering your product to harried office workers in your area.

Things You'll Need

- ❏ Previously written sections of the business plan
- ❏ Your existing risk-related research

Describing Your Risk Management Strategy

When you write your Risks section, you need to do more than just identify and discuss the risks and threats to your new company. You must convey to the reader how you confront and minimize them.

Small Business Notes at http://www. smallbusinessnotes.com has compiled a five step process of managing risks. They are

- Identify the risk
- Measure the risk
- Formulate ways to limit the risk
- Formulate tasks to implement the risk
- Monitor the process to evaluate the mitigation of the risk

> **note** When you think about insurance, the normal types of insurance, such as fire, theft, and flood, come to mind. But a business needs to consider another type of insurance—*key man insurance*. This type of insurance is for those people in your business who are critical to its operations. If they die or are disabled, the company is reimbursed for the loss of that critical person. The money paid is used to recruit and compensate another person to replace the one who is disabled or passed away.

Other risks to your particular business could include people risk. A service company especially depends upon having certain employees or certain kinds of employees to supply a service. A technology company might need a special type of programmer that's not easily available. If you're writing a plan for a business that requires specialized personnel, identify these types of personnel and describe how you plan to deal with the problem of recruiting and retaining them.

Remember, if you don't show the reader you are aware of the risks facing your new business venture, or state that no appreciable risks exist, she will dismiss you and your business idea as naïve.

Write the Plan!

Answer the following questions as they apply to your business plan; all questions apply to all plan types.

Answer these questions as you identify your business and describe your risk-management strategy:

1. How will you keep your competitive advantage? Will you be introducing improved products or services, price cutting, expanding into new geographical areas, or adding new product lines?

INSURANCE CONSIDERATIONS

Many risks to your business can be covered by insurance policies. But what should you consider when choosing a policy? In addition to determining which types of insurance you need (such as theft, fire, or flood) you must also decide how much coverage you will require. Don't forget to consider the cost of the coverage; the cost of premium payments is a concern for any small- to medium-size businesses.

Shop around for competitive bids. Better yet, find an independent insurance agent who represents several different insurance companies and have him find you the best price.

Consider reducing your premium for the insurance coverage you need by taking a high deductible.

Finally, make sure you have the insurance coverage in place before you open your doors for business.

2. What risks do you face in producing your product or service? Are there any possible health and safety risks in your business or work site? How will you mitigate them?

3. What risks do you face with a totally new product or service? How will you test its viability in the marketplace? Surveys? Focus groups?

4. What risks do you face with the marketing plan you have outlined? Will you be creating new promotional opportunities that are untried and untested? What are your plans if they fail?

5. What human resource risks do you face? Consider your management team, advisors, and employees. What if your key employees quit? What if they get seriously hurt on the job? How will you retain key employees?

6. What if your major vendor can no longer supply you with parts or goods? What other suppliers exist? At what cost? What kind of relationship will you have with them?

Summary

Like life, establishing a business involves risks. These risks cannot be entirely eliminated but they can be reduced to a manageable level. By seriously considering the risks to your business model, you can mediate their effects and show the reader that you have realistically evaluated your business model. The reader of your plan who needs to make a decision on whether to support your business idea with money or resources is looking for an explanation of these risks and how you will manage them.

Remember, if you don't show the reader you are aware of the risks facing your new business venture, or state that no appreciable risks exist, he will dismiss you and your business idea as naïve.

The next chapter will show you how to describe the implementation plan for your new business.

Part IV

When and How Much?

Creating Your Implementation Plan

12

In this chapter:

✳ Set objectives in each phase of your implementation plan

✳ Outline what tasks or actions must be performed in each phase

✳ Describe the overall milestones to be reached in each phase of implementation

According to some Asian philosophies, the journey is more important than one's destination. In a way, that's true of business plans, too. How you implement your business venture is as important as the venture itself.

An *implementation plan* is important because it provides a way of planning your time and resources so all the necessary tasks are carried out within a given timescale. It also describes what future plans you have for your company after initial success. Identifying future plans is one way of telling the reader how you will stay competitive and one step ahead of the competition. In other words, it provides a snapshot of how you intend to set up your company and implement your plan over time.

To do this, you need to break down the phases of your implementation plan into three parts:

- The objective or target to reach in each phase
- What tasks or actions must be performed in each phase
- The overall milestones to be reached

The implementation plan does not need to be complex. Just a few pages or so in your document outlining the important phases of your company startup and development is enough.

You can see a sample of an implementation plan in Appendix A, "Sample Business Plan."

All issues and questions in this section pertain to all plan types, with a few minor exceptions occurring in the internal plan. An internal plan probably does not require facility rental costs, utility deposits, build outs, new telecommunications equipment, office equipment, company website, or legal and bookkeeping setup because these items have already been accounted for by the existing company.

To do list

- ❏ Establish startup goals for your company
- ❏ Define, list, and describe startup tasks and expenses

Detailing the Startup Phase—The Zero Months

Even before you open your doors for business, you perform tasks that should be described in your plan. Even if you're writing an internal plan for an existing company, you still have startup tasks to perform.

Many of these tasks incur expenses and these expenses are reflected in the Financial Plan section of your plan under columns in your *pro forma* (your estimate of revenue, expenses, and profits) called zero month(s). They're called *zero month(s)* because you are not generating any revenue during the first months of operation, although your company is in existence, spending money or using resources.

As mentioned, the Implementation Plan section of your plan must detail your startup goals, the tasks involved in attaining those goals, and the related expenses. Your overall objective, of course, is to prepare to open your doors for business. But you need to reach a number of secondary goals in the process. Here are some examples:

- **Preparing the physical plant**—During startup, one of your goals will be to prepare to do business within your physical space, whether office, retail, or warehouse space, or some combination of all three. If you are planning to work out of a home office, you need to consider startup needs such as office equipment. Your plan's readers will assume you have already acquired the necessary space to do business. But during these zero months, you will be occupying your physical location and paying rent even before you generate revenue. You'll also want to pay any necessary deposits on water, electricity and/or phone service, build-out expenses for office and warehouse space, and so on during this startup phase. In the Implementation Plan section of your business plan, be sure to list and describe these goals, plans, and expenses.

- **Acquiring office equipment**—You'll also have the startup goal of acquiring all necessary office equipment. During the zero months, you will be installing and paying for all the office equipment and telecommunication technology you need to run your company. As you list and describe the tasks and expenses associated with accomplishing this goal, be sure to include telephones, office computers, copy and fax machines, and office furniture and, if a retail store, displays and signage.

- **Establishing an Internet storefront**—You might also have the startup goal of opening an Internet storefront. In this case, you will most likely have to pay for the creation and hosting of your e-tail storefront on the Web. Even if you will not sell on the Web, you might require a company website that will need to be designed and hosted. The design of your digital presence will incur a cost during these months. If you're hosting your website yourself, you will need to buy and install the necessary web servers and Internet connection. Your Implementation Plan section must include a description of your goals for your Web presence and the tasks and expenses necessary to attain them.

- **Establishing your company's legal and market presence**—In preparing to begin business operations, you'll also need to legally establish your company and its market presence. To accomplish this goal, you will most likely use the services of a number of professionals, all of which will be zero month expenses. If you're incorporating your company, you probably will have to pay for incorporating expenses. You also might need to hire a service to design and print your business cards, letterhead, sales brochures, and direct mail pieces. You might also incur the costs of deposits and marketing materials for your initial direct mail or email marketing campaign, as well as print and Internet advertising. There might be banking fees such as credit card merchant account setup and the purchase of checks that must be paid for during these zero months, as well. Be sure to clearly and completely list and describe all tasks and expenses associated with the goals you set for establishing your company as a legal and market entity.

- **Hiring personnel**—It goes without saying that you must have your initial management and staff in place before sales start and this will incur costs in salaries and wages during the zero months. You're going to need people to work on opening the doors of your new enterprise, so clearly describe your personnel goals and the tasks and expenses associated with bringing them onboard.

note These tasks required for the zero months need to be described in this section of your plan, but the expenses associated with them must also be conveyed in your pro forma. You learn how to write the Pro Forma section of your business plan in Chapter 13, "Writing Your Financial Plan."

To do list

- ☐ List and describe first-year objectives
- ☐ Establish milestones within the first year for accomplishing the objectives

Describing the First Year

After you have your zero months' goals, tasks, and associated expenses, you need to describe your plan for running your company during its first year of operation. You must describe to the reader your objectives for your first year in business. This is where you can explain step-by-step how you will implement your business plan.

Be prepared to describe

- What volume or number of products or services you want to produce or sell during the first year
- Expected revenue, quarter by quarter
- Your first-year break-even point, in regard to dollars of revenue, units of sales, number of clients, and so on
- Your advertising plan, where you'll be placing ads quarter by quarter, the types of marketing material you will use, and when
- Growth of personnel count, at what point you will add staff and/or management personnel, and how you'll use added personnel to advance your business
- What kinds of direct mail or email programs you initiate, and when you plan to initiate them

Don't forget to be specific in your plan for implementing your goals. Be sure your implementation plan outlines each major objective for your first year of operation, and all tasks and expenses associated with the objectives. Also, be certain to set specific milestones for when you plan to achieve each objective in your plan. In other words, after you have listed your tasks for the first year, you must show when they will be started and finished.

USING A GANTT CHART

A number of tools can help you detail the implementation tasks you outline for your company. Though sometimes these planning tools result in more detail than is necessary in your business plan, these tools can help you put together a detailed project plan that will be extremely useful after your company is up and running.

One such planning tool is called the Gantt chart. A *Gantt chart* is a horizontal bar chart used in project scheduling and management that shows the start date, end date, and duration of tasks within a project. Gantt charts allow you to assess how long a project should take, lay out the order in which tasks need to be carried out, manage the dependencies between tasks, and determine the resources needed.

With a Gantt chart, you can monitor the progress of a project or your company and see immediately what should have been achieved at any given point in time.

You can download free weekly and monthly Gantt chart templates at http://www.mfep.co.uk/plan/gantt_chart.html.

To do list

- [ ] List and describe your company's three to five year expansion plan
- [ ] Define and describe your company's long-term product or service strategy

Outlining the Three to Five Year Plan

The majority of business ventures (at least those that are successful) reach the break-even point and start showing a profit sometime within the first and third year of operation. The Implementation Plan section of your business plan should describe the expected revenue, quarter by quarter and year by year, of your third to fifth year of business. Your three to five year plan should also identify your company's future plans and how you intend to remain competitive over that period of time.

You should convey briefly in a few paragraphs any future additions to your company in terms of new products and services. For example, in my business plan for a home concierge service, I describe to the reader the medium to long range objectives of the business. At first, the company would provide any and all services that can be performed exclusively in or around the home. Then, a few years later, we expand those services to those that can be performed for or at a business location.

Also in this section of the plan, describe how you'll develop new or improved products over the next 3–5 years, and any relationship between market segments, market demand, market needs, and product development. Perhaps you will combine a service along with the products you sell. For example, if you sell business computers, you might also offer a way to lease the computers you sell. Or perhaps you have a company selling bridal gowns and plan to offer a way for your customers to recover some of the cost of their gowns by auctioning them off on your website.

You might also have plans to expand a product line you manufacture or add a new line of product or service to capitalize on the customer base you have serviced over the years. Add these ideas to your implementation plan and show the reader you have thought of ways to increase the value of your business and stay ahead of the competition.

Things You'll Need

- ❏ Previous sections of your business plan
- ❏ All relevant research regarding the physical plant, equipment, personnel, and other expenses associated with your business operation

Write the Plan!

Answer the following questions as they apply to your type of plan to write the implementation plan portion of your business plan—startup, full, or internal plan.

The Startup Business Plan

Answer these questions to describe your startup phase goals, tasks, and expenses:

1. What utility deposits or down payments for build outs will you be making? What tasks will you perform in those efforts, and what expenses will ensue?
2. What telecommunications equipment will you need to purchase? Telephones, computers, or servers? What kind? How many? Will you lease or buy? What will the costs be?
3. What kind of office equipment will you need? Copy machines, fax machines, or office furniture? What kind? How many? How much will they cost?
4. Will you need retail displays? What kind of signage will you need on your building? Where will you get it? How long will it take to receive and install? What will it cost?
5. What kind of digital presence will you have? An online storefront or a company website? Who will design it? In-house or outsource? How long will it take? What will it cost?
6. What legal and bookkeeping setup will you require? If you're incorporating, what tasks and expenses will be involved in that process? Will you be setting up company books with an accounting firm? How long will it take? How much will it cost?
7. What kind of collateral materials will you need? Letterhead, business cards, brochures, menus, checks, and so on? Where will you get them? How long will it take? How much will they cost?
8. Will you need to hire a firm to create your marketing materials? What will be involved in finding that firm? How long will it take to get the materials? How much will the firm charge?

9. Will you need any deposits for your initial direct marketing campaign? Direct mail or telemarketing deposits? Postage for catalogs or bulk rate postage permits?

10. Will you need a deposit or upfront fee for a credit card merchant account? How much?

11. What initial personnel will you require? Who are they? How many? What will it cost to find and hire them?

Answer these questions to describe your first year of operation:

1. What do you want to accomplish during the first year as to the products and services you will sell?

2. What is your expected revenue, quarter by quarter?

3. What is your break-even point in the first year? How many dollars in revenue, units of sales, number of clients, and so forth?

4. Describe in general your advertising plan, where you'll be placing ads quarter by quarter, the types of marketing material you will use, and when.

5. How many new personnel do you intend to hire, and in what roles? How will they advance your company? At what point will you add staff and management personnel? In what positions? How many?

6. What kinds of direct mail or email programs will you initiate? When do you plan to initiate them, and what will these programs cost?

Answer these questions when outlining your three to five year plan:

1. At what point do you plan to break even? How many dollars in revenue, units of sales, number of clients, and so on, will you need to reach that point?

2. What is your expected revenue, quarter by quarter and year by year, of your company?

3. What are your plans for expanding the company and remaining competitive?

4. Will you be adding new products or services? When do you plan to add them? What are these new products or services, and what tasks will be involved in adding them? How will they make you more competitive?

5. Will you add new features to your product or service? What are they? How will they make you more competitive?

The Full Business Plan

Answer these questions to describe your startup phase goals, tasks, and expenses:

1. What utility deposits or down payments for build outs will you be making? What tasks will be involved in those efforts, and what expenses will ensue?

2. What telecommunications equipment will you need to purchase? Telephones, computers, or servers? What kind? How many? Will you lease or buy? What will the costs be?

3. What kind of office equipment will you need? Copy machines, fax machines, or office furniture? What kind? How many? How much will they cost?

4. Will you need retail displays? What kind of signage will you need on your building? Where will you get it? How long will it take to receive and install? What will it cost?

5. What kind of digital presence will you have? An online storefront or a company website? Who will design it? In-house or outsource? How long will it take? What will it cost?

6. What legal and bookkeeping setup will you require? If you're incorporating, what tasks and expenses will be involved in that process? Will you be setting up company books with an accounting firm? How long will it take? How much will it cost?

7. What kind of collateral materials will you need? Letterhead, business cards, brochures, menus, checks, and so on? Where will you get them? How long will it take? How much will they cost?

8. Will you need to hire a firm to create your marketing materials? What will be involved in finding that firm? How long will it take to get the materials? How much will the firm charge?

9. Will you need any deposits for your initial direct marketing campaign? Direct mail or telemarketing deposits? Postage for catalogs or bulk rate postage permits?

10. Will you need a deposit or upfront fee for a credit card merchant account? How much?

11. What initial personnel will you require? Who are they? How many? What will it cost to find and hire them?

Answer these questions to describe your first year of operation:

1. What do you want to accomplish during the first year as to the products and service you will sell?

2. What is your expected revenue, quarter by quarter?

3. What is your break-even point in the first year? How many dollars in revenue, units of sales, number of clients, and so on?

4. Describe in general your advertising plan, where you'll be placing ads quarter by quarter, the types of marketing material you will use, and when.

5. How many new personnel do you intend to hire, and in what roles? How will they advance your company? At what point will you add staff and management personnel? In what positions? How many?

6. What kinds of direct mail or email programs will you initiate? When do you plan to initiate them, and what will these programs cost?

Answer these questions when outlining your three to five year plan:

1. At what point do you plan to break even? How many dollars in revenue, or units of sales, or number of clients, and so on, will you need to reach that point?

2. What is your expected revenue, quarter by quarter and year by year, of your company?

3. What are your plans for expanding the company and remaining competitive?

4. Will you be adding new products or services? When do you plan to add them? What are these new products or services, and what tasks will be involved in adding them? How will they make you more competitive?

5. Will you add new features to your product or service? What are they? How will they make you more competitive?

The Internal Business Plan

Answer these questions to describe your startup phase goals, tasks, and expenses:

1. Will you need retail displays? What kind of signage will you need on your building? How long will it take to receive and install? What will it cost?

2. What kind of digital presence will you have? An online storefront or a company website? Who will design it? In-house or outsource? How long will it take? What will it cost?

3. What kind of collateral materials will you need? Letterhead, business cards, brochures, menus, checks, and so on? Where will you get them? How long will it take? How much will they cost?

4. Will you need to hire a firm to create your marketing materials? What will be involved in finding that firm? How long will it take to get the materials? How much will the firm charge?

5. Will you need any deposits for your initial direct marketing campaign? Direct mail or telemarketing deposits? Postage for catalogs or bulk rate postage permits?

6. Will you need a deposit or upfront fee for a credit card merchant account? How much?

7. What initial personnel will you require? Who are they? How many? What will it cost to find and hire them?

Answer these questions to describe your first year of operation:

1. What do you want to accomplish during the first year as to the products and services you will sell?

2. What is your expected revenue, quarter by quarter?

3. What is your break-even point in the first year? How many dollars in revenue, units of sales, number of clients, and so forth?

4. Describe in general your advertising plan, where you'll be placing ads quarter by quarter, the types of marketing material you will use, and when.

5. How many new personnel do you intend to hire, and in what roles? How will they advance your company? At what point do you add staff and management personnel? In what positions? How many?

6. What kinds of direct mail or email programs will you initiate? When do you plan to initiate them, and what will these programs cost?

Answer these questions when outlining your three to five year plan:

1. At what point do you plan to break even? How many dollars in revenue, units of sales, number of clients, and so on, will you need to reach that point?

2. What is your expected revenue, quarter by quarter and year by year, of your company?

3. What are your plans for expanding the company and remaining competitive?

4. Will you be adding new products or services? When do you plan to add them? What are these new products or services, and what tasks will be involved in adding them? How will they make you more competitive?

5. Will you add new features to your product or service? What are they? How will they make you more competitive?

Summary

An implementation plan sets out the logical steps, or phases, you need to go through to turn your business idea into reality.

Your implementation plan also provides a well-thought-out roadmap for applying your time and resources in the critical early stages of your business operation, and it enables you to lay out a timeframe for accomplishing all of the tasks necessary for reaching your business goals. As you've learned in this chapter, you need to break down the phases of your implementation plan into three parts. What is the objective or target to reach in each phase? What tasks or actions must be performed in each phase? And what overall milestones have you set for accomplishing those tasks and reaching those goals?

In the next chapter of this book, you learn how to detail your capital requirements.

Writing Your Financial Plan

We've all heard the quote, "The opera is not over until the fat lady sings." Conversely, a business plan is not finished until you can show your new venture can break even in the short term and become profitable over time. All your business strategies, marketing plans, product or service descriptions, and sales tactics are for naught if you can't prove to the reader that you have a viable company.

Except for the Executive Summary, you will note that the Financial Plan section of your plan is written last, after you've made your marketing, selling, or production plans. Keep in mind that you are not creating a full-blown accounting statement here. Elements such as stockholders' equity, general ledgers, and so on are best left up to the accounting firm you hire to do your books. Here, your job is to give the business perspective of your financial plan that an investor or loan officer wants to see. Although the information you learn in this chapter helps you draft your own financial plan, I strongly advise you to have an accountant review the financials in your draft and then create the final version of this section for your finished business plan.

note All questions in this section pertain to all three types of business plans.

Presenting Persuasive Financials

After you catch your reader's interest with your business concept, she wants to see if your business plan is a viable entity. Will it make enough money to reach break-even and then sustain profitability? Readers are also looking to see if your numbers are real and make sense. Anyone can slap a spreadsheet together, make projections, and show a wild profit. The challenge is to show that these profit projections are based on solid business assumptions. These assumptions come from the ideas, concepts, and strategies you've described throughout your entire business plan, which form the basis for your financial statements and projections.

You can see a sample of a financial plan in Appendix A, "Sample Business Plan." There are four comprehensive reports included in the financial plan. You need to include these in your plan, as well:

- **Three- to five-year pro forma**—An estimate of revenue, expenses, and profits over three to five years of company operations.
- **Income statement**—The actual income generated by your company.
- **Cash flow statement**—Revenue is not money in the bank. This statement shows if your company has enough cash on hand to cover your monthly expenses.
- **Balance sheet**—Uses the information from your pro forma projections to show yearly projections from year one to year three.

note Palo Alto Software, at http://www.bplans.com/bc/, has a nice set of financial calculators you can use when creating your financial sections of your plan. They include cash flow, starting cost, and break-even calculators.

note Remember, you can use the financial plan in your business plan not only to raise investment capital, but to guide you as you operate your business. If you have done your homework, the financial documents you have prepared can help you assess the ongoing operation of your business and the business assumptions you've made.

Things You'll Need

- ❑ Market research for your company
- ❑ Estimates of necessary goods and expenses for your company
- ❑ Computer and spreadsheet software

Creating a Draft of Your Financial Plan

Even though I suggest you have an accountant review and finalize your financial plan, you should prepare a first draft of your financials yourself. Only you know the intimate details of your business concept and understand viable assumptions that have to be made when constructing your financial statements. Further, a potential lender or equity investor wants to see not only that the numbers look good, but also that you understand them. If you can't answer highly detailed questions about how you arrived at your numbers, you aren't going to get your funding.

Your financial statements and projections should follow generally accepted accounting standards. Investors and bankers are familiar with these standards and expect to see them reflected in your financial statements. So don't attempt to devise your own method of presenting your financials. Stick to the tried and true, as described in this section.

Investors and loan officers expect to see financial projections—your *pro forma*—for a three- to five-year period and two or three pro forma scenarios. Your pro forma, therefore, should include at least two possible financial projections for your company—a minimum of one scenario with sales coming in under expectation, and another scenario with sales over expectation. Revenue, more than expenses, drive a hypothetical pro forma scenario, so the revenue projections are a critical component of your plan. If you're an existing company, you should show historical statements.

Creating the Financial Assumptions

If this is a new venture, you're probably asking yourself how you are going to create financial statements that show pro forma scenarios, profit and loss, cash flow, and a balance sheet on a company or division that doesn't exist yet. You do this by making some well-informed assumptions about the revenue and expenses of your company during the years of operation. Picking sales and revenue numbers and expenses out of the air because they sound good is not the way to impress the reader of your plan. Readers want to see if you have properly conveyed the reasons behind the numbers you've chosen for your financial projections.

So, you have to first include in this section of your plan the financial assumptions you will use. These assumptions can be described in as little as one page to as much as several pages, depending on the complexity of your business. Sometimes they are included at the bottom of the pro forma scenarios themselves. The assumptions are then cross-referenced to the different line items on the pro forma.

You should always begin your financial assumption with projected sales because this number drives all others. Then describe your cost of goods.

Describing Your Revenue Assumptions

Here's a simple example of creating financial assumptions.

Suppose you're opening a pizza parlor and from the market research you performed in Chapter 7, "Describing Your Marketplace," you found that the average pizza parlor sells 50 pizzas a day. This number includes both individual pies and slices. Your research also shows that it costs an average of $5.00 in ingredients to create a single pizza that can be sold at an average of $12.00. So, when you create the revenue line in your pro forma, you state that your monthly revenue in pizza sales is $18,000 (50 pizzas per day, for 30 days, at an average sale of $12.00).

You state in your assumptions that the monthly revenue of pizza sales is arrived at by the above assumptions and calculated based on your market research. You then duplicate this process for all revenues from all other sales. After that's done, you then compute your cost of goods and expenses and enter them into your pro forma.

Describing Your Cost of Goods Assumptions

Let's look at the cost of goods assumption next. We said the ingredients to make an average pizza costs $5.00. This is your *cost of goods* and this number is included in your assumptions. You then calculate the expense items, such as rent, utilities, payroll, supplies, and so forth, on your pro forma in the same way.

Remember that the object here is to keep your pro forma simple. If you'll be selling many types of products from the same category, like books or CDs or pizzas, use the average sale number backed by solid assumptions. It makes your income statement easier to read, yet gives the reader what they need to know to decide if your business venture can financially succeed.

Some business plans suffer from too many spreadsheets. Today's spreadsheet software makes it too easy to create multiple variations of financial documents. In the case of financial projections, less is more.

HOW CAN YOU BENCHMARK YOUR ASSUMPTIONS?

So where can you get the data to benchmark your assumptions? You can get some of the data you need from industry associations. You can find a list of them at Yahoo! under Business and Economy > Organizations > Trade Associations. Also, trade magazines and newsletters publish statistics for their industries. You can find them at Bacon's Media Directories at http://www.bacons.com/research/directoryoverview.htm. Compare your numbers with similar sized firms in the same industry. Keep in mind, Bacon's charges for this information.

You might consider hiring a consultant to do the benchmarking for you. He puts together a study of a half-dozen or more firms very similar to yours. Being a disinterested third party, the consultant keeps each firm's individual numbers confidential by providing only average or median cost information and then gives each company the common information as an incentive for participating.

Adding Expense Assumptions

If you're a startup or creating a new division for your company, you need to first consider startup expenses before diving into your operating expenses. Your *startup expenses* are the total of all expenses you will need to open your doors to business and start generating revenue. These expenses take place in the zero months discussed in Appendix D, "Funding Your Business." The startup expenses are one-time expenditures and may include

- Major equipment purchases
- Utility deposits (phone, electric, water)
- Down payments (rent or leases)
- Personnel costs prior to opening, including payroll expenses
- Legal and professional fees (corporate set up, insurance)
- Licenses and permits
- Occupancy costs of materials and build outs
- Initial supplies
- Initial advertising and promotional costs

When creating your startup expense, keep your salaries and office expenses reasonable. You may eventually become a big company some day, but don't fall into the trap of acting like one before you open your doors.

Some additional simple assumptions to add to your financial plan are assumptions about interest expenses, capital expenditures, your projected employee head count, and office or warehouse space requirements and why you need them.

Remember, investors and bankers give as much credence to the assumptions your projections are based on as they do the numbers themselves. So your assumptions must be based on solid information.

To do list

- [ ] Choose a format for your pro forma
- [ ] Project personnel costs
- [ ] Create pro forma using cost and revenue estimates

Writing the Pro Forma

An investor or lender wants to first know when you will start to make money on your venture. The pro forma gives the reader a clear view of the financial viability of your company. The pro forma shows where your money comes from and where it will be spent over a specific period of time, normally three to five years. It could be based on an annual calendar—January through December—or your tax year. You can see a sample of a pro forma in Appendix B, "Sample Elements."

As mentioned earlier, your financial plan should include a minimum of two (but no more than three) pro forma scenarios—one based on sales revenues below your expectations, and one showing sales revenue above those expectations. In either case, your plan's readers expect the company to show profitability within a year to 18 months. As a rule of thumb, angel investor Cal Simmons, coauthor of *Every Business Needs an Angel*, advises that "entrepreneurs should plan to reach profitability within half as much time as they're raising money to cover. For example, six months if they're raising a year's worth of funding."

WILL YOUR COMPANY MAKE MONEY?

Preparing a break-even analysis can help you determine whether your company can succeed. A *break-even analysis* shows you the amount of revenue you need to bring in to cover your expenses before you make any profit. If you can bring in more than the amount of revenue you need to meet your expenses, your company stands a good chance of making money.

To do the analysis, look at the assumptions you created. Take your annual fixed costs and divide them by your gross profit percentage. This determines the revenue you'll need to generate to break even. For example, Joe's Plumbing Supplies has fixed costs of $9,000 per month. He expects his average profit margin on the items he sells to be 25%. Thus, his break-even point is $36,000 in revenue per month ($9,000 divided by .25). In other words, Joe must make $36,000 each month just to pay his fixed costs and his product costs. Note that the $36,000 does not include any profit, or even a salary for Joe.

If your analysis shows your break-even point is higher than the expected revenues, you need to decide if you can change your plan to create an achievable break-even point. Perhaps you can find a less expensive source of products, do with fewer employees, save rent by working out of a less expensive physical space, or even sell your product or service at a higher price.

If after making these changes to your product costs and expenses, you still can't reach the break-even point, you may need to rethink your business plan or even change your idea.

Following the Standard Format

The pro forma spreadsheet must follow an accepted format and contain these basic categories:

- **Gross income**—This is the gross sales from revenue from your products or services. Includes all the income generated by the business and any additional revenue sources.

- **Cost of goods sold**—This is the actual cost of the products, materials, or ingredients you purchase or manufacture for resale.

> **tip** As a rule of thumb, you should overstate your expenses and understate your revenues in your pro forma. This gives you a conservative pro forma and one that could be closer to reality.

- **Gross profit or gross revenue**—This is the difference between your gross income and your cost of goods sold. Gross profit can be expressed in dollars, as a percentage, or both. As a percentage, the gross profit is always stated as a percentage of revenue. For example, if you sell a product for $10.00 and it costs you $9.00 to make, your gross profit is $1.00 or 10%.

- **Expenses**—These include your startup and ongoing operating expenses, including all overhead and labor required for the operation of the company. This category includes the fixed expenses that must be paid at the same rate, regardless of the volume of business (such as rent, utilities, salaries and wages, and so on) as well as variable expenses that change based on the amount of business you do (such as advertising, sales commissions, freight, supplies, and so forth).

- **Total expenses**—The total of all expenses.

- **Net profit (or loss)**—Gross profit or gross revenue minus total expenses before taxes.

If your company will manufacture its own products, be careful to include all production costs. Review the production process you created earlier in your plan. Account for all your manufacturing costs, including shipping materials and the installation and maintenance of equipment.

Use a spreadsheet program like Microsoft Excel to enter your line items and quantitative numbers. Here's an outline of the items the spreadsheet should contain:

Income

1. Gross sales
2. Cost of sales
3. Gross profit (1 minus 2)

Expenses

1. Variable expenses
   a. Advertising
   b. Freight
   c. Shipping costs
   d. Credit card costs
   e. Parts and supplies

   f. Sales salaries

   g. Postage

   h. Legal and accounting fees

2. Fixed expenses

   a. Insurance

   b. Licenses and permits

   c. Office salaries

   d. Rent

   e. Utilities

   f. Fixed salaries and wages

   g. Phone

   h. Equipment lease

Total expenses

Income from operations (gross sales minus expenses)

Income before taxes

This is just a simple statement. Your pro forma could be different and have many more line items depending upon the complexity of your business. You can an example of a detailed pro forma in Appendix B.

Projecting Your Personnel Costs

Within your pro forma, you must calculate your personnel costs. To calculate these costs, you must determine how many employees you will need, and how many of those will be full-time. You also need to decide the functions of all personnel, the number of hours they'll work, and whether they'll be salaried or hourly employees.

If you are planning a large company, you need to have executive positions, such as CEO, president, and vice-presidents of various departments, such as production, sales, marketing, operations, and administration. Plan to list these people in the Personnel section of your pro forma. Small- to medium-size companies typically don't have executive titles, but do list management positions, such as operations manager, sales manager, marketing manager, and bookkeeper. Under the managers might be supervisors, and under them staff personnel, including shippers, warehouse and accounting personnel, clerks, or cashiers. Executive and managerial positions are paid a fixed salary, and supervisors and staff are normally paid an hourly wage.

Your personnel expenses include direct compensation in the form of salaries and wages, along with indirect costs that include payroll taxes and any medical benefits. Ask your accountant or state employment board what percentage of salaries and wages are to be set aside for payroll taxes. A rule of thumb is 10%–15% for payroll taxes and another 3%–5% for medical benefits if you offer them.

There are two approaches for creating the personnel table in your pro forma. The first is the standard personnel plan and the second is the detailed personnel plan. The *standard personnel plan* is just a simple list of names or functions, titles, and employee groups, each of which is assigned a monthly cost and is added to your pro forma under personnel costs. Here is an example:

- Management, $5,000 per month
- Consultants, $3,000 per month
- Graphics personnel, $7,500 per month
- Sales personnel, $4,000 per month
- Office manager, $4,000 per month
- Receptionist, $3,000 per month
- Warehouse personnel, $10,000 per month
- Other, $5,000 per month

When using this format, you next calculate the indirect expenses of payroll costs and medical benefits of all employees and add that as a separate single line in your pro forma.

The *detailed personnel plan* breaks out the departments of your company into categories such as sales and marketing, general and administrative, and so on, as in this example:

- **General and administrative**—President, administrative assistant, clerical, bookkeeping ($20,000 per month)
- **Production and operations**—Operations and production managers, warehouse, fulfillment ($15,000 per month)
- **Sales and marketing**—Sales and marketing managers, technical support, salespeople ($15,000 per month)
- **Other personnel**—($8,000 per month)

As before, take the indirect expenses of payroll costs and medical benefits and add that as a separate line on your pro forma.

Sometimes you will find that a pro forma lists not only departments or functions of the personnel, but their actual positions. For example, look at the pro forma in Appendix B and you will see that the payroll, or personnel expenses, are listed as functions or employee groups using the standard personnel plan approach. But under each function is a list of each individual employee who will perform the function. This format gives the reader more detail as to personnel costs.

KNOW THE CREDIT CARD COSTS

A company that does not take and process credit cards in today's business environment is a company running on only one cylinder. But setting up a merchant account to accept and process credit cards presents a series of costs that need to be reflected in your income statement.

The costs contained in accepting and processing credit cards may include some or all of the following:

- **Setup fees**—The cost to you for the bank setting up your account.
- **Sizable deposit**—If you are a new company, the bank might require a deposit of up to six months of projected credit card sales.
- **Discount rate**—The percentage of the sale the bank charges for processing the credit card. This discount rate can be between 1% and 5% of your sale.
- **Transaction fees**—Another fee added per credit card charge processed.
- **Monthly statement fee**—Some banks charge to print and mail a monthly statement to you.
- **Minimum processing fee**—Some banks charge a minimum processing fee if the transaction fee is too low.
- **Charge backs**—The fee a bank charges if a customer disputes a charge and the bank refunds their money.

The discount rate, fees, and setup costs go under credit card expenses on your pro forma.

To do list

- ☐ Create an income statement
- ☐ Create a cash flow statement
- ☐ Create a balance sheet

Organizing Your Financial Statements

At first, you might be intimidated by the task of forecasting the finances of your new venture. But in reality, this task isn't so bad if you plan well. Valid financial projections consist of making educated guesses as to how much money you'll take in and how much you'll need to spend, and then using these estimates to calculate whether your company will be profitable. If your company is already established, you need to include past annual balance sheets and income statements in your financial plan.

Here are the financial projections you should have in this section of y

* Income statement
* Cash flow statement
* Balance sheet

Remember: Stick to these main statements because more spreadsheets do not help the readability of your plan.

Creating Your Income Statement

Your *income statement* is a synopsis of revenue, expenses, and profits for the first three years of the operations of your company, as listed in your pro forma statement. Existing companies should provide income statements for the last three years if available. The income statement gives the reader of your plan a quick bird's-eye view of the expected performance of your business.

You can see a sample of an income statement in Appendix B.

If your assumptions are correct and your business plan is written for success, your income statement and pro forma should show the reader that your business venture is viable and can make a profit year after year.

Creating Your Cash Flow Statement

A faulty cash flow statement can tank the most successful-looking business pro forma or income statement. Projected profits don't guarantee money in the bank. Even if your pro forma tells you your company will become profitable, those projections can't tell the reader, investor, or lender who is considering your business plan if you have enough cash on hand at any given time to cover your monthly expenses. Your readers want to see you've taken into account the funds you'll need to pay these expenses, including your inventory and the materials, equipment, and personnel necessary to offer the products or services you sell.

That's the purpose of a *cash flow statement*, one of the most critical tools for the evaluation of your business. It tells you how much money you must have on hand or available to draw on to stay in business while you are becoming profitable. You can see a sample of a cash flow statement in Appendix B.

Many a company has failed because of a lack of cash flow. These companies' accounts may show a profit, but their cash is tied up in inventory and in clients that owe them money on sales. A necessary amount of working capital is critical to a company's success.

Like the income statement, the numbers and projections from the pro forma statement flow into the cash flow statement. You begin your cash flow statement by

listing the money you have on hand and what
is available for you to draw on. For example,
the amount of money you have in the bank,
the cash available on your credit cards, a business loan, or a personal credit line from your
bank are all part of the money available
to you.

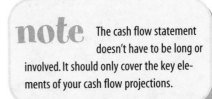

After you've determined the cash resources you have on hand or available to you,
make a list of projected expenses for your company, including any expenses
incurred in manufacturing a product for sale. You then subtract the expenses from
the total cash available. The result is a *net cash flow*—positive or negative. If the net
cash flow is negative, you need to increase the cash available for the business, even
if your pro forma and income statement show profit.

The cash flow statement is created on a monthly basis for the first year and then
quarterly projections are created for years two through five. Here are the basic steps
for calculating a simple cash flow statement:

1. Calculate a beginning cash balance for your company in month one. As
   mentioned before, this balance is the total of cash on hand plus the monetary resources you can draw on.
2. Add the cash receipts from sales or the revenue generated for the month from
   all sources.
3. List the total of the beginning cash balance and cash receipts from sales as
   your *total cash available*.
4. From your total cash available, subtract your monthly expenses and all
   accounts payable (the money you owe suppliers for inventory or manufacturing materials).
5. This gives you a total cash disbursements amount.
6. Subtract the total cash disbursements from the total cash available and you
   end up with a net cash from operations total for the month.
7. Carry this net cash from operations to the next month and that becomes
   your new beginning cash balance.
8. From here you create the next month of your cash flow statement. Create all
   following months the same way.

A simple cash flow statement or projection is included in the examples in
Appendix B.

Creating Your Balance Sheet

Like the income statement and cash flow statement, the balance sheet uses the information from your pro forma projections and should show yearly projections from
year one to year three.

Existing companies should provide balance sheets from the prior two years, if available.

You can see a sample of a balance sheet in Appendix B.

A balance sheet consists of three basic parts:

- Company assets
- Company liabilities
- Company equity

The *company assets* is anything a company owns that has a monetary value, such as cash on hand, receivables (customers and vendors who owe your company money), the value of a company's inventory on hand, other inventory items such as office, shipping, or manufacturing supplies, and any prepaid expenses or deposits. *Prepaid expenses* are those fully paid for in advance—for example, insurance premiums and maintenance contracts. *Deposits* are funds paid but a company fully expects to have returned after a period of time, such as deposits on equipment rentals. Also included in the company assets are the long term assets, or *fixed assets*, such as manufacturing equipment, and long term investments in financial instruments not readily converted to cash.

Company liabilities are monies owed to vendors and creditors—accounts payable, accrued liabilities (accrued expenses not paid out yet such as salaries and overhead), and city, state, and federal taxes. There are also long term liabilities like bonds payable that are due at the end of the year, mortgages or loans, and any amount still owned on long term debts such as notes.

A *company's equity* is equal to the company's net worth. After the assets and liabilities are entered into the balance sheet, you can then compute the equity of your company. You arrive at this number by subtracting the company liabilities from your company assets. This number is important to investors because this is how they calculate the amount they invest in your company.

A simple balance sheet is shown in the examples in Appendix B.

Write the Plan!

Answer the following questions to write the financial plan portion of your business plan. This portion of the plan has the same contents, whether you're writing a startup, full, or internal plan.

Creating Your Pro Forma

1. Do you have any startup expenses? What are your startup equipment purchases, utility deposits, down payments, personnel costs prior to opening (including payroll expenses), legal and professional fees, licenses and permits, occupancy costs of materials and/or build outs, initial supplies, and initial advertising and promotional costs? Place them in to the zero month(s) of your pro forma (the months where you incur expenses but have not opened your doors for business).

2. What is your gross sales income or other revenue per month from your products or services? Include all the income generated by the business and any additional revenue sources.

3. What are your costs of goods sold per month? Include here the actual cost of the products, materials, or ingredients you purchase or manufacture for resale.

4. What is your gross profit or gross revenue per month? Determine this by calculating the difference between your gross income and your cost of goods sold, and list it in dollars, as a percentage, or both. As a percentage, the gross profit is always stated as a percentage of revenue.

5. What are your variable expenses per month (variable expenses are those which change based on the amount of business you do, such as advertising, sales commissions, freight, supplies, and so on)?

6. What are your fixed expenses per month (expenses paid at the same rate, regardless of the volume of business, like rent, utilities, salaries and wages, and so on)?

7. What are your total expenses per month (fixed plus variable expenses)?

8. What is your net profit or loss per month (gross profit or gross revenue minus total expenses before taxes)?

Creating Your Income Statement

1. What are your total sales for each year?

2. Do you have revenue from other types of sales? If so, add them into your income.

3. What are your costs of goods sold for each year?

4. What is the gross profit for each year?

5. What are your variable expenses for each year?

6. What are your fixed expenses for each year?

7. What is your net income for each year?

Creating Your Cash Flow Statement

1. What is the beginning cash balance for the month?

2. What are the cash receipts from sales for the month?

3. What is the total cash available (add the beginning cash balance to cash receipts from sales)?

4. What are the different cash disbursements for the month (the monthly expenses and all accounts payable)?

5. What are the total cash disbursements for the month?

6. What is the net cash from operations (subtract the total cash disbursements from the total cash available)?

7. What is your beginning cash balance (carry the net cash from operations to the next month and that becomes your new beginning cash balance)?

Creating Your Balance Sheet

1. What are your company assets? Include all cash, receivables, inventory, pre-pays, and fixed assets.

2. What are your total company assets?

3. What are your company liabilities? Include all payables, taxes, notes, bonds, and other debts.

4. What are your total company liabilities?

5. What is the equity of your company (total assets minus total liabilities)?

Summary

A business plan is not finished until you can show you have a firm plan for how your new venture can break even in the short term and become profitable over time. The Financial Plan section of your plan is written last, after you've made your marketing, selling, or production plans.

There are four comprehensive reports that need to include in your financial plan. They are the three- to five-year pro forma, income statement, cash flow statement, and balance sheet. Don't attempt to devise your own method of presenting your financials. Stick to the tried and true, as described in this chapter.

The next chapter will describe how to create your Executive Summary.

Part V

The Pitch

14

Presenting Your Executive Summary

Now that you have written the bulk of your business plan, there's one last section you need to write. The Executive Summary is the final and most important section of any business plan.

The Executive Summary is the first thing read by investors and supporters. It might also be the last thing they read in the plan; if your Executive Summary is poorly written or incomplete, busy investors and lenders might decide to save their time and reject the plan outright. Many readers form their basic conclusions about your business idea from the pages of your Executive Summary.

You can see a sample of an Executive Summary in Appendix A, "Sample Business Plan."

Besides giving readers their first impression of your business concept, the Executive Summary is also the primary place for your salesmanship to come shinning through. So the summary should be written very carefully and—like a good novel— revised and rewritten several times. Use succinct and clear language in your Executive Summary to give readers the best possible summary of your business idea and why it

In this chapter:

* Learn the parts of an Executive Summary
* Organize your Executive Summary

note All techniques and information in this chapter pertain to all plan types.

should be funded or supported. This is your chance, and maybe the only chance, for you to get the reader excited about the business concept you are presenting.

To do list

- ☐ Write a summary of your business opportunity and concept
- ☐ Write a summary of your marketing and promotion plan
- ☐ Write a summary of your plan's financial elements

Organizing Your Executive Summary

An Executive Summary is not an abstract, an introduction, or a preface to your business plan. This is a mistake most business plan writers make. In fact, the Executive Summary is a compact, miniature version of your total business plan and should stand alone. The Executive Summary should "sell and tell" everything about your business concept in no more than two to three pages. Think of it as a business plan within a business plan.

You might be thinking that summarizing your business plan in just a few pages is quite a task. It is. That's why the Executive Summary is written last—after you've thought through your entire business concept and nailed down all the details. Your task is to hook the reader immediately within the first few sentences of your summary. Get to the point of your plan and get to it quickly. Tell the reader about your unique selling position, why your idea differs from others in the market, the size of your marketplace, the percentage of the market you intend to capture, and when you intend to capture it.

Like a solid building, your business plan must stand firmly on the foundation of the Executive Summary. Your summary also should convey the excitement and essence of the rest of the plan. Your objective is to make someone reading your Executive Summary say, "Wow! This is a great idea!"

ONLINE SAMPLE EXECUTIVE SUMMARIES

The sample business plan provided by Palo Alto Software (http://www.paloalto.com) in Appendix A contains an Executive Summary. But the more Executive Summaries you see, the better you can construct an effective summary for your plan.

Palo Alto Software offers three online sample Executive Summaries for your review. Each one has a little different take on what information to include in an Executive Summary. They are

* Studio67 Executive Summary—http://www.bplans.com/spv/3259/index.cfm
* AMT Computers Executive Summary—http://www.bplans.com/spv/3015/1.cfm
* Javanet Internet Cafe Executive Summary—http://www.bplans.com/spv/3142/index.cfm

Begin preparing your Executive Summary by setting its priorities. Your list of the most important goals for this element of your business plan might include items like these:

- Summarize the opportunity in a way that catches the reader's interest right from the start and explains clearly what the opportunity is.
- Summarize the business concept by describing the company and its objective, product or service description, and unique selling position.
- Summarize the marketplace, your marketing strategy, and the competition.
- Summarize the financial sections of your plan, including key elements of your development plan, capital requirements, exit strategy, and summary of projected profits.

The priorities you've listed represent the major sections of your Executive Summary, each of which requires a heading. At the very least, your Executive Summary should have the following section headings:

- The Opportunity
- Business Concept
- Marketing and Promotion
- Sales and Profitability
- Funds Sought and Exit Strategy

> **tip**
> Your Executive Summary is there to sell your idea. *So ask for the sale!* After you've sold the reader in your summary, tell them what you want—an investment, a loan, or departmental resources. State your need and make it very clear to the reader. Focus on the opportunity you're presenting and make it clear why it's unique.

Things You'll Need

❑   The other sections of your business plan

Summarizing the Opportunity and Business Concept

Your Opportunity section should explain, in no more than half a page or so, the unique opportunity your business concept offers to the reader. It should clearly explain to the reader what's in it for them. What's the payoff to the reader for supporting your plan with either money or resources?

State the name of your company, its objective, and the company mission statement you created in Chapter 3, "Getting Started: Introducing Your Plan and Identifying Your Mission and Goals". If you're looking for funding or company resources, state the objective or goal of the business plan. Is it to acquire investors, get a loan, or gain support within your company? Make it very clear what the opportunity is for the reader. Here's an example of some of the text from the Opportunity section of the Executive Summary from one of my business plans:

"The One Minute Shopper has created the most unique and innovative affiliate network selling system on the Internet today."

The section went on to cite figures supporting the opportunity, which were pulled from the Market Analysis section of the plan:

"Affiliate selling accounts for 11% of the $5.8 billion consumer transactions online. Forrester Research projects that figure will grow to 24% or $37.5 billion total sales by 2002."

The Opportunity section finished by saying that the One Minute Shopper takes this successful affiliate selling concept to a new level with its unique network selling system. In less than half a page, the Opportunity section of this Executive Summary informed the reader of the name of the company, what it does, and the opportunity it offers for making money.

After you've described and supported the opportunity, you can write the Business Concept section of the summary. I suggest no more than a page for this. First, briefly and succinctly describe the unique selling position you created in Chapter 5, "Describing Your Product or Service," perhaps using bulleted lists. Sell, don't tell, here. Use this opportunity to sell your business idea. If you've hooked them on the opportunity, sell them on how your product or service will achieve it. Next, describe briefly describe your product or service, the market your company serves, what it offers the consumer, and how it differs from the competition. Finish the Business Concept section by describing the goal or reason for your business plan.

note You might consider using bullet points where appropriate in your Executive Summary to indicate the key points of your plan.

Summarizing Your Marketing and Promotion Plan

The third section of your Executive Summary should summarize your marketing and promotion strategy. In a half page or so, very briefly describe the marketing and promotion plan you created in Chapter 8, "Crafting Your Marketing Strategy." Describe your marketing objectives, your marketing strategy for meeting the competition, and your sales and distribution strategies. Then briefly describe your customer acquisition, retention, and monetization plans. Give the reader some idea of your expected percent of market penetration and the frequency and quantity of marketing and advertising required to reach that percentage.

This is a good place to include the company slogan you developed in Chapter 8. Again, sell, don't tell. A good company slogan will help you along the way.

> **note** If you have room in your Executive Summary, you might want to add the top members of your management team. Even a list of their names and a short bio could lend more credence to the success of your business venture.

Summarizing the Financial Elements of Your Plan

The last section of your Executive Summary is where you ask for the sale—tell the reader exactly what you want from them in the area of funding or support—and highlight the important financial points of the business you're proposing. The Sales and Profitability section should define your financial objectives (sales and profitability projections); the Funds Sought and Exit Strategy section should summarize your funding or company resource request.

Begin the Sales and Profitability section by briefly discussing your immediate and long-term sales goals for your company. Go on to outline the activities necessary to achieve those goals, such as expanding your sales goals, new market niches, research and development needs, or whatever activities you'll need to undertake in order to meet your company's financial objectives.

For example, "The company is projected to turn a profit in the third quarter of the second year. Year two projections show gross revenues of $1.5 million dollars with a net profit before taxes of $75,000, and year three projections show gross revenues of $2.75 million with a net profit of $150,000 before taxes."

In the Funds Sought and Exit Strategy section, you should describe your capital requirements. That is, the amount of funding or company resources you will need to meet your financial objectives and to expand.

For example, "$2,000,000 is needed to establish the company and have it reach break even. The company might seek additional funding for expansion 18 months in the future."

Don't make the mistake of forgetting the details of any investments or loans you are asking for. If the purpose of your business plan is to seek investment capital, the last part of this section should describe an exit strategy. How will your investors get their money back with a reasonable return on their investment? If you are offering an equity position, you might state that the investors would get a full return on their investment, along with some profits, when the company goes public. If you are asking for a loan, explain what dividends or interest payments you will pay and when you plan to pay off the loan.

Write the Plan!

Answer the following questions to write the Executive Summary portion of your business plan.

Summarize the Opportunity and Business Concept

1. What is the name of your company?
2. What opportunity for making money does your business offer?
3. What is your business concept? What is your company mission statement?
4. Briefly describe what your company offers the consumer and how it differs from the competition.
5. Briefly describe your unique selling position.
6. What is the goal of your business plan? What do you want the reader to do?

Summarize the Marketing and Promotion Plan

1. Briefly explain your marketing and promotion plan.
2. What are your marketing objectives?
3. What is your marketing strategy for meeting the competition?
4. What are your sales and distribution strategies?
5. Briefly describe your customer acquisition, retention, and monetization plans.
6. If you have a company slogan, include it here.
7. What is your expected percent of market penetration?
8. Briefly describe the frequency and quantity of marketing and advertising needed to reach that percentage.

Summarize the Financial Elements

1. Briefly describe your immediate and long-term sales goals for your company.
2. What are the activities necessary to achieve those goals?
3. What are your sales and profitability projections? When will you break even?
4. What are your revenue and profit projections after you break even?
5. What are your capital requirements? How much money or what type of company resources will you need to break even and show a profit?
6. Will you be looking for additional funding down the line?
7. What is your exit strategy for investors or lenders? How will your investors get their money back with a reasonable return on their investment? If you are asking for a loan, explain what dividends or interest payments you will pay and when you plan to pay off the loan.

Summary

The Executive Summary is the last thing you write and it's the first thing read by investors and supporters. Besides giving the readers their first impression of your business concept, it also is the primary place for your salesmanship to come shinning through. The Executive Summary conveys the excitement and essence of the rest of your plan.

A good Executive Summary should summarize the opportunity, the business concept, the marketplace, the competition, the capital requirements, the exit strategy, and the projected profits of your company. Like a solid building, your business plan rests on the firm foundation of the Executive Summary.

15

Presenting Your Plan

Your plan is done and ready for prime time. But your work is not over yet. Now you have to present your business idea in a way that grabs the listener's attention, quickly communicates your idea, and gets your listeners interested enough to buy into your new venture.

An ill-prepared presentation can turn off a potential supporter or investor. A well-prepared presentation is crucial in gaining the attention and support for your business venture, and a well-prepared pitch lets you take maximum advantage of this situation.

Business presentations come in two types—print or verbal. You need to be prepared to do both. You need the print version, which includes your formal business plan, a PowerPoint slide presentation, a summary of your business idea, and so on for formal sit-down meetings with investors or bankers, and the verbal presentation to take advantage of an unexpected opportunity to make a pitch.

In this chapter:

* Create an elevator pitch
* Prepare your business plan presentation
* Learn effective techniques for presenting your business plan to investors

To do list

- [ ] Create a compelling outline for a short presentation of your business idea
- [ ] Practice the presentation for content and length

Creating the Elevator Pitch

The first place to start in creating your presentation, whether it is to be written or verbal, is the elevator pitch. An *elevator pitch* is a very succinct explanation of your business idea (about 200 words or less) that you can deliver to potential investors or those who are interested in your business model at the outset of a formal meeting, over lunch, or on the phone when pitching your idea to a prospect.

The idea is to pretend you're in an elevator and you run into a potential investor and only have the time between floors (about 30 seconds) to grab their attention and make them want to know more. What would you say, and how would you say it?

So what goes into an elevator pitch? Your pitch must quickly and succinctly answer these questions:

- What is your business? What is your industry?
- What is your market? Who will you be selling to? How big is your market?
- What is your product or service? Describe it briefly. Don't go into detail.
- What is your revenue model? How will you make money?
- Who's the management team? Tell about the team's background and success in the past. Remember, investors invest in people, not just ideas.
- Who is your competition? You will have some. They prove your business idea can work. What is your competitive advantage?

All this information should, by now, be in your business plan. Use it to craft your elevator pitch.

When determining what to include in your elevator pitch, remember you are *not* creating a sales pitch. An elevator pitch sells your business—not your product or service.

The elevator pitch is not easy to create. You will have to write and rewrite it many times until you get it just right. When you think you have it, try it out on your family and friends who know little or nothing about your business idea. Ask them, does it make sense? Can they understand why such a product or service is needed?

To do list

- ☐ Research the backgrounds of the people in your audience
- ☐ Outline key presentation points
- ☐ Create appropriate graphics
- ☐ Prepare written notes, PowerPoint, or video presentation materials
- ☐ Review and practice the presentation
- ☐ Tailor the presentation to venture capitalists, if appropriate

Presenting Your Plan to Investors and Management

So your elevator pitch hooked them and got you through the door. Now it's time for your formal presentation. You have less than 60 minutes to sell them on your idea and you need to make every one of these minutes count. The presentation to an investor group or banker not only gives you a chance to sell them on the next big thing, but also an opportunity for them to ask questions.

Things You'll Need

- ❑ 3"×5" cards
- ❑ Computer and Internet access or other research tools
- ❑ Word processing, presentation, and video recording software and tools, as appropriate

Preparing Your Presentation

Careful and thorough preparation is essential to making a successful presentation. This section offers some simple steps and techniques for preparing your presentation.

First, do your homework. Analyze the people you'll be presenting to. Find out who will be in the meeting by calling ahead. If you're presenting to investors, do some research on them. Google (http://www.google.com) is a great resource. Type in their names or their venture firm and get some background on them and their firm. Find out what other businesses they are invested in and what's in it for them in your company. What do they already know about your industry and target market? The information you dig up on Google will help.

Next, get organized. Outline your key points. Organize your presentation in the same order as your business plan, using the major sections as your key points.

Organize your actual presentation to be compelling and memorable by providing an introduction, body, and conclusion. To do that, first tell them what you are going to tell them, then tell them, and finally tell them what you told them. This process makes up the introduction, body, and conclusion of your presentation.

> **tip** This book's Table of Contents lists all the major sections of your business plan and can be a big help to you in pulling together the outline of key points for your presentation.

Charts, tables, and other graphics can be compelling elements in either traditional or PowerPoint presentations, but don't use inappropriate graphics that might be distracting rather than informative. Avoid animated graphics that take the audience's attention away from your message.

If you're using PowerPoint or any other type of presentation software, keep the number of slides to no more than 10 to 15. The same number applies if you're using overheads. Handouts are good to support your remarks but keep them to a minimum; too many handouts can be distracting and confusing. If you need a number of illustrations, consider using a flipchart or overhead to display the illustrations, and giving the audience all the handouts in a packet for later reference.

tip Keep in mind the technical expertise of your audience. Use plain technical terms and avoid three-letter acronyms.

Errors to Avoid

You might want to show a corporate video, but if you do, keep it to 5 minutes or less. And no matter what presentation style you use, in the end, summarize your high points.

SOME POINTERS ON POWERPOINT PRESENTATIONS

Keep these pointers in mind when preparing PowerPoint presentation or overheads:

* Use large fonts (22 points is minimum size for text). A title should be 32 points or larger.

* Use a sans serif font, such as Helvetica or Arial, for normal text. Use a serif font, such as Times Roman or Book Antigua, in titles to show good contrast. For emphasis, use bold, italic, or all caps, but never more than one at the same time.

* Use no more than 36 words per slide. Use bullet points as "talking points" and avoid paragraphs. Try to use three to six points per slide.

* Be consistent and correct in capitalization. As with any writing, use proper grammar, phrases or sentences that make sense, and no misspelled words.

* Avoid bright colors. Use light colors on a dark background.

* Don't use primary colors (red, yellow, and blue) together, such as red text on a blue background.

* Don't read your material from the slide or talk to the screen.

* Establish eye contact with the audience on a regular basis.

And, of course, dress professionally. You want your appearance to match your professional presentation.

Prepare what you are going to say. Jot down key points of your presentation on 3"×5" cards and refer to them if need be, but don't read from your materials. Be conversational in your tone. Try to anticipate questions and be ready to answer them. If your audience wants to ask questions, answer them and then get back to your presentation.

And finally, review your presentation and practice it before you present your business idea to an audience.

Presenting to Venture Capitalists

If you've chosen the venture capital route, you need to use some special techniques to get a venture capitalist's interest. You can improve your odds of being accepted by a venture firm if you provide certain types of information within your presentation. Venture capitalists look at these key things:

- **Can they make big bucks?** If venture firms are going to risk millions of dollars on your business idea, they want to know what chances you offer them for a big payoff. They'd rather invest five, ten, twenty million or more in a $20 billion market than in a $100 million market. The bigger the market, the bigger the payoff—if the company works. To get a venture capitalist's attention right away, show him your business idea can exploit a big market.

- **Do they invest in your specific market?** Even if your idea is a good one, if you pitch your idea to a venture firm that doesn't invest in your market, you're wasting your time. Venture firms usually specialize in one area. Make sure your business area coincides with theirs. Also, if you're looking for *early stage* capital (money to start up your company and finance it to break even), don't pitch to venture firms that only invest in mature companies that have reached break even or are turning a profit, and are looking to expand or implement the next phase of their development.

- **Whose pain are you solving?** You have to make very clear not only the market you will serve but also the niche you're targeting. If you have a well-defined unique selling position, you'll have a better chance of getting a venture firm's attention. Don't make claims you can't deliver. A venture capitalist picks up on that real fast. Also, state your weaknesses. This shows the venture capitalist that you have thoroughly thought through your business concept.

- **Can you do what you say?** When you pitch your business idea, be specific on why you can execute it. Remember, ideas are easy. The proper execution of them is the hard part. Be sure you mention your competition, who they are, and how you plan to stay ahead of them.

- **Do you have the team?** Venture firms say they invest in people, not ideas. This tells you that the management team you've assembled or plan to assemble is of vital importance to a venture capitalist. Be specific in presenting your team's skills. The venture capitalist wants to know you can deliver on the promise of your business idea.

- **Do the numbers make sense?** Do your homework. Be sure your assumptions on your market, your expenses, and your revenue are airtight, and be ready to defend them. Also, provide clear milestones to measure your success. When will you start to make sales? When will you break even and turn profitable?

Answer these questions to a venture capitalist's satisfaction and you will have her attention.

MEET POTENTIAL INVESTORS

Instead of finding investors, have the investors find you. There are several sites on the Internet, such as VentureDirectory.com (http://www.venturedirectory.com), that enable you to meet potential investors. Some even post your business plan and then match you up with investors looking for new business opportunities. There's a catch, though. Many of them are not free. Prices or annual fees range from less than a hundred dollars to a few hundred dollars.

Here are a few other sites to consider:

* Capital Match at http://www.capmatch.com
* NVST.com at http://www.nvst.com
* Venture Capital Access Online at http://www.vcaonline.com
* VC Experts at http://vcexperts.com

Summary

In this chapter, you learned how to prepare and present your business plan to potential investors. Business presentations can be presented either verbally or in print; you need to be prepared to do both. You also learned some general guidelines for creating and delivering an elevator pitch.

By this point in the book, you should have your business plan organized, written, and nearly ready to go. If you have any areas that need further work or assistance, refer to the appropriate chapters or check out the appendixes in the back of this book. There you'll find ample examples and resources to help you hone your plan for success.

Part VI

Helpful References

Sample Business Plan

This sample business plan is used by permission of Palo Alto Software (http://www.paloalto.com/). Palo Alto Software—The Planning People—develops, publishes, and markets software products for use with personal computers. Its products offer task-oriented, "know how" solutions for small-business and home-office entrepreneurs, professionals, and middle managers. The company is a privately-owned corporation in Eugene, Oregon.

Acme Consulting

January, 1996

This sample business plan has been made available to users of Business Plan Pro, business planning software published by Palo Alto Software. Our sample plans were developed by existing companies or new business startups as research instruments to determine market viability or funding availability. Names, locations, and numbers might have been changed, and substantial portions of the original plan text might have been omitted to preserve confidentiality and proprietary information. Although this has been revised for our Business Plan Pro 2002 version, we've had to leave the original dates because otherwise the discussions of market conditions and industry would seem off base. This plan was written before the Internet had exploded in 1998 and 1999 and fallen back again in 2000 and 2001.

You are welcome to use this plan as a starting point to create your own, but you do not have permission to reproduce, publish, distribute, or even copy this plan as it exists here.

Requests for reprints, academic use, and other dissemination of this sample plan should be emailed to the marketing department of Palo Alto Software at marketing@paloalto.com. For product information, visit our website at http://www.paloalto.com or call 1-800-229-7526.

Confidentiality Agreement

The undersigned reader acknowledges that the information provided by _____ in this business plan is confidential; therefore, reader agrees not to disclose it without the express written permission of

_____.

It is acknowledged by reader that information to be furnished in this business plan is in all respects confidential in nature, other than information which is in the public domain through other means and that any disclosure or use of same by reader, might cause serious harm or damage to _____.

Upon request, this document is to be immediately returned to _____.

_____
Signature

_____
Name (typed or printed)

_____
Date

This is a business plan. It does not impl

1. Executive Summary

Acme Consulting will be a consulting company specializing in marketing high-technology products in international markets. The company offers high-tech manufacturers a reliable, high-quality alternative to in-house resources for business development, market development, and channel development.

Acme Consulting will be created as a California C corporation based in Santa Clara County, owned by its principal investors and principal operators. The initial office will be established in A-quality office space in the Santa Clara County Silicon Valley area of California, the heart of the U.S. high–tech industry.

Within the United States and European high–tech firms that Acme plans to target, we will focus on large manufacturer corporations such as HP, IBM, and Microsoft. Our secondary target will be the medium-sized companies in high growth areas, such as multimedia and software. One of Acme's challenges will be establishing itself as a *real* consulting company, positioned as a relatively risk-free corporate purchase.

Industry competition comes in several forms, the most significant being companies that choose to do business development and market research in-house. There are also large, well–known management consulting firms such as Arthur Anderson, Boston Consulting Group, and so forth. These companies are generalist in nature and do not focus on a niche market. Furthermore, they are often hampered by a flawed organizational structure that does not provide the most experienced people for the client's projects. Another competitor group is the various market research companies, such as Dataquest and Stanford Research Institute. Acme Consulting's advantage over such companies is that Acme provides high-level consulting to help integrate market research data with the companies' goals.

Acme Consulting will be priced at the upper–edge of what the market will bear, competing with the name-brand consultants. The pricing fits with the general positioning of Acme as providing high-level expertise. Sales estimates project revenues of approximately $159,000 in the first year, and $289,000 by year three.

The company's founders are former marketers of consulting services, personal computers, and market research, all in international markets. They are founding Acme to formalize the consulting services they offer. Acme should be managed by working partners, in a structure taken mainly from Smith Partners. In the beginning we assume three–five partners.

The firm estimates profits of approximately $65,000 by year three with a net profit margin of 6%. The company plans on taking on approximately $130,000 in current debt and raise an additional $50,000 in long-term debt to invest in long-term assets by 1998. The company does not anticipate any cash flow problems arising.

1.1 Objectives

- Sales of $550,000 in 1996 and $1 million by 1998.
- Gross margin higher than 70%.
- Net income more than 5% of sales by 1998.

1.2 Mission

Acme Consulting offers high-tech manufacturers a reliable, high-quality alternative to in-house resources for business development, market development, and channel development on an international scale. A true alternative to in-house resources offers a very high level of practical experience, know-how, contacts, and confidentiality. Clients must know that working with Acme is a more professional, less risky way to develop new areas even than working completely in-house with their own people. Acme must also be able to maintain financial balance, charging a high value for its services, and delivering an even higher value to its clients. Initial focus will be development in the European and Latin American markets, or for European clients in the United States market.

2. Company Summary

Acme Consulting is a new company providing high-level expertise in international high-tech business development, channel development, distribution strategies, and marketing of high-tech products. It will focus initially on providing two kinds of international triangles:

- Providing United States clients with development for European and Latin American markets
- Providing European clients with development for the United States and Latin American markets

As the company grows, it will take on people and consulting work in related markets, such as the rest of Latin America, the Far East, and similar markets. It will also look for additional leverage by taking brokerage positions and representation positions to create percentage holdings in product results.

2.1. Company Ownership

Acme Consulting will be created as a California C corporation based in Santa Clara County, owned by its principal investors and principal operators. As of this writing, it has not been chartered yet and is still considering alternatives of legal formation.

2.2. Startup Summary

Total startup expense (including legal costs, logo design, stationery, and related expenses) comes to $18,350. Startup assets required include $32,000 in short-term assets (office furniture, and so on) and $25,000 in initial cash to handle the first few months of consulting operations as sales and accounts receivable play through the cash flow.

2.3. Company Locations and Facilities

The initial office will be established in A-quality office space in the Santa Clara County Silicon Valley area of California, the heart of the U.S. high-tech industry.

3. Services

Acme offers the expertise a high-tech company needs to develop new product distribution and new market segments in new markets. This can be taken as high-level retainer consulting, market research reports, or project-based consulting.

3.1. Service Description

- **Retainer consulting**—We represent a client company as an extension of its business development and market development functions. This begins with complete understanding of the client company's situation, objectives, and constraints. We then represent the client company quietly and confidentially, sifting through new market developments and new opportunities as is appropriate to the client, and representing the client in initial talks with possible allies, vendors, and channels.
- **Project consulting**—Proposed and billed on a per-project and per-milestone basis, project consulting offers a client company a way to harness our specific qualities and use our expertise to solve specific problems, develop and/or implement plans, and develop specific information.
- **Market research**—Group studies available to selected clients at $5,000 per unit. A group study is a packaged and published complete study of a specific market, channel, or topic. Examples might be studies of developing consumer channels in Japan or Mexico, or implications of changing margins in software.

3.2. Competitive Comparison

The competition comes in several forms:

- The most significant competition is no consulting at all, companies choosing to do business development, channel development, and market research in-house. Their own managers do this on their own, as part of their regular business functions. Our key advantage in competition with in-house development is that managers are already overloaded with responsibilities and they don't have time for additional responsibilities in new market development or new channel development. Also, Acme can approach alliances, vendors, and channels on a confidential basis, gathering information and making initial contacts in ways that the corporate managers can't.
- The high-level prestige management consulting groups, such as McKinsey, Bain, Arthur Anderson, Boston Consulting Group, and so forth. These are essentially generalists who take their name-brand management consulting into specialty areas. Their other very important weakness is the management structure that has the partners selling new jobs, and inexperienced associates delivering the work. We compete against them as experts in our specific fields, and with the guarantee that our clients will have the top-level people doing the actual work.

- The third general kind of competitor is the international market research companies such as International Data Corporation (IDC), Dataquest, Stanford Research Institute, and so forth. These companies are formidable competitors for published market research and market forums, but cannot provide the kind of high-level consulting that Acme will provide.
- The fourth kind of competition is the market-specific smaller house. For example, Nomura Research in Japan and Select S.A. de C.V. in Mexico (now affiliated with IDC).
- Sales representation, brokering, and deal catalysts are an ad-hoc business form that will be defined in detail by the specific nature of each individual case.

3.3. Sales Literature

The business will begin with a general corporate brochure establishing the positioning. This brochure will be developed as part of the startup expenses.

Literature and mailings for the initial market forums will be very important.

3.4. Fulfillment

The key fulfillment and delivery will be provided by the principals of the business. The real core value is professional expertise, provided by a combination of experience, hard work, and education (in that order).

We will turn to qualified professionals for freelance backup in market research and presentation and report development, which are areas that we can afford to subcontract without risking the core values provided to the clients.

3.5. Technology

Acme Consulting will maintain the latest Windows and Macintosh capabilities including

- Complete email facilities on the Internet, Compuserve, America Online, and Applelink, for working with clients directly through email delivery of drafts and information.
- Complete presentation facilities for preparation and delivery of multimedia presentations on Macintosh or Windows machines, in formats including on-disk presentation, live presentation, or video presentation.
- Complete desktop publishing facilities for delivery of regular retainer reports, project output reports, marketing materials, and market research reports.

3.6. Future Services

In the future, Acme will broaden the coverage by expanding into coverage of additional markets (for instance, all of Latin America, Far East, Western Europe) and additional product areas (for instance, telecommunications and technology integration).

We are also studying the possibility of newsletter or electronic newsletter services, or perhaps special on-topic reports.

4. Market Analysis Summary

Acme will be focusing on high-technology manufacturers of computer hardware and software, services, and networking, who want to sell into markets in the United States, Europe, and Latin America. These are mostly larger companies, and occasionally medium-sized companies.

Our most important group of potential customers is executives in larger corporations. These are marketing managers, general managers, sales managers who are sometimes charged with international focus and sometimes charged with market or even specific channel focus. They do not want to waste their time or risk their money looking for bargain information or questionable expertise. As they go into markets looking at new opportunities, they are very sensitive to risking their company's name and reputation.

4.1. Market Segmentation

Large manufacturer corporations: Our most important market segment is the large manufacturer of high-technology products, such as Apple, Hewlett-Packard, IBM, Microsoft, Siemens, or Olivetti. These companies will be calling on Acme for development functions that are better spun off than managed in-house, for market research, and for market forums.

Medium-sized growth companies: Particularly in software, multimedia, and some related high-growth fields, Acme will offer an attractive development alternative to the company that is management constrained and unable to address opportunities in new markets and new market segments.

Market Analysis

Potential Customers	Growth	1996	1997	1998	1999	2000	CAGR
U.S. High Tech	10%	5,000	5,500	6,050	6,655	7,321	10.00%
European High Tech	15%	1,000	1,150	1,323	1,521	1,749	15.00%
Latin America	35%	250	338	456	616	832	35.07%
Other	2%	10,000	10,200	10,404	10,612	10,824	2.00%
Total	6.27%	16,250	17,188	18,233	19,404	20,726	6.27%

4.2. Target Market Segment Strategy

As indicated by the previous table and illustration, we must focus on a few thousand well-chosen potential customers in the United States, Europe, and Latin America. These few thousand high-tech manufacturing companies are the key customers for Acme.

4.3. Service Business Analysis

The consulting industry is pulverized and disorganized, with thousands of smaller consulting organizations and individual consultants for every one of the few dozen well-known companies.

Consulting participants range from major international name-brand consultants to tens of thousands of individuals. One of Acme's challenges will be establishing itself as a *real* consulting company, positioned as a relatively risk-free corporate purchase.

4.3.1. Business Participants

At the highest level are the few well-established major names in management consulting. Most of these are organized as partnerships established in major markets around the world, linked together by interconnecting directors and sharing the name and corporate wisdom. Some evolved from accounting companies (for instance, Arthur Andersen and Touche Ross) and some from management consulting (McKinsey and Bain). These companies charge very high rates for consulting, and maintain relatively high overhead and fulfillment structures based on partners selling and junior associates fulfilling.

At the intermediate level are some function-specific or market-specific consultants, such as the market research firms (IDC and Dataquest) or channel development firms (ChannelCorp, Channel Strategies, and ChannelMark).

Some kinds of consulting are little more than contract expertise provided by somebody who, while temporarily out of work, offers consulting services.

4.3.2. Distribution Patterns

Consulting is sold and purchased mainly on a word-of-mouth basis, with relationships and previous experience being, by far, the most important factor.

The major name-brand houses have locations in major cities and major markets, and executive-level managers or partners develop new business through industry associations, business associations, chambers of commerce and industry, and so forth, and in some cases social associations such as country clubs.

The medium-level houses are generally area specific or function specific, and are not easily able to leverage their business through distribution.

4.3.3. Competition and Buying Patterns

The key element in purchase decisions made at the Acme-client level is trust in the professional reputation and reliability of the consulting firm.

4.3.4. Main Competitors

1. The high-level prestige management consulting

Strengths—International locations managed by owner-partners with a high level of presentation and understanding of general business. Enviable reputations which make purchase of consulting an easy decision for a manager, despite the very high prices.

Weaknesses—General business knowledge doesn't substitute for the specific market, channel, and distribution expertise of Acme, focusing on high-technology markets and products only. Also, fees are extremely expensive, and work is generally done by very junior-level consultants, even though sold by high-level partners.

2. The international market research company

Strengths—International offices, specific market knowledge, permanent staff developing market research information on a permanent basis, and good relationships with potential client companies.

Weaknesses—Market numbers are not marketing, not channel development, and not market development. Although these companies compete for some of the business Acme is after, they cannot really offer the same level of business understanding at a high level.

3. Market-specific or function-specific experts

Strengths—Expertise in market or functional areas. Acme should not try to compete with Nomura or Select in their markets with market research, or with ChannelCorp in channel management.

Weaknesses—The inability to spread beyond a specific focus, or to rise above a specific focus, to provide actual management expertise, experience, and wisdom beyond the specifics.

4. Companies that do in-house research and development

Strengths—No incremental cost except travel; also, the general work is done by the people who are entirely responsible and the planning is done by those who will implement it.

Weaknesses—Most managers are terribly overburdened already, unable to find incremental resources in time and people to apply to incremental opportunities. Also, there is a lot of additional risk in market and channel development done in-house from the ground up. Finally, retainer-based antenna consultants can greatly enhance a company's reach and extend its position into conversations that might otherwise never have taken place.

5. Strategy and Implementation Summary

Acme will focus on three geographical markets (the United States, Europe, and Latin America) and in limited product segments: personal computers, software, networks, telecommunications, personal organizers, and technology integration products.

The target customer is usually a manager in a larger corporation, and occasionally an owner or president of a medium-sized corporation in a high-growth period.

5.1. Pricing Strategy

Acme Consulting will be priced at the upper-edge of what the market will bear, competing with the name-brand consultants. The pricing fits with the general positioning of Acme as providing high-level expertise.

Consulting should be based on $5,000 per day for project consulting, $2,000 per day for market research, and $10,000 per month and up for retainer consulting. Market research reports should be priced at $5,000 per report, which will, of course, require that reports be very well planned, focused on very important topics, and very well presented.

5.2. Sales Strategy

The sales forecast monthly summary is included in the Appendix. The annual sales projections are included here.

Sales Forecast

	1996	1997	1998
Sales			
Retainer consulting	$200,000	$350,000	$425,000
Project consulting	$270,000	$325,000	$350,000
Market research	$122,000	$150,000	$200,000
Strategic reports	$0	$50,000	$125,000
Other	$0	$0	$0
Total sales	$592,000	$875,000	$1,100,000
Direct cost of sales	1996	1997	1998
Retainer consulting	$30,000	$38,000	$48,000
Project consulting	$45,000	$56,000	$70,000
Market research	$84,000	$105,000	$131,000
Strategic reports	$0	$20,000	$40,000
Other	$0	$0	$0
Subtotal direct cost of sales	$159,000	$219,000	$289,000

5.3. Milestones

Our detailed milestones are shown in the following table.

Milestones

Milestone	Start Date	End date	Budget	Manager	Department
Business plan	10/1/1995	11/19/1995	$5,000	HM	Devpt
Logo design	1/1/1996	2/1/1996	$2,000	TAJ	Marketing
Retainer contracts	2/1/1996	12/31/1996	$10,000	HM	Sales
Stationery	3/1/1996	4/15/1996	$500	JD	G&A
Brochures	3/1/1996	4/15/1996	$2,500	TAJ	Marketing
Financial backing presentations	4/1/1996	9/15/1996	$10,000	HM	Devpt
Initial mailing	6/1/1996	7/1/1996	$5,000	HM	Sales
Office location	1/15/1996	2/9/1996	$5,000	JD	G&A
Office equipment	1/15/1996	2/19/1996	$12,500	JD	G&A
Other	1/1/1996	12/31/1996	$10,000	ABC	Department
Totals			$62,500		

6. Management Summary

The initial management team depends on the founders themselves, with little backup. As we grow, we will take on additional consulting help, plus graphic/editorial, sales, and marketing help.

6.1. Organizational Structure

Acme should be managed by working partners, in a structure taken mainly from Smith Partners. In the beginning we assume three–five partners:

- Ralph Sampson.
- At least one, probably two, partners from Smith and Jones.
- One strong European partner, based in Paris.
- The organization has to be very flat in the beginning, with each of the founders responsible for his or her own work and management.
- One other strong partner.

6.2. Management Team

The Acme business requires a very high level of international experience and expertise, which means that it will not be easily leveragable in the common consulting company mode in which partners run the business and make sales, while associates fulfill. Partners will necessarily be involved in the fulfillment of the core business proposition, providing the expertise to the clients. The initial personnel plan is still tentative. It should involve three–five partners, one–three consultants, one strong editorial/graphic person with good staff support, one strong marketing person, an office manager, and a secretary. Later, we will add more partners, consultants, and sales staff. Founders' resumes are included as an attachment to this plan.

6.3. Personnel Plan

The detailed monthly personnel plan for the first year is included in the Appendix. The annual personnel estimates are included here.

Personnel Plan

	1996	1997	1998
Partners	$144,000	$175,000	$200,000
Consultants	$0	$50,000	$63,000
Editorial/graphic	$18,000	$22,000	$26,000
VP marketing	$20,000	$50,000	$55,000
Sales people	$0	$30,000	$33,000
Office manager	$7,500	$30,000	$33,000
Secretarial	$5,250	$20,000	$22,000
Other	$0	$0	$0
Other	$0	$0	$0
Total People	7	14	20
Total Payroll	$194,750	$377,000	$432,000

7. Financial Plan

Assumptions, projected profit and loss, cash flow, balance sheet, and pro forma are included in the Appendixes.

B

Sample Elements

Full Pro Forma

Synergy Icons Confidential

12 Month Performa

Revenue	1	2	3	4	5	6	7	8	9	10	11	12	TOTAL	Year 3	Year 5
Sales Revenue															
1 Site Banner Advertising	$0	$500	$1,550	$6,705	17,376	39,113	68,024	124,827	212,309	333,540	491,894	641,084	$1,936,923	$5,810,769	$8,716,153
2 Pay-As-You-Go	$0	$0	$500	$1,000	$5,000	$10,000	$15,000	$25,000	$50,000	$75,000	$100,000	$150,000	$431,500	$1,294,500	$1,941,750
3 Non-Traditional Revenue	$0	$0	$0	$5,000	$10,000	$30,000	$50,000	$50,000	$60,000	$80,000	$80,000	$100,000	$460,000	$1,380,000	$2,070,000
4 Icon Development	$0	$1,500	$5,000	$5,000	$10,000	$20,000	$25,000	$30,000	$50,000	$60,000	$75,000	$85,000	$366,500	$1,099,500	$1,649,250
5 Icon Sponsorship	$0	$0	$250	$500	$2,500	$5,000	$7,500	$12,500	$25,000	$37,500	$50,000	$75,000	$215,750	$647,250	$970,875
6 Special Events	$0	$0	$5,000	$5,000	$10,000	$10,000	$15,000	$20,000	$20,000	$25,000	$25,000	$30,000	$165,000	$495,000	$742,500
7 Memberships	$0	$0	$100	$250	$500	$750	$1,000	$1,250	$1,500	$2,000	$2,500	$3,000	$12,850	$38,550	$57,825
Hardcopy Publishing															
8 Web Development	$0	$2,000	$4,000	$5,000	$8,000	$10,000	$12,000	$16,000	$25,000	$35,000	$40,000	$50,000	$207,000	$621,000	$931,500
9 Kit Publishing	$0	$250	$500	$2,500	$5,000	$35,000	$7,500	$10,000	$50,000	$12,500	$15,000	$50,000	$188,250	$564,750	$847,125
10 CD Publishing	$0	$250	$500	$2,500	$5,000	$20,000	$7,500	$10,000	$11,000	$12,500	$15,000	$50,000	$134,250	$402,750	$604,125
11 Book Publishing	$0	$0	$0	$0	$0	$0	$0	$25,000	$10,000	$25,000	$10,000	$25,000	$95,000	$285,000	$427,500
Total Revenue	$0	$4,500	$17,400	$28,455	$73,376	$179,863	$208,524	$324,577	$514,809	$698,040	$904,394	$1,259,084	$4,213,023	$12,639,069	$18,958,603

Payroll	1	2	3	4	5	6	7	8	9	10	11	12	TOTAL	Year 3	Year 5
Sales															
12 VP Sales & Marketing	$6,000	$6,090	$6,290	$6,427	$7,101	$8,518	$8,919	$10,544	$13,207	$15,773	$18,662	$23,627	$131,158		
13 Director of Sales	$0	$0	$0	$0	$0	$7,518	$7,919	$9,544	$12,207	$14,773	$17,662	$22,627	$92,250		
14 Sales Rep - Banner Ads	$4,000	$4,010	$4,041	$4,154	$4,448	$4,982	$5,660	$6,997	$9,246	$12,171	$15,838	$19,822	$95,368		
15 Sales Rep - Icon	$0	$0	$4,000	$4,110	$4,250	$4,500	$4,650	$4,850	$5,500	$5,950	$6,500	$7,200	$51,510		
16 Sales Rep - NTR	$0	$0	$0	$4,000	$4,400	$4,800	$5,300	$5,400	$5,600	$6,100	$6,100	$6,600	$48,300		
16 Sales Rep - Publishing	$0	$0	$0	$0	$0	$4,000	$4,300	$4,900	$5,420	$5,000	$4,800	$6,500	$34,920		
17 Sales Clerical	$2,500	$2,500	$2,500	$2,500	$2,500	$2,500	$2,500	$2,500	$2,500	$2,500	$2,500	$2,500	$30,000		
Technical															
18 Web Master	$5,500	$5,500	$5,500	$5,500	$5,500	$6,000	$6,000	$6,000	$6,000	$6,500	$6,500	$6,500	$71,000		
19 Programming - HTML	$0	$0	$0	$4,000	$4,000	$4,000	$4,500	$4,500	$4,500	$4,500	$4,500	$4,500	$39,000		
20 Programming - Flash	$0	$0	$0	$0	$4,000	$4,000	$4,000	$4,000	$4,500	$4,500	$4,500	$4,500	$34,000		
21 Programming - Web Design	$0	$0	$0	$0	$0	$4,000	$4,000	$4,000	$4,000	$4,000	$4,000	$4,000	$28,000		
22 Graphics Design 1	$3,000	$3,000	$3,000	$3,500	$3,500	$3,500	$3,500	$3,500	$3,500	$3,500	$3,500	$3,500	$40,500		
23 Graphics Design 2	$0	$0	$0	$3,000	$3,000	$3,000	$3,000	$3,000	$3,000	$3,000	$3,000	$3,000	$27,000		
General & Administration															
24 President	$8,000	$8,000	$8,000	$8,000	$8,000	$8,000	$8,000	$8,000	$8,000	$8,000	$8,000	$8,000	$96,000		
25 Admin. Clerical	$3,000	$3,000	$3,000	$3,000	$3,000	$3,000	$3,000	$3,000	$3,000	$3,000	$3,000	$3,000	$36,000		
26 Reception Clerical	$2,500	$2,500	$2,500	$2,500	$2,500	$2,500	$2,500	$2,500	$2,500	$2,500	$2,500	$2,500	$30,000		
Total Payroll	$34,500	$34,600	$38,831	$50,691	$56,198	$74,818	$77,749	$83,235	$92,681	$101,766	$111,561	$128,376	$885,006	$1,327,509	$1,991,264
27 Salary Burden	$12,075	$12,110	$13,591	$17,742	$19,669	$26,186	$27,212	$29,132	$32,438	$35,618	$39,046	$44,932	$309,752		
Total Payroll Expense	$46,575	$46,710	$52,422	$68,433	$75,867	$101,005	$104,961	$112,367	$125,119	$137,384	$150,607	$173,308	$1,194,758	$1,792,137	$2,688,206

Expenses

	1	2	3	4	5	6	7	8	9	10	11	12	Year 1	Year 2	Year 3
Property															
28 Rent	$2,000	$2,000	$2,000	$2,000	$2,000	$3,000	$3,000	$3,000	$3,000	$3,000	$3,000	$3,000	**$11,000**		
29 Asset Tax	$6,500	$700	$600	$1,800	$700	$1,800	$200	$200	$500	$200	$200	$100	**$8,750**		
Insurance															
30 General	$800	$800	$800	$800	$800	$1,000	$1,000	$1,000	$1,000	$1,000	$1,000	$1,000	**$11,000**		
31 Liability	$700	$700	$700	$700	$700	$750	$750	$750	$750	$750	$750	$750	**$8,750**		
Communications															
32 Telephone & Fax	$5,000	$500	$750	$1,000	$1,500	$1,700	$1,800	$1,800	$1,800	$1,800	$1,800	$1,800	**$21,250**		
33 Cellular & Pager	$250	$250	$250	$350	$350	$350	$500	$500	$500	$500	$500	$500	**$4,800**		
34 ISP	$2,500	$2,500	$2,500	$2,500	$2,500	$2,500	$3,500	$3,500	$3,500	$3,500	$3,500	$3,500	**$36,000**		
Assets															
35 Equipment, fax, copier, etc.	$15,000	$5,000	$0	$0	$1,000	$0	$0	$1,000	$0	$1,000	$1,000	$0	**$23,000**		
36 Furniture	$15,000	$1,000	$2,500	$7,500	$2,500	$7,500	$0	$0	$0	$0	$0	$0	**$38,000**		
37 Computer/Printer/Network	$35,000	$1,000	$3,500	$10,500	$3,500	$10,500	$1,000	$1,000	$5,000	$1,000	$1,000	$1,000	**$74,000**		
38 Software	$8,000	$0	$0	$3,000	$0	$3,000	$0	$0	$1,000	$0	$0	$1,000	**$16,000**		
Travel															
39 Travel General	$3,500	$3,500	$3,500	$3,500	$5,000	$5,000	$5,000	$7,500	$7,500	$8,500	$8,500	$10,000	**$71,000**		
40 Automobile	$250	$250	$250	$350	$350	$350	$500	$500	$500	$650	$650	$650	**$5,250**		
Administration															
41 Office Supplies	$3,000	$500	$500	$1,000	$500	$500	$500	$500	$500	$1,000	$500	$500	**$9,500**		
42 Postage & Shipping	$300	$300	$300	$300	$400	$400	$400	$400	$500	$600	$600	$600	**$5,100**		
43 Printing	$1,500	$1,000	$1,000	$1,000	$2,500	$2,500	$2,500	$2,500	$5,000	$5,000	$5,000	$5,000	**$34,500**		
44 Maintenance & Repair	$150	$150	$150	$150	$200	$200	$200	$200	$250	$250	$250	$250	**$2,400**		
Promotion & Advertising															
45 Advertising	$0	$0	$1,000	$1,000	$1,000	$1,000	$1,500	$1,500	$1,500	$2,000	$2,000	$1,000	**$13,500**		
46 Promotion	$0	$0	$500	$500	$500	$500	$1,000	$1,000	$1,000	$1,500	$1,500	$2,000	**$9,000**		
47 Public Relations	$0	$0	$500	$500	$500	$500	$1,000	$1,000	$1,000	$1,500	$1,500	$1,500	**$9,000**		
Professional															
48 Legal	$15,000	$500	$1,000	$500	$1,000	$8,000	$1,000	$1,000	$500	$1,000	$2,000	$1,000	**$30,500**		
49 Accounting	$2,000	$1,000	$1,000	$1,000	$1,000	$2,000	$1,000	$1,000	$1,000	$1,000	$2,000	$1,000	**$15,000**		
50 Miscellaneous	$1,000	$1,000	$1,000	$1,000	$1,500	$1,500	$1,500	$1,500	$2,000	$2,000	$2,000	$2,000	**$18,000**		
Total Expenses	$176,100	$81,470	$88,313	$127,125	$125,537	$181,741	$160,524	$172,849	$195,857	$211,252	$228,404	$257,889	$1,982,310	2,973,466	4,460,198
Total Revenue	$0	$4,500	$17,400	$28,455	$73,376	$179,863	$208,524	$324,577	$514,809	$698,040	$904,394	$1,259,084	$4,213,023	6,319,534	9,479,302
Total Expense	$176,100	$81,470	$88,313	$127,125	$125,537	$181,741	$160,524	$172,849	$195,857	$211,252	$228,404	$257,889	$1,982,310	2,973,466	4,460,198
EBIT	($176,100)	($76,970)	($70,913)	($98,670)	($52,161)	($1,878)	$48,001	$151,728	$318,952	$486,788	$675,991	$1,001,195	$2,230,713	3,346,069	5,019,103
Private Placement	$250,000	$100,000	$100,000	$100,000	$100,000				($100,000)	($100,000)	($100,000)	($100,000)	($100,000)	(425,000)	
Cumulative Cash	$73,900	$96,930	$26,017	$27,348	$75,186	$73,308	$121,309	$273,037	$491,989	$878,777	$1,454,768	$2,355,963	$2,230,713	2,921,069	5,019,103

Assumptions

1 Site Banner Advertising: partners @1M Visitors w/ 1% click through +10% bleed over, DoubleClick type, & direct sales, @5¢/impression (4¢ to 7¢).

2 Pay-as-you-go assumes assumes $1 per download. Click through are currently paying between 50¢ and $5.

3 Non-Traditional Revenue is very conservative. Expected to exceed projections. Gross sale = $20,000 * .5 = $10,000.

4 Icon Development is basically cost recovery at approximately $5,000 per icon.

5 Icon Sponsorship is assumed at 50¢ per icon download.

6 Special Events are: Lindbergh, British Airways, & Air Resource Fire Fighter and are assumed at $5,000 per event.

7 Memberships are where teachers, parents, and kids sign up through ecommerce for curriculum materials.

8 Web Development generate revenue as clients hire us as content consultants. Handled as a subsidiary.

9 Kit sales are assumed to be partnered with McGraw Hill or Michael's type partner. Conversations with McGraw Hill in process. Revenue assumed at $1 per $10 kit.

10 CD Publishing is realized immediately due to sales through ecommerce on SI web page ecommerce, sales through museum & city stores and publishing partners.

11 Book Publishing doesn't start until month 7, due to the time to locate a partner, and print, includes ecommerce.

12 VP Sales base of $6,000 plus 2% commission on his sales, plus 1% commission on all sales.

13 Director of Sales is added in month 6 with a $5,000 base plus 2% commission on his sales, plus 1% commission on all sales.

14 Sales Representatives are added with a specialty in specific revenue source with a base of $4,000 plus 2% commission on their sales, no sales in their first month.

15 Sales Representatives are added with a specialty in specific revenue source with a base of $4,000 plus 2% commission on their sales, no sales in their first month.

16 Sales Representatives are added with a specialty in specific revenue source with a base of $4,000 plus 2% commission on their sales, no sales in their first month.

17 Sales Clerical is needed immediately to support sales.

18 Web Master - Server, network, html, flash at first, delegating responsibilities as more technical is added.

19 Programming - HTML is added in month 4.

20 Programming - Flash is added in month 5.

21 Programming - Web Design is added in month 6.

22 Graphics 1 are necessary immediately to design models and web site graphics.

23 Graphics 2 is necessary in the 4th month to design models and web site. graphics.

24 President receives annual bonus based on profitability, to be terminated.

25 Administrative Clerical added at start up.

26 Reception Clerical added at start up to assist in set up.

27 Salary burden assumed at 35%, and includes benefits.

28 Rent is 3,000 S.F., standard low profile, but attractive office space with option to grow, assume a 3 year lease. Storage also included in month 6.

29 Asset tax, assumed at 10%.

30 General Insurance includes, fire & theft, etc.

31 Liability Insurance includes liability, errors & omission, etc.

32 Telephone & Fax includes deposits & installation of telephone system and dedicated fax line.

33 Cellular & Pager includes 12 month contract.

34 ISP assumes one T! or at least dsl service.

35 Equipment includes fax, copier, etc.

36 Furniture is assumed at 2,500 per person.

37 Computers & Software are assumed at $3,500 per person

38 Software assumed at $1,000 per person.

39 Travel & Entertainment includes, client & vendor meetings, tradeshows, etc.

40 Automobile reimbursements.

41 Office Supplies is standard.

42 Postage is standard, USPO, UPS, FedEx, and includes ecommerce shipping.

43 Printing includes, business cards, stationary, reports, proposals, and client mass color reproduction.

44 Mantenence & Repairs is standard for all office equipment.

45 Advertising should remain low due to media partnering, includes trade shows, & specialty promotion, but will include some advertisements in specialty trades.

46 Promotion includes freebies that incur payroll & hard costs..

47 Public Relations include creating articles in trades, and specialty publications.

48 Legal includes start up incorporation, agreement review, and patent / copyright.

49 Accounting / Legal is standard.

50 Miscellaneous is standard.

51 GENERAL - Although Banner Clients are assumed at 1m total visitors, * 10% click through, and 5¢ per impression, a significantly lower value was used.

52 GENERAL - Year 3 revenues increase at an assumed rate of 300% of Year 1.

Pro Forma Income Statement

	YEAR 1	YEAR 2	YEAR 3	YEAR 4
	SALES			
Systems	24	250	500	1,000
Revenue	246	3,750	6,750	12,000
Cost of Sales	93	750	1,350	2,400
Gross Income	153	3,000	5,400	9,600
	EXPENSES			
Salaries	281	1,088	1,796	2,708
Notes Payable	37	163	270	417
Travel and Entertainment	16	307	483	653
Automobile	8	9	12	15
Consulting	104	20	30	50
Advertising and Promotion	9	94	187	375
Trade Shows	—	24	24	44
Contractor Installation	—	—	—	625
Legal and Accounting	7	20	40	60
Insurance	—	20	22	24
Office Rent	47	66	83	103
Communications	7	34	62	114
Office Supplies	4	5	10	10
Postage	2	3	5	6
Miscellaneous	1	10	18	20
Depreciation	10	40	45	50
Total Expenses	533	1,903	3,087	5,274
Income Before Tax	(380)	1,097	2,313	4,326
Provision for Income Tax	—	200	925	1,730
NET INCOME AFTER TAX	(380)	897	1,388	2,596

Pro Forma Statement of Cash Flow

	YEAR 1	YEAR 2	YEAR 3	YEAR 4
CASH FLOW FROM OPERATIONS				
Net Income (Loss)	(380)	897	1,388	2,596
Adjustments				
Add Depreciation	10	40	45	50
Change in Accounts Receivable	—	(500)	(200)	(950)
Change in Inventory	(20)	(30)	(60)	
Change in Accounts Payable	(43)	30	30	75
Change in Notes Payable	(128)	(165)	(140)	
Total Adjustments	(161)	(615)	(295)	(885)
NET CASH FROM OPERATIONS	(541)	282	1,093	1,711
CASH FLOW USED FOR INVESTMENT				
Furniture and Fixtures	50	50	30	40
Equipment	40	30	30	30
CASH USED FOR INVESTMENT	90	80	60	70
CASH FLOW FROM FINANCING				
Notes Payable	305			
Sale of Common Stock	1,100	—	—	—
NET CASH FROM FINANCING	1,405	—	—	
NET INCREASE (DECREASE) IN CASH	774	202	1,033	1,641
BEGINNING CASH BALANCE	5	779	981	2,014
ENDING CASH BALANCE	779	981	2,014	3,655
NET INCREASE (DECREASE) IN CASH	774	202	1,033	1,641

Balance Sheet

ASSETS

Current Assets	
Checking/Savings	
Checking—Scripps Bank	$4,314
Checking—Virtual Account	$374
Total Checking/Savings	$4,688
Total Current Assets	$4,688
TOTAL ASSETS	$4,688

LIABILITIES AND EQUITY

Equity	
Retained Earnings	($3,979)
Net Income	($7,194)
Total Equity	$4,688
TOTAL LIABILITY AND EQUITY	$4,688

References and Resources

In addition to the online and offline resources mentioned in the body of this book, here is a list of additional places to find help in writing your plan and running your business. This list of online resources was compiled by this book's technical editor, Gina Woods, a business advisor with the Central Indiana Small Business Development Center (http://www.isbdc.org/index.cfm).

Marketing Websites

- **http://www.powerhomebiz.com/vol77/marketing.htm**—How to develop your marketing plan.
- **http://www.jcotterill.com**—Information regarding business, marketing, and strategic plans.
- **http://www.marketitright.com**—Everything you need to know about marketing a business. Also has a free e-newsletter.
- **http://www.targetonline.com**—Target Marketing Magazine.
- **http://www.netsol.com**—Website design. The Network Solutions site allows you to develop inexpensive and attractive websites and is very user friendly. For $129,

get a five-page website package, including your domain name and a matching email address.

- **http://www.valueweb.com**—Website design, like netsol.com, but does not allow pop-ups. Cost is a $25 set-up charge and $19.95 per month.

Free Marketing E-Newsletters

- **http://www.marketingprofs.com**—Marketing know-how from professionals.
- **http://www.marketingangel.com**—All types of marketing information.
- **http://www.marketingsherpa.com**—Practical know-how and case studies.
- **http://netbusiness.netscape.com**—Fortune Small Business News.

Financial Information

- **http://www.key.com/smallbiz**—Key Bank's Solution Center has resources, online tools, and account and service suggestions to help your business grow. You'll find a library filled with news and articles, interactive calculators and tools to help you strategize, and information on accounts and services specific to your needs.
- **http://www.vfinance.com**—Venture capital, angel investors, and lenders.
- **http://www.springboardenterprises.org**—Venture and angel capital forum.

Business Plans and General Business Information

- **http://www.sba.gov/starting/wideindexbusplan.html**—The SBA's business plan outline and how to write the plan. Includes a Spanish version.
- **http://www.businessownersideacafe.com**—Small business ideas and information, including starting and running a business, free trade publications, funding venture capital, marketing, and so on.

Technology Solutions

- **http://www.smallbiztechnology.com**—Technology solutions for small businesses

Legal Information

- **http://www.alllaw.com**—Legal information, links, and resources

Tax Information

- **http://www.irs.gov/businesses/small/index.html**—The Internal Revenue Service site. You can order a free CD that gives information regarding taxes and other topics.

National Association for the Self-Employed

- **http://www.nase.org**—Offers many services to its members, such as health insurance, discounts, and an informative quarterly newsletter. In addition, they have a huge small business lobby in Washington. (1-800-232-NASE)

Minority Business Information

- **http://www.mbda.gov (Minority Business Development Agency) and http://www.evn.org (Emerging Venture Network)**—The Emerging Venture Network is a nonprofit organization that was formed to help connect minority entrepreneurs with funding sources. Both organizations launched the MBDA Equity Access Capital program, which offers equity capital training, as well as business plan competition with an equity "boot camp" for winners.

Women's Business Information

- **http://www.onlinewbc.gov**—Small Business Administration's Women's Business Center
- **http://www.entrepreneur.com/franchisezone/women**—Valuable advice and insight from current women franchise leaders
- **http://www.nfwbo.org**—Statistics on women-owned businesses

Funding Your Business

The old saying goes, "It takes money to make money." That doesn't necessarily mean it takes lots of money, but it does take some.

Some entrepreneurs tend to believe that revenue and sales can handle all their money requirements, thinking they can fund the growth of their company out of profits. That scenario rarely occurs, however.

As we've seen throughout *Write a Business Plan In No Time*, there can be substantial startup costs involved when starting a new venture. Beyond startup, your plan also must account for cash flow considerations. If you're selling a product, you most likely have to pay for your inventory or the costs of manufacturing the product before you can generate enough sales to cover the costs of the product and your normal overhead. The same upfront financial needs exist for a service company. You have overhead and personnel costs to cover before you make your first service sale.

In most cases, this means you need money or investment capital right off the bat. To detail these needs in your business plan, you need to show you have taken the following items into account:

- How much money you need in general and how you use it
- Where you acquire necessary funds
- How you plan to repay the loan or compensate the investors (if you have a loan or investors)

In this appendix

* Itemize and describe the funds you require for your company
* Identify and describe your funding sources
* Create an exit or payback strategy

Outlining Your Use of Funds

Though you are not writing your financial plan in this section, you should give a general overview of how the money you need will be used. Even if you're using your personal capital resources, you should still outline how you plan to use the funds you require for your business. Why? Because the exercise is important for gaining a clear picture of your funding needs and plans, and it helps prepare you for writing your pro forma (you learn about writing the pro forma in Chapter 13, "Writing Your Financial Plan").

Things You'll Need

- ❑   Previous sections of your business plan
- ❑   Research related to operational and startup requirements and expenses

Based on what you have written so far, you should have a rough idea of how much money you need for the following:

- Advertising and marketing
- Salaries and wages
- Office equipment
- Manufacturing equipment
- Physical plant expenses
- General operating expenses

An investor wants to know how you plan to use the funds or company resources requested in your business plan and expects you to back up your funding assumptions with hard data. That is, you are expected to support all your financial assumptions with realistic numbers. That's where your pro forma comes into play.

A very simple, free budget calculator can be found at http://www. businessownersideacafe.com/ financing/budget_calculator.html.

> **tip**
>
> When doing your budget, be realistic. Underestimate your revenue and overestimate expenses. When budgeting expenses, think of the unexpected—higher than expected phone expenses because of high personnel needs or increased customer service expenses because of more sales. It's these types of expenses that kill a budget quickly.

To do list

- ❑ Understand the use of personal funding sources
- ❑ Determine how to borrow money from a bank
- ❑ Learn how to fund your company using equity investors

Describing Funding Sources

Love might make the world go 'round, but if you're starting a company, it's money you need. So where do you find it and how do you get it?

First, you have to ask yourself a few important questions. How much money do you need? What kind of financing is right for your business? Where do the funds come from? What are you willing to give up for an investment in your company? Basically, start by asking yourself what kinds of financing you're likely to need and what you are willing to accept in exchange. Each kind of financing has different characteristics you should take into consideration when writing your plan.

To secure some types of investment funding, you are asked to give up a piece of your company in exchange for the funds. Are you willing to give up control? Giving up controlling interest in your company could lead to your removal from management if your investors think you're doing a shoddy job.

If you want to maintain control of your company, you have to give away less for less money, dip into your own pocket, or borrow the cash. If you borrow the money, how much can you afford? You have to make payments on any loans. Your budget can tell you what you can afford and how much you can pay back over time.

WHAT KIND OF FINANCING IS RIGHT FOR YOU?

The Business Owners' Idea Café is an easy-to-understand source of information on company financing. At this site, you can educate yourself on the different kinds of company financing. You can also test your own attitudes toward the consequences of using various funding sources. You can find the information on financing options and the quick attitude test at http://www.businessownersideacafe.com/financing/kind_of_financing.php.

Personal Funding Sources

The most obvious source of capital is from your own pocket. Many a small company was started on personal savings, home equity loans, and personal credit cards. Your credit cards are a ready source of unsecured loans. If your credit limit is $5,000 to $20,000 or more, you already have at your disposal a preapproved loan. Okay, so the interest rate is not so great. But if you shop around (or just look in your mailbox), you'll find many credit cards offering short-term introductory interest rates at a fraction of the rates credit cards normally charge.

 Bank Rate Monitor lists a lot of frequently updated information on which banks and credit card companies are offering the best rates. Check it out at http://www.bankrate.com/brm/rate/cc_home.asp.

Another way to raise cash is sell what you don't use. Remember eBay (http://www.ebay.com)? It's a great place to sell unused stuff collecting dust in your closet or basement that can be turned into funds.

Then there's your family and friends. But borrowing money from friends and family takes some courage. You're about to take their hard-earned savings and invest it in your online startup with no guarantee of success. If you want to earn the trust of your friends and family, you should be risking most of the needed capital yourself. After all, if you don't have confidence in your new company by putting in the maximum you can, why should anyone else? The downside to the friends and family option is that family members might show a sudden, zealous, hands-on interest in your company.

If you've exhausted yourself, family, and friends, you have to go on to the next set of funding sources—banks and investors.

Borrowing Money from a Bank

Bankers are a nervous bunch. Unlike venture capitalists or individual investors, they avoid risk whenever possible. Including a well-thought-out business plan with your loan application considerably increases your chances of getting a loan. A formal business plan shows you are serious enough to do formal planning. That's a message bankers like to see. To them, individuals who plan are better risks than those who don't.

So what does a banker look for when deciding to loan you money for your company? The *three Cs*—character, credit, and collateral.

Character for bankers means stability in the community. They want to know that if your company runs into trouble, you're not going to suddenly disappear for parts unknown. They want to see that you have ties to the community such as long residence, family ties, and home ownership. A good *credit rating* is another thing that bankers look for. Missing a couple of credit card payments shouldn't be a factor, but if you miss a few mortgage payments, that could hinder your chances at a bank loan.

Finally, bankers want to see a good character and good credit, but they live for solid *collateral*. Physical assets such as lists of equipment, ownership of buildings or other real estate, company vehicles, the inventory you currently carry, and the raw materials you might use in manufacturing your products are the kinds of collateral they look for.

Can you get a business loan for your type of business? If you have what is mentioned above, you should. If you're a service company that traditionally has little or no physical assets, getting a bank loan might be a problem. If so, you might be required to put up a personal guarantee on your business loan. That means if your company defaults on the loan, the bank can go after your personal assets. A personal guarantee would most certainly be required if you are a small startup.

If you are an existing company, two years or more of a profitable operation greatly increases your loan chances. If you're a startup, the larger your personal investment is in the company, the better your chances of getting a loan.

tip   Get a home equity loan line of credit. This is much easier than trying to get a business loan because your home is the collateral. Then use the funds from the line of credit to invest in your company.

Funding Through Equity Investors

There are two types of equity investors—the angel investor and the venture capitalist. If you choose the *venture capitalist*, you need to decide the amount of control you might have to surrender. Venture capitalists usually invest millions of dollars and are looking for companies that will make a fast profit. They might also demand equal control of your company. Venture capitalists often expect significant input into management decisions. They might demand you place an executive of their choosing on your staff or place one or more of their people on your board of directors.

There are many good sources of information on venture capital on the Web. For example, vFinance Investments, Inc. at http://www.vfinance.com has the links to everything from locating a venture capital firm to details of security law to articles related to getting investors.

Angel investors, on the other hand, might be very involved or not involved at all, depending on their personal style. But most times they stay out of your company and act as guides and counselors. That's why they're called "angels."

To do list

❑ Formulate a plan for repaying loans and investments
❑ Outline the strategy, including milestones

Creating an Exit or Payback Strategy

You don't get something for nothing. Individuals or organizations who invest in your company want a way to recoup their investment—and make a profit in the process. This is known as an *exit strategy*. They're putting money in at some risk and want to know how they will be rewarded. *Equity investors*, those to whom you sell shares of your company, hope that your company is successful and can *go public* (selling a portion of your company shares to individuals or institutions on the open market) within five years, or at least they hope to make the company successful enough that a larger company buys or merges with your company at a substantial value.

But don't automatically assume your company has the potential to go public. More importantly, don't fail to devise and fully describe in your business plan an exit strategy for your company.

Venture capitalists, for example, don't invest in small companies to lend a helping hand. They invest to make money. That means you need to convince them that you can get them a 10 times or more return on their investment with your exit strategy. Venture capitalists are typically looking for a company that has a realistic possibility of becoming a very large company within five to seven years, large enough for a major public offering or for sale to a Fortune 500-size company.

So, if you're funding your company with investment capital, you need to state in your plan your exit strategy. That is, how the investor gets back his money with a reasonable return on his investment. Whatever your exit plan might be, you should state it in this section and be sure it appears realistic.

For example, I was involved in the venture capitalist funding of an e-commerce startup in California. The venture capitalist firms put up millions of dollars. The exit strategy was either to go public and sell a portion of the company's shares, or accept a buyout offer from another company. The latter is what transpired. The venture capitalists put in several million dollars, and the company was sold for $700 million dollars. A nice little return on their investment.

The Exit Strategy section of your business plan should also outline your long-term plans for your company. Begin by asking yourself why you are getting into business. Do you see yourself running your company several years from now, or do you plan to move on to other opportunities? Are you in it for the big bucks or interested in running a long–term, solid, family business?

Summary

Some entrepreneurs tend to believe that revenue and sales can handle all their money requirements, thinking they can fund the growth of their company out of profits, but this is rarely the case. There can be substantial startup costs involved when starting a new venture.

You must decide how much money you need in general and how you use it, where you acquire the funds you need, and if you have investors or are looking for a loan, how you plan to repay the loan or compensate the investors.

Index

D

Q - R

How can we make this index more useful? Email us at indexes@quepublishing.com.

X - Y - Z